DILEMMAS OF CARE IN THE NORDIC WELFARE STATE

Dilemmas of Care in the Nordic Welfare State

Continuity and Change

Edited by

HANNE MARLENE DAHL
Roskilde University, Denmark

and

TINE RASK ERIKSEN
University of Copenhagen, Denmark

ASHGATE

Published by
Ashgate Publishing Limited
Gower House
Croft Road
Aldershot
Hants GU11 3HR
England

Ashgate Publishing Company
Suite 420
101 Cherry Street
Burlington, VT 05401-4405
USA

Ashgate website: http://www.ashgate.com

British Library Cataloguing in Publication Data
Dilemmas of care in the Nordic welfare state : continuity
    and change
    1.Welfare state - Scandinavia 2.Public welfare -
    Scandinavia
    I.Dahl, Hanne Marlene II.Rask Eriksen, Tine
    361.9'48

Library of Congress Cataloging-in-Publication Data
Dilemmas of care in the Nordic welfare state : continuity and change / [edited] by
Hanne Marlene Dahl and Tine Rask Eriksen.
        p. cm.
    Includes bibliographical references and index.
    ISBN 0-7546-4266-6
    1. Social service--Scandinavia. 2.Welfare state--Scandinavia. I. Dahl, Hanne
Marlene. II. Rask Eriksen, Tine.

    HV318.D55 2004
    361.948--dc22

2004022610

ISBN 0 7546 4266 6

Printed and bound by Athenaeum Press Ltd.,
Gateshead, Tyne & Wear.

Contents

PART IV: DIFFERENT FORMS OF KNOWLEDGE AND DILEMMAS OF CARE EDUCATION

List of Figures and Tables

List of Contributors

Karen Christensen (born 1959) is Associate Professor at the Department of Sociology, University of Bergen. On a thesis: *Care and Work. A Sociological Study about Changes in Norwegian Home Based Care Services* she became Dr. Polit. of Sociology in 1997 at the University of Bergen. She has since made research in several projects about social care and services to the elderly and disabled people of the Norwegian welfare state. Among several articles she has been a co-author of a status report on Norwegian care services. At present she is editor of the Norwegian *Journal of Sociology*. Her central interests are social care and services, social policy, the challenges of the welfare state and qualitative methodology.

Hanne Marlene Dahl (born 1963) is an Associate Professor at Roskilde University, where she teaches and researches in the field of feminist social and political theory, feminist ethics, care, the welfare state professions and the Danish welfare state including (feminist) discourse analysis. She has studied in the USA and Great Britain, and has an MA in Political Theory (Essex) and a Ph.D. degree in Political Science from Århus University. She has published extensively in Danish and English in journals such as *Acta Sociologica*, *The European Journal of Women's Studies*, *The International Journal of Feminist Politics* (forthcoming, 2005) and in various edited works such as a contribution to the Danish commission on Power, and is currently the co-editor of the Danish feminist journal *Kvinder, Køn & Forskning*. Her current research is about caregiving work in the state, and theories of justice.

Rannveig Dahle (born 1940) is Dr. Philos. and senior research fellow at NOVA (Norwegian Social Research). Her research interests are in the field of gender, professions and health care organizations. Her publications include being co-editor of a forthcoming book on *Welfare Services in Transition* (2004) in a Norwegian context and several other papers on these issues. She is currently conducting research on flexibilization of professional work and temporary health care providers in medical institutions, and also doing research on the health sector as a multicultural arena, focusing at gender, ethnicity and class.

Betina Dybbroe (born 1952) is an Associate Professor, Ph.D. at the Department of Educational Research, University of Roskilde in Denmark. Her research includes qualification studies and the learning in care in work as well as in education, in a gender perspective. Additionally institutional analyses of the welfare state specifically regarding the caring professions and health sector, and changes in working identities and working comunities in relation to modernization of the public sector. For five years she has been part of the Life History Research Project of her department, funded by the research council of the humanities. Here she is focusing on methodological questions concerning psychoanalytical and socializational approaches in lifehistory research, in combination with biographical and narrative approaches.

Tine Rask Eriksen (born 1945) is an Associate Professor, Ph.D. at the Department of Education, Philosophy and Rhetoric University of Copenhagen. Head of the Master of Education and Professional Development Programme. Her research interests include questions related to nurses' and students' care socialization in the meeting with a female care education 1987-1991. 1991-1996 she developed a theory on how the sick handle life with cancer and the care relations they established with professionals. The project was supported by the Danish Cancer Association. Presently she is exploring the skills of practical professions and how they fare when they are rendered academic. She has published three books and several articles from 1979 in the Nordic countries.

Lea Henriksson (born 1954), Ph.D., Docent in Social Policy, works at Tampere School of Public Health, University of Tampere, where she has held university positions as a researcher and a teacher in sociology and health research. Her doctoral thesis, published in 1998, was entitled *Women's Heath Work and the Politics of Professionalisation* (in Finnish). She has led an Academy of Finland research project on Service Professions in Transition (2000-2003) and is currently leading an Academy of Finland research project entitled *The Politics of Recruitment*.

Karen Jensen (born 1952) is Professor at the Institute for Educational Research, University of Oslo. She is also Joint Professor at the Centre for the Study of Professions, Oslo University College. Her research interests include questions related to professional identity and learning, value commitments, transitions from school to working life, as well as to the more overall challenges related to professional development within a society characterized by rapid institutional and cultural shifts. Jensen is currently scientific leader for two research projects within the field of professional learning. *The Desire to do Good – an analysis of moral motivation among health and social care personnel* and *Professional learning in a changing society*. Both projects are supported by the National Council for Research in Norway.

Kristian Larsen (born 1958), nurse, Master of Educational Studies and Ph.D. Associate Professor at The Danish University of Education, Department of Educational Sociology, Denmark. Areas of interest are empirical research based on sociological theory about relations and positions within a medical field (patient, nurses, doctors).

Marta Szebehely (born 1950) is Professor of Social Work at Stockholm University. Her main fields of interest are in gender, social policy and care, especially care for elderly people in Sweden and in Scandinavia. Between 1999 and 2001 she was a member of the Swedish Welfare Commission appointed by the Swedish Government and since 2002 she is holding a six-year fellowship in gender equality studies financed by the Swedish Research Council. Together with Professor Rosmari Eliasson-Lappalainen at Lund University, she is heading the research programme *Care for the elderly: Conditions and everyday realities*, financed by the Swedish Council for Working Life and Social Research. Among her recent publications is an edited book in Swedish based on a qualitative comparative study, examining the public home care services for elderly people in four Scandinavian countries.

Helle Timm (born 1959), Msc in cultural sociology and Ph.D. in medicine, is Senior Researcher at The University Hospitals Centre for Nursing and Care Research (UCSF), Copenhagen. Main topics of research and education: Lay perspectives on health, serious diseases and death – and on the Health Care System, user involment, rehabilitation and palliation. Topics of research, education and supervision: methodology, evaluation and qualitative methods.

Bodil Tveit (born 1961) is a nurse and Assistant Professor in nursing at Diakonhjemmet College, Oslo. Currently she is working on a Ph.D. thesis on student motivation and self-identity in nursing, at the Centre of the Study of Professions, Oslo University College.

Sirpa Wrede (born 1963), D.Soc.Sc., finished her doctoral thesis entitled *Decentering Care for Mothers: The Politics of Midwifery and the Design of Finnish Maternity Services* in 2001 (Åbo Akademi University Press, Turku). She is one of the editors of *Birth by Design: Pregnancy, Maternity Care, and Midwifery in North America and Europe* (Eds. Raymond DeVries et al., Routledge, New York). She presently works as Academy Research Fellow at Academy of Finland and Åbo Akademi University and leads a research project entitled *New Dynamics of Professionalism within Caring Occupations*.

Kari Wærness (born 1939) is Professor of Sociology at the University of Bergen since 1987 and Fil.Dr.Hon. University of Uppsala 2004. Her research has covered the areas of social policy and family sociology, with particular emphasis on the work on women, and the relation between unpaid care in family and the formally organized health and social services. For the time being she is also engaged in a research project connected to the Institute of African Studies, University of Legon, Ghana, Globalization and changes in the cultures of survival and care.

Introduction

Dilemmas of Care in the Nordic Welfare State

Tine Rask Eriksen and
Hanne Marlene Dahl

Care, dilemmas and the Nordic model

The purpose of this anthology is to bring together contributions from various professional disciplines that constitute the wealth of Nordic research on social care. The anthology develops insights into the *conditions, practices, and tendencies* in the area of paid care in the social and health care sector. Insights that aim to expose tensions and dilemmas within paid care. The book consists of previously unpublished contributions by Nordic anthropologists, political scientists, educationalists and sociologists. In the book, fundamental conditions for the research into care and related theories are examined, rejected and/or clarified, thus facilitating a more comprehensive overview of the complex state of paid work in social care within the Nordic welfare states. The focus of this book is upon care and treatment in institutions including educational institutions. The main area of interest is the health and social policy field, but other fields are referred to when deemed relevant, for example, child care.

Hitherto the Nordic countries have been referred to as 'Women's Paradise' (Johansson, 2000). However, there is an increasing awareness, even among feminists, about dilemmas in care. Not understood as general dilemmas or trade-offs in care that might apply to various kinds of welfare state regimes (Knijn and Kremer, 1997), but as more specific dilemmas present in the comparary Nordic welfare state.

In order to explore the dilemmas of paid care work in the Nordic countries, it is essential to clarify the ontology of care, as well as expose how the gendered and social division of labour is constitutive of the institution of care work. The *contrast* between private and public care must be explored in order to sharpen one's understanding of political discussions of care and to recognize the professionals (nurses, pedagogues, teachers, doctors and so on) understanding of themselves. This exploration is similarly necessary in unveiling types of care incorporated in the knowledge and work forms at play in paid care work. One of the *dilemmas* is that care skills on the one hand function as experience-based knowledge in a number of work communities, and on the other hand are incorporated into the scholarly skills of care training programmes. Here care is communicated through textbooks, in the form of research-based professional skills. A number of Nordic care researchers have attempted to clarify such *contrasts*, and they have shown how modernization processes, in a broad sense of the term, and power relations contribute to the specific work conditions of today (amongst others Christensen, 2003; Dahl, 2000a; Dybbroe, 1999; Eriksen, 1992; Heggen, 1995; Jensen, 1992; Larsen, 2000; Martinsen, 1989; Wærness, 1980).

In daily speech, care is understood as interest in the other, the caring for and worrying about the other. It is thus something that takes place between people where one cares for the other, and where the recipient of care shows gratitude through a form of mutuality in the relation. Care can be constituted in family relations based on (loving) feelings, where the life of the family promotes that the older, the strong, and the experienced take interest in and care for those that are on their way in life, and those that can no longer care for themselves. These are the bodily, emotional, and cognitive powers of care, where the one part acts (as action, as language, and/or as feeling) and through intimacy, empathy, and responsibility relates to the other and 'nurtures' the other's situation (and perhaps thereby his or her own situation). The 'familiar' care skills are thus culturally determined everyday abilities that through centuries have been handed over in families, as well as been differentiated by the historical and socially determined structures and values that influence human interaction and caring.

Philosophical theories of care

Various philosophers have developed theories of care. The German philosopher Martin Heidegger has described the basic structure of human existence as: the ability to understand and care about what happens to oneself and others (Heidegger 1967). He argues that human beings are thrown into life in a state of mutual dependency, and that our existence presupposes the existence of others. Danish theologian and philosopher Knud Ejler Løgstrup proposes that human understanding is constituted in what we have in common: that is, humans' dependency upon each other (Løgstrup 1956, 1972). This is an element of any meeting between individuals. Our reference to each other consists in what Løgstrup calls manifestations of life. Fundamental aspects of such manifestations of life are trust, compassion, and mercy. Manifestations of life are indispensable, as human life cannot be sustained without them. They are spontaneous by nature, but they often 'live' a hidden life. In each unique and complex, concrete relation of care, judgment is introduced in order to find out how to act, given the situation and the other's manifestations of life.

American pedagogue, philosopher, and feminist Nel Noddings presents care as a form of behaviour or way of relating, which, in the meeting with another, consists in a fundamental movement from the self to an engagement with the other. Care consists of relations in a community where there is an ethical commitment to care for the fellow human being, just as it consists in meeting the other's needs in a 'face-to-face' relation. It is a function that cannot be fulfilled by the one needing care, and there is thus an asymmetrical process of relation and learning between the experienced and the inexperienced. Elements of presence, openness, reception, mutuality, and verbal and bodily forms of expression form part of the process/ relationship that Nel Noddings, however, does not present in a social context (Noddings 1984). The phenomenological philosophers' expositions of human existence are important in order to gain insights into the nature of care. However, they seem ideological in their context independent approach to humans' ability to participate in care relations and the circumstances for such human participation. Many of the theories, furthermore, lack explanatory power in regards to the gendered dimension of care.

The contextualization of care

Historical, social scientific, and feminist approaches must be utilized in order to provide a more detailed exposition of care. These can contribute greatly to the analysis of the culturally, socially, and biologically determined division of labour between the sexes, and they can expose how women through time have given birth, nursed, and provided care in order to ensure the continuation of the family. That is, how women's 'natural' position in the family has been controlled by men's (and children's) interest in their performance of the many more or less visible tasks of everyday life. The division of labour was/is maintained by values, which dictate that a 'real' woman accepts her chores and performs them with a sense of responsibility and understanding of the importance of maintaining the family. Here the political, economic, and ideological context was/is constitutive for the formation of women's abilities to care and the care needs of the family. Already in the 1980s, Norwegian sociologist and gender researcher Kari Wærness depicted care as a unique relation, as well as work: that is, as care services. She distinguishes between spontaneous care services such as personal services based on a balanced mutuality and care work as paid labour (Wærness 1980). Norwegian philosopher and care researcher Kari Martinsen distinguishes between care in daily life and care as a professional skill (Martinsen 1989). Learning care as a professional skill requires an understanding of the importance of practical skills.

In order to develop an understanding of care that can also account for the life historical and subjective aspects of care, the care constructions of Danish education and care researcher Tine Rask Eriksen must be mentioned. These are based on theories of culture that can capture the gender-determined division of labour and its objective structures, as well as the phenomenological and subjektive aspects of care. The empirical material of the constructions is taken from the life conditions of young girls. These constructions expose the practical sense of care incorporated into the girls' relations to their mothers or other persons of care in familiar female communities around 1970 (1992: 142). These skills were, at the same time, differentiated according to class in the sense that girls from the middleclass and lower middleclass were avaible to others in a higher degree than girls from the dominating class. These skills were produced and reproduced in a given community where the necessity of care entails that they were passed on from one generation to the next.

Care abilities, gender and the Nordic welfare state

There are, as indicated, a number of *contrasts* in the familiar care abilities and in what is treated thematically as care in the professionalized paid care work of the Nordic welfare institutions. The expansion of the Nordic welfare states, caused an increase in the institutionalization of familiar care funktions such as rearing children, educating youths, and taking care of the elderly and the sick. These changes happened quickly after the Second World War. In the 1960s under 1/4 of all women in Denmark were employed, while this figure had risen to 3/4 in the 1990s. In this regard, the processes of change varied among the Nordic countries. Women in Denmark and Sweden started gaining employment earlier than those in Norway. The working women were mostly employed in reproductive professions where the work consisted in 'creating and recreating' humans and relations between humans. Thus, middleclass women in particular (through the gender determined division of labour) had a double function as care workers in the public sector, as well as working mothers in the families. The question is, therefore, what consequences this double placement of women has had for the care in families and for the public care services from the 1960s until today.

The answer must from the outset consider the changes in time and space that have happened in the public care work, as well as the services these communities 'produce' for the relations between the ones needing care and the wage-earners. In particular, increased expenses in connection to public care work have contributed to the fact that work principles of the productive sector, such as intensification, maximization of efficiency, division of labour, specialization, and computerization have come to control the work and production of social relations in public institutions. Further, the development of bureaucratic institutions has supported certain power structures in paid care work.

Profession research

The unique character of care work has been explored and described by the various welfare professions through profession research.[1] This is required by the immanent demands of professionalization: the professions must develop their own 'theory-based' area of knowledge, they must monopolize their own professions, and they must be autonomous within their 'own' field. This profession specific form of research thus functions in continuation of the rational logic of the social space. It is result-oriented, determined, and prescriptive research of each profession's understanding of its own professional identity. Research that does not give any insights into the complex conditions of paid care work in institutional contexts in Nordic welfare states (Eriksen 2001).

Parts of the profession research developed in the 1990s thus have no explanatory power in regards to the distinct conditions of paid care work, given the pres-

---

[1] Research has also been undertaken more generally by research on professions such as by sociologists on the various professionalization processes (Brante, 1988, Evertsson, 2001; Selander, 1989).

ence of technical service relations between a manufacturer and a user in an asymmetrical face-to-face relation with built-in conflicts of interest. If the relation includes a sick person, the asymmetry consists, for example, in the fact that the sick person's body is undermined by a biological dysfunction, just as the person's life situation is marked by disorder (as shown by Timm in the contribution to this book). These relations take place in hospitals where the professional (who is healthy and at work) meets the sick person through time-restricted routine care services. The asymmetry of the relation causes, among other things, the situation where the professional possesses the power to impose standardised care routines 'produced' in the social space upon the sick. The relations are, however, differentiated by whether the sick are of a high or low social position, whether they are young or old, and whether they are men or women (Eriksen 1996). The conflicts of interest between the ones needing care and the professional can be blurred by the fact that the professionals' self-understanding is often based on the idea that they establish trusting (loving) care situations with the sick or the suffering. Or, it can be blurred by the fact that the professionals 'from inner compulsion are forced to' participate in care relations with the weak, as part of their own struggle against an 'inner' powerlessness, or as part of a wish to confirm their own omnipotence.

One of the *paradoxes* of care work in the new millennium is that taking care of each other is fundamental to being human, while the social and cultural changes of family and working life have changed humans' relations with one another dramatically. The individual has become more isolated from the community, partly due to values that dictate that the individual must take care of him/herself. Families are decreasingly the space for intimacy, mutuality, and responsibility, as large parts of family care have been institutionalised as part of women's struggle for 'equality'. The gender struggle has thereby, in regards to women, produced a form of self-repression of the female care potentials. Instead, the familiar care ideology functions as symbolic capital for the professionals in the public sector, in what is increasingly 'care deprived' work between professionals of the female dominated professions and the users in need of care. Today there is a weak tendency towards these *dichotomies* taking on different forms, for instance in day-care centres, where a minor part of the paid care work is performed by male pedagogues (Baagøe Nielsen 2002). Finally, it should be noted that a significant *dilemma* of public care work is that the professionalization of this work, so to speak, is a consequence of what we call development; the continuous exploitation of labour and of nature creates a higher standard of living and changed ways of living, which in turn lead to the professionalization of more and more inter-human relations.

The editors and the process of the book

As our biographies indicate, it is clear that we, as editors, represent two different generations of researchers and feminists and that we have our origins in different scientific backgrounds. Tine Rask Eriksen participated in the early feminist struggle in 1968. This was partly due to her experiences of working at Denmark's largest hospital Rigshospitalet in Copenhagen. There she experienced the patriarchal and medical forms of domination prevalent in the hospital sector at the time. In

1979 she commenced her theoretical pedagogy studies at the University of Copenhagen. Here her work experiences, her participation in a basis group for the women's liberation movement, and her life in a family with husband and children have all influenced her continued academic research on welfare institutions and care work. Hanne Marlene Dahl is a feminist political theorist and has continuously been involved in feminist issues from her early days as a student.

We met at a conference organised by Danish women and gender research in 1996, in a workshop organised around the theme of care. Our collaboration from then onwards has been marked by a shared passion for gaining insights into the institutionalised care work. Hanne Marlene Dahl is characterized by academic stringency and great productivity, and she generally publishes her work in English. Tine Rask Eriksen's work is particularly marked by a departure from the established ways of exploring and understanding paid care work. These differences work as the dynamo for our continuous habit of diving into challenging projects. One of these projects is based on our opinion that Nordic care research must be brought out into a larger international context. Nordic research on care should no longer merely have to refer to international care research; international care research should similarly be enriched by Nordic care research. Therefore we have initiated the particularly demanding project of publishing this book, which began as an idea in 1999, and resulted in a symposium held in 2002.

At the symposium 'Modern Care Work in the Nordic Welfare States' which took place in August 2002 in Copenhagen, the plan of the book was presented, 16 papers were presented and discussed among 20 distinguished Nordic scholars in the field.

Our position and the pluralist approach

Our focus on the Nordic countries is linked to our belief in situated knowledge(s) inspired by the feminist philosopher Donna Haraway (1984). Our position within the Nordic welfare states means thinking through our locations as mothers, daughters and researchers in relation to the object of investigation: the care and health services, and gives us a unique access to studying the golden image often presented by feminists from abroad. The Nordic welfare state is not a homogenuous entity. In our presentation in the book, our perspective is Danish which frames our understandings of the changes occurring within the last twenty years in the Nordic welfare states.

Methodologically, researchers from the Nordic countries have often applied a double perspective in contrast to scholars from the Anglo-American world (Dahl, 1997). The perspective of the Nordic researchers has often been a bottom-up. However, a new plurality of approaches seems to have become prevalent in the field. Constructivism, top-down approaches and life historical perspectives are applied as approaches and research techniques. This plurality is beneficial for the investigation of a subject matter as complex as care in an institutional context. Interesting new work on boundaries between the clean and the dirty work as well as research on ambiguities in care work raise new questions for the scientific agenda.

The Nordic model

The Nordic model consists of the welfare states of Denmark, Finland, Norway and Sweden,[2] and it has inspired researchers, politicians and feminists around the world due to its success in reducing class and gender inequalities. Its status as a normative ideal is often related to its universal and generous benefits (Petersen, 1997), such as unemployment and housing benefits as well as free access to education, health and care services. Feminists in particular have focussed upon the high (and full time) female participation rates in the labour market enabled by state run daycare facilities for pre-school children, generous parental leave arrangements as well as extensive and state financed elderly care.

A feature of the Nordic model is the 'passion for equality' that is often related to the importance of social democratic parties and labour movements for the universalistic oriented institutional design of the welfare states (Esping-Andersen, 1985). The model has been characterized as being based upon comprehensive, principally tax-financed, redistributive and universal social and welfare policies (Kuhnle, 2000). These characteristics are the result of political struggles in and outside the state apparatus between political parties, social movements, philanthropists and state agents all of whom act according to their interpretative horizons and interests in their understanding of the contemporary socio-economic situation.

The struggle for social rights resulted in a new gender contract (Hirdman, 1994) with a new ideal for gender relations supported by a process of reproduction going public. The state was supposed to relieve women of some of the caregiving tasks due to their increased participation rates in the labour market. The 'potentially women friendly state' (Hernes, 1987) determines the level of services and the conditions of its production. The increased 'verstaatlichung' seems to be related to an increased number of professions as well as their increasing strength (Petersen, 1997) up to the implementation of new orders of regulation in the 1990s. The expansion of the welfare state in the end of the 1960s was, among others, built on an understanding of expertise as improving care (Petersen, 1997).

This expansion of the Nordic welfare state which took place in the late 1960s resulted in a feminization of the welfare state (Borchorst, 1989). Unpaid caregiving work in the home became paid in state institutions and the women were primarily employed at the bottom of the welfare state, i.e. in the caregiving services towards preschool children, sick and the elderly.

However, any model is necessarily a construction drawing on some similarities and leaving out some differences. Lately, the similarities between the four countries have been questioned from a feminist perspective (Leira, 1992; Bergqvist et al., 1999) and the concept of universalism has itself become an object of investigation, since it has been argued that universalism has been a premise rather than an empirical fact in the studies concerning the Nordic model (Anttonen, 2002). More generally, there has been an increased skepticism towards the usefulness of models (Petersen, 1997). It has also been argued that the Nordic model is moving away

---

[2] The Nordic model also comprises Iceland, The Faroese Islands and Greenland.

from its defining feature of universalism and adopting more selective measures (Anttonen, 2002). In this volume Szebehely's contribution shows this to be the case for Swedish pre-school and elderly care.

Globalization, retrenchment and new public management

During the 1980-90s the Nordic welfare states experienced a financial crisis[3] and simultaneously, through its publications, the OECD as an ideological agent of change legitimized skepticism about the welfare state (Kuhnle, 2000). The supposed need for change was later linked to globalization and the altered demographic profile of the population (Andersen, 2000) and these claims for retrenchment of the welfare state have grown more insistent (Pierson, 2001). Among politicians, globalization is widely believed to pose a deterministic threat to the survival of the welfare state and its present institutional design (Marcussen, 2001).[4] Politicians in need of solutions to this complex set of problems were looking for a solution, a cure for the problems. In the marketplace of ideas they found one, that of New Public Management (NPM).

NPM is a new paradigm for administrative reform predicated on a substantial, if varying transfer, of private-sector rationalities and techniques into the public sector (Bislev et.al, 2002). As a complex of ideas, it originated in the USA and traveled through international organizations like the OECD, and its Public Management Committee, and became the new orthodoxy in 1995 (Marcussen, 2001). It combines neo-liberal ideas with Human Resource Management (HRM) (Clarke and Newman, 1997), and is often described with concepts of marketization, managerialization (or more precisely a management of change) and 'doing more with less' (read: efficiency) (Ashburner et al., 1996). Compared to Britain, the Nordic countries in general have implemented a softer version of NPM using new management techniques and the drive for efficiency, rather than the element of marketization. Within the Nordic countries, however, differences exist in the NPM versions applied. Denmark has adopted a NPM light where NPM has been combined with strategies of decentralization and democratization (Sehested, 2002), whereas Sweden has applied a more traditional NPM cure using marketization more than has been done by its Danish counterpart. Some of these differences are described in the contributions of Dahl and Szebehely in the present volume.

In a sense, NPM is more than just a neutral tool of restructuring the state, since it can be argued that it basically redefines the logic of the Nordic welfare state. Within health care services NPM on one hand implies an increased focus upon 'quality', and on the other hand results in worsened conditions for the caregiving person employed in a hospital. NPM results in an increased focus upon documentation of performed tasks and in doing so, it transfers resources from the concrete

---

[3] The financial crisis appeared in Denmark in the 1980s whereas in Sweden and Finland it occurred a decade later.

[4] Social researchers have disagreed upon the effects of globalization upon the autonomy of the welfare state and the characteristics of globalization as such (Hirst and Thompson, 1999).

caregiving work to its documentation (Hamram, 1996). This constitutes a dilemma, since the political aim to ensure quality of services seems to produce an opposite result.

Such dilemmas can also be identified within elderly care in Denmark, where new tools of management like 'Mutual language' aims to produce a governable and better (and more visible) quality of home help, but instead produces dissatisfaction with a bureaucratic and inflexible system (Petersen and Schmidt, 2003). When analyzing the discourses on care themselves, it becomes obvious that they are also contradictory. An example is the expressed policy aims within Danish elderly care in the period 1980-95. In this period, there was an increased stress upon self-determination of the elderly person and simultaneously an ideal of care being meticulously described, which hinders the self-determination of the elderly person (Dahl, 2000b). The ideal of care describes the obligations of the elderly person in the sense of her/his obligation to care for her/himself and to develop her/his abilities. In this sense, the discourse is paradoxical, since there is both a withdrawal of the state and an increased regulation of the elderly.

NPM and professionalization

NPM is often believed to challenge the traditional autonomous role of professionals (Sehested, 2002), since the field for the power and knowledge game changes. However, this view is more ambiguous if we consider less traditional professionals such as the welfare state engineered professions. The professions that Johansson (1995) describes as mass, female and subordinate are often wrongly referred to a semi-professions by the dominant male and mainstream view, as their theoretical paradigm is based upon a gendered notion of the professional (Witz, 1992). Examples of such less elitist, female dominated and often state engineered professions are publicly paid home helpers and practical nurses. These new types of professions are, on the one hand, colonised by the foreign logic of NPM, and on the other hand, NPM offers as a new logic opportunities for enlarging their field of expertise at the expense of more traditional professions such as nurses.

NPM changes the field where the professionals and their professional organizations can position themselves, since new values such as flexibility and documentation of tasks accomplished dominate the field. This new set of values brought forward by NPM inspired techniques and policies has several more general implications whereas more specific ones depend upon the national context of other government strategies. Firstly, NPM redraws the boundaries of the established professions, since specialization is no longer an absolute virtue giving that the new professions are more in line with the stress upon flexible and more general qualifications. Secondly, NPM leads to an internal differentiation of the professionals since a new strata of managerial professionals is generated (Sehested, 2002). Thirdly, a new ideal of the professional is generated, i.e. that of a specialised generalist (Dahl, 2000a) and, finally, NPM provides input for new professions to arise such as shown by Henriksson and Wrede in the present book.

References

Andersen, J.G. (2000): 'Welfare Crisis and Beyond', in: Kuhnle, S. (ed.): *Survival of the European Welfare State*, London: Routledge

Anttonen, A. (2002): 'Universalism and Social Policy: A Nordic-feminist Revaluation', in: *NORA*, 10 (2): 71-80.

Ashburner, L. et al. (1996): *The New Public Management in Action*. Oxford: Oxford University Press.

Baagoe Nielsen, S. (2002): '"Modernisering" og "Feminisering" i velfærdsstaten – omsorg, professionalisering og kønsmagt under forandring', in: *Kønsmagt under forandring*. Copenhagen: Hans Reitzel.

Bergqvist, C. et. al. (1999): *Likestilte demokratier?* Oslo: Universitetsforlaget.

Bislev et al, (2002): 'The global Diffusion of Managerialism: Transnational discourse Communities at Work', in: *Global Society*, 16 (2): 199-212.

Borchorst, A. (1989): 'Kvinder, velfærdsarbejdet og omsorgsarbejdet', in: *Politica*, 21 (2): 132-148.

Brante, T, (1988): 'Sociological Approaches to the Professions', *in: Acta Sociologica* 31 (2): 119-142.

Christensen, K. (2003): 'De stille stemmer', in: *Omsorgens pris*. Oslo: Gyldendal, Akademisk.

Clarke, J. and Newman, J, (1997): *The Managerial State*. London: Sage.

Dahl, H.M. (1997): 'Mellem kærlighed og arbejde. Omsorgsteori: Traditioner og centrale temaer', in: *Kvinder, Køn & Forskning*, 6 (2): 56-65.

Dahl, H.M. (2000a): *Fra kitler til eget tøj – Diskurser om professionalisme, omsorg og køn.* Århus: Politica.

Dahl, H.M. (2000b): 'Fra den "store" til den lille "omsorg"?', in: *GRUS*, 21 (61): 5-17.

Dybbroe, B. (1999): 'Vi er alle mødre for vor herre – omsorgskundskaber hos arbejderkvinder i Danmark og Andalusion', in: *Social Kritik*, 11 (63): 22-37.

Eriksen, T.R. (1992): *Omsorg i forandring*. Copenhagen: Munksgaard Danmark.

Eriksen, T.R. (1996): *Livet med kræft – i et støtte og omsorgsperspektiv*. Copenhagen: Munksgaard.

Eriksen, T.R. (2001): 'Omsorgsteori i et kritisk og videnskabsteoretisk perspektiv', in: *Filosofi-Etik-Videnskabsteori*. Copenhagen: Akademisk Forlag.

Esping-Andersen, G. (1985): *Politics against Markets – The Social Democratic Road to Power*. Princeton: Princeton University Press.

Evertsson, L. (2001): *Välfärdspolitik & Kvinnoyrken – Organisation, Välfärdsstat och professionaliseringens villkor*. Umeå: Umeå Universitet.

Hamran, T. (1996): 'Effektivisering versus omsorgsansvar', *Kvinneforskning*, 2: 35-46.

Haraway, D. (1984): 'Situated knowledges: The Science Question in Feminism and the Privilege of Perspective', in: *Feminist Studies*, 3: 575-599.

Heidegger, M. (1967): *Sein und Zeit*. Germany: Max Niemeyers Verlag.

Heggen, K. (1995): *Sykehuset som 'klasserum'*. Oslo: Universitetsforlaget.

Hernes, H. (1987): *Welfare State and Woman Power – Essays in State Feminism*. Oslo: Universitetsforlaget.

Hirst, P. and Thompson (1999): *Globalization in Question*, Cambridge: Polity Press (2. revised edition).

Hirdman, Y. (1994): *Women – From Possibility to Problem?* Stockholm: The Swedish Center for Working Life (Research Report Series no. 3)

Jensen, K. (1992): *Hjemlig omsorg i offentlig regi. En studie av kunnskapsutviklingen i omsorgsarbeitet*. Oslo: Universitetsforlaget.

Johansson, S. (1995): 'Introduktion', in: Johansson, S. (ed.): *Sjukhus og hem som arbetsplats*. Stockholm: Universitetsforlaget.

Johansson, S. (2000): 'Women's Paradise lost? Care in the Quasi-Markets in Sweden', in: Hobson, B (ed.): *Gender and Citizenship in Transition*. London: Macmillan.

Knijn, T. and Kremer, M.: 'Gender and the Caring Dimension of Welfare States: Toward Inclusive Citizenship', in: *Social Politics*, 4 (3).

Knudsen, A.: *Her går det godt – send flere penge*. Copenhagen: Gyldendal.

Kuhnle (2000): 'The Scandinavian Welfare State in the 1990s: Challenged but Viable', in: *West European Politics*, 23, 2: 209-228.

Larsen, K. (2000): *Praktikuddannelse, kendte og miskendte sider*. Universitetshospitalernes Center for Sygepleje og omsorgsforskning. Danmark.

Leira, A. (1992): *Welfare States and working Mothers*. Cambridge: Cambridge University Press

Løgstrup, K.E. (1956): *Den etiske fordring*. Copenhagen: Gyldendal.

Løgstrup, K.E. (1972): *Norm og spontanitet*. Copenhagen: Gyldendal.

Marcussen, M. (2001): *OECD og idéspillet – Game over?* Copenhagen: Hans Reitzel.

Martinsen, K. (1989): *Omsorg, Sykepleie og Medisin. Historiske filosofiske essays*. Oslo: Tano.

Noddings, N. (1984): *Caring. Feminine Approach to Ethics and Moral Education*. University of California Press.

Petersen, K. (1997): 'Fra ekspansion til krise- udforskning af velfærdsstatens udvikling efter 1945', in: *Historisk tidsskrift* 2: 356-375.

Petersen, L. and Schmidt, M (2003): *Projekt Fælles Sprog*. Copenhagen: Akademisk Forlag.

Pierson, P. (2001): 'Introduction', in: Pierson, P. (ed.): *The New Politics of the Welfare State*. Oxford: Oxford University Press.

Sehested, K. (2002): 'How New Public Management reforms challenge the Roles of Professionals', in: *International Journal of Public Administration*, 25 (12): 1517-1541.

Selander, S. (ed.) (1988): *Kampen om yrkesutövning, status og kunskap: professionaliseringens sociala grund*. Lund: Studentlitteratur.

Witz, A. (1992): *Professions and Patriarchy*. London: Routledge.

Wærness, K. (1980): 'Omsorgen som lönearbete en begrebsdiskussion', in: *Kvinnovetenskabelig tidsskrift* nr. 3.

PART I
CARE AND FEMINIST THEORY IN
A GLOBAL PERSPECTIVE

Chapter 1

Social Research, Political Theory and the Ethics of Care in a Global Perspective

Kari Wærness

Introduction

What kind of social research should be argued for in relation to the enormous challenges that problems of globalization and changes in the cultures of survival and care represent for all of us? I will discuss this question here in light of my experiences as a feminist researcher in the field of care for nearly three decades. This research interest developed when in the 1970s I worked as a politically elected leader of the board of public social care and child protection services in my community – a community that is part of the Norwegian city of Bergen. In this political work we had to cope with a lot of challenging problems related to the care of children, disabled and elderly. I often felt a strong lack of relevant scientific knowledge when having to argue for more resources, new public services or reorganization of existing ones. I found the dominant scientific perspectives or paradigms in the political planning discourse on public services to be defective and inadequate for describing the problems in the real world of care in a way that would matter in the political and planning process.

In the context of a well-developed Scandinavian welfare state, many political feminists and feminist researchers found it necessary to develop new perspectives in research on care in order to strengthen the welfare of women and of those dependent on care and help in everyday life. The problem of how to carry out research that would really matter in policies and practice of care was, and still is, a challenging one, even in the Scandinavian context and even more in a global context. And many of the problems in the relationship between practice and policy relevant research are the same. Therefore I will argue that some of the experiences from development of this research field in Scandinavia are relevant to most researchers who want to carry out social research that matters with respect to policies and practices in the field of care and survival.

In this chapter I will first give a brief description of the field of 'research on care' in Scandinavia and then of how this research field in Scandinavia and Britain has developed since the 1970s. Thereafter, I will give a very short presentation of the international theoretical discourse on gender and care and present some thoughts from the new emerging field, feminist ethics of care. And finally I will argue that researchers need to take on more responsibility than they have done hitherto, to develop knowledge that could be a more relevant and influential tool in creating better care policies and practices, not only in the context of modern welfare states, but also from a global perspective.

Scandinavian research on care in the 1990s – two parallel discourses with different influence

'Care', as a definition of different types of activities in the welfare state, was common long before we had any women's studies. In connection with such activities we have established research activities, which in part go further back in time and which are based on other perspectives than feminist research. Research on care for the elderly is a good illustration of the differences between these lines of research. In this area we find a development where dominant paradigms in established gerontology – strengthened by socio-economic welfare expertise and market economic thinking – have contributed to an increasing extent towards defining the elderly and care of the elderly as a *socio-economic problem* (Eliasson 1996). Based on this view of the problem, efficiency and rational solutions are in demand and are attractive qualities in welfare services for the elderly. Feminist researchers[1] see other sides of the welfare services and have formulated perspectives that go against this established perspective. The new perspective is that researchers are more concerned about the real world of care – and do research on concrete care actions, skills, knowledge and ways of thinking on the practical level, at the bottom of the welfare services organizations' hierarchy. Based on this perspective, questions about what care really is and what it means both to those giving and those receiving care, become of key importance. Feminist researchers have criticized the established planning perspective, because it is not based on an adequate understanding of the distinctive nature of care and therefore often generates proposed reforms and measures, which aggravate the situation both for care workers and for those receiving care (Thorsen and Wærness 1999). Both planning research and feminist research in this area are normative in the sense that researchers speak both about the facts and what is good, desirable and possible. The normative perspective is, however, the most clearly expressed in many of the feminist inspired reports, as it is in such research studies that moral, human values and own views on values are most often discussed.

Today, we find these perspectives as parallel discourses in research on the welfare services (Wærness 1999). With the so-called 'quality assurance' way of thinking also becoming a dominant trend in the health and welfare sector, it seems clear that it is the planning perspective, which has the dominant influence on how these services become organized (Slagsvold 1999). The fundamental critique of this new

---

[1] Not everyone here, who I have defined as feminist researchers, has been or defines themselves as feminists. It is appropriate however to call their research 'feministic inspired research on care'.

way of thinking appears so far not to have had any effect on the public authorities' implementation of so-called quality assurance programmes in this sector. Based on the feminist inspired perspective, the problem with these quality assurance programmes is not just that they appear to be irrelevant to the concrete problems on a practical level. They can also sometimes help to create what Slagsvold (1995) calls *quasi-quality*, which means making the quality of care worse than it was before. The knowledge from feminist inspired research has not hitherto had any effect on the structure of the care organizations. The public discussion on how the health and welfare services should be changed is still dominated by academic experts who mainly use a language based on economic, technical and legal rationality – a language that is usually considered to be far removed from the experiences in the real world of care. For several years now, this real world has had key position in Scandinavian and British feminist research on care.

Scandinavian and British feminist research on care – development over time[2]

In the earliest phase of the Anglo-Saxon feminist research on care we can distinguish between two different discourses; one that places emphasis on care as work and one that places emphasis on the emotional aspects of care (Abel and Nelson 1990). Studies, which placed emphasis on the work content, analysed care as a woman-suppressing practice, full of routine and alienating tasks. Studies that placed emphasis on the emotional aspects, considered care to be a meaningful activity which makes women better people. We might name these perspectives 'the perspective of misery' and 'the perspective of dignity' respectively. In feminist research it is always easy to criticize studies based on one of these perspectives with the other perspective as a point of departure. To develop scientific knowledge on care that should matter in policy and planning it is still a great challenge how to balance these perspectives.

In the anthology *Caring: A Labour of Love* (Finch and Groves 1983) these perspectives are combined. All the authors in this book have been important participants in the British discourse on care and common to them all is that they study care as a physically and emotionally demanding *unpaid* job that women carry out in the home. The purpose of this book was to show the hidden care work in the family, how it is shared between men and women and what it costs the caregivers. Criticism was raised against this research, because it was too one-sided, both in the sense that it only focused on the caregivers and not on those receiving the care and that it only discusses informal care and not care as a paid and professional work (Baldwin and Twigg 1991, Morris 1991/92, Qureshi and Walker 1989).

Scandinavian feminist research on care included both unpaid and paid care from the start. Care was also defined as work and feelings and dealt with caregivers and those receiving care. The first research seminar on the subject was arranged

---

[2] I have based much of this paragraph on Szebeheley (1996) and Eliasson (1996).

in 1978 by the then Research Council of Norway's Secretariat for Social Research on Women under the heading 'Paid and unpaid care', and the topics discussed had a broad basis; care work in the private and public sector, children and care, women's self-organised help arrangements, care functions in families with small children, new roles for children, men and women, emotional fatigue in good-natured caring women in the welfare services and the development of professional nursing at the end of the 19th century. The seminar was based on the understanding that women had the main responsibility for care both in private relations and in the public sector and the following reasons were given for why it is necessary to look more deeply into the care phenomenon:

> in order to proceed in the work of extending the social scientific knowledge in this area, based on a women's liberation perspective, and to give the authorities a broader basis with respect to planning and implementing a care organization *that takes into consideration the needs of those giving and receiving care* (NAVF's Secretariat for Social Research on Women 1979, Foreword, my italics).

Norwegian feminist researchers appear here to be quite typical representatives of modernity in the sense that they show great optimism both with respect to faith in the importance of knowledge and to the friendliness of the Norwegian welfare state towards women. New definitions and distinctions in the field of care were gradually created, definitions that were intended to give clarification in the debate on welfare policy and thereby was believed to have an influence on welfare policy (Wærness 1982). Involvement in welfare policy was included in this research from the start. 'The social service state' and its importance from women's perspective became an important supplement to mainstream research on welfare, which up to the 1990s was mainly concerned with financial support, social security systems and the economic redistributive aspects of the welfare state.

The Anglo-Saxon and Scandinavian feminist-oriented research on care have gradually approached each other and today we can point to three lines of development in this research with respect to the understanding of what care is:

- from either feelings or (manual) work to both/and eventually also intellect-tual work
- from the family via unpaid women's work in the government's service, to the state as either a women-friendly and/or shaky social service state
- from focus on women as carers and care workers to a perspective that also includes those who need and receive care.

The main emphasis is still on care being 'something good', which is threatened by male, scientific, bureaucratic and market economic rationalities, values and interests and on care as being women's work. However, we can also see the outline of a few new development trends: The risk of encroaching on the other's freedom, which care gives the possibility for, has become a more important topic and there is increasing interest in studying possibilities for service schemes that may be good or better alternatives to more person-oriented and continuous care relations

(Gough 1996). There has also been increased focus, inter alia in studies of what is called 'the new paternity', on whether there is a 'masculine kind of care', which is different from the feminine kind (Brandth and Kvande 1996).

One risk of these expansions considered from a feminist viewpoint is that they can lead to the basis for the feminist-oriented research being forgotten, namely the desire to make visible the traditional female work and the social importance of this and thus help to raise women's marginal status in society. Though perhaps there is no great risk of this happening today in the *close to practice* research on care, i.e. research based on the real world of care. In such research activities one is constantly being reminded, in the same way as documented in the above-mentioned seminar report from 1978, that care obligations are not just distributed according to gender, but also according to social class (and what is becoming more visible in Scandinavia in the recent years also according to ethnicity), that the division of labour among women in this area has changed very much over time and that care-givers can have great power with respect to those dependent on care, even if they have little power and influence in other relations.

The political-sociological and empirically rooted research on care has had a strong position in Scandinavian feminist research. Scandinavian feminist researchers have participated very little, however, in the international development of political-normative theory on care. This does not mean that there are no important contributors in this area. Both the Swedish sociologist Rosmari Eliasson and to an even greater extent, the Norwegian nurse, philosopher and historian, Kari Martinsen, have given important theoretical contributions to care ethics, contributions, which in addition to being based on important philosophers, are also based on women's public care work in the past and present (Eliasson 1987, Eliasson-Lappalainen 1999 and Martinsen 1989, 1993, 1996, 2000). However, this work has still not reached the international theoretical debate on care and gender. Thus their influence on the care discourse in general, also in the Nordic countries, has hitherto been more limited than the influence of leading American feministic theorists in the field. The American feminist theorists have not been so much concerned about specific dilemmas and problems that the welfare state's care workers face. This is perhaps not so strange, if we take into consideration the big differences between the Scandinavian and American welfare state model. Greater understanding of this dominant division in feministic theory and research on care may contribute, however, to a more relevant insight into the care crisis that late-modern societies now appear to be in, regardless of which welfare state model they use as a basis.

The international theoretical discourse regarding care and gender

At the same time as the more close to practice and feminist welfare policy research on care grew in Scandinavia and in the UK, several pioneering feminist studies of a more theoretical and philosophical nature were published in the US. The most internationally known and influential study of a moral philosophic nature was Carol

Gilligan's book *In a Different Voice: Psychological Theory and Women's Development* (1982).[3]

One main focus in the debate following this book (the so-called Kohlberg-Gilligan controversy) has been the question whether women and men have a fundamentally different approach to morality, or expressed in today's terminology in feminist research; is morality linked to gender? Even if Gilligan has never clearly expressed that 'the different voice' she studies is always a female one, most people have interpreted her as describing a different approach to morality between the sexes. An important part of the rejection of her argumentation has been results from empirical studies, partly based on the same methodology as that used by Gilligan. These empirical studies show that other differences (class, ethnicity) may be as significant to differences in moral development as gender. In addition to these empirical studies, we also have got analyses based on other theories and ways of thinking that support the same argument.

The reason why it was so important for American feminists to reject Gilligan's argumentation was that it could be used to support the correctness of traditional gender roles in American (and Western) culture and thereby strengthen an understanding of men and women as fundamentally different. Several feminist theorists have strongly opposed Gilligan's argumentation and her book has been interpreted as a part of the 1980s backlash of feminism (Faludi 1991). Male theorists (see for instance Habermas 1990, Puka 1990) have claimed that the 'different voice', which Gilligan has identified, is a private and personal voice and that it represents a constricted, less universal type of moral thinking than the male theorists in this field present. This kind of argumentation reduces Gilligan's ethics of care to belonging only to the private sphere and thus expresses that it does not deserve to be dealt with as a part of moral theory.

What then about the public care services? Has Gilligan's ethics of care no relevance in this context? Based on the reality, which close to practice research on public care has shown and focuses on, theoretical conclusions like this seems very strange and make it difficult to see what relevance theoretical and philosophical discourses on morality and ethics have to empirical research in this field. The fundamental problem, which I was concerned about when I read Gilligan's book for the first time, was the following: Does Gilligan's book show a way of thinking about morality and ethics, which is very important, but which philosophy and modern social science suppress or ignore to a great extent? And can her distinction between an ethic of care and an ethic of justice be used as a conceptual tool to identify a number of important development trends in several different social institutions, which we otherwise would easily overlook? And furthermore: Are these development trends that we should be aware of, because they are development trends that most of us would consider to be negative and undesirable? With respect

---

[3] Other such works I can mention are Hochschild (1975), Chodorow (1989), Noddings (1984). There are also some very good empirical studies from the US that deal with gendered division of labour in the family with respect to care, but naturally enough these were related to the welfare state discussion that characterised the Scandinavian and British studies.

to such questions – the discussion of 'essentialism' in relation to Gilligan's work becomes irrelevant and limitation of care ethics to the private sphere directly outrageous. This academic discourse gives no theoretical tools with which to understand the care workers' problems in being able to provide human and personal care in a public sector that sets increasingly higher efficiency requirements. It also does not help us to understand the modern child family's problems and dilemmas in combining gender equality ideals with the demands of a fast-changing working life. It is hardly likely that the breadwinner-housewife family can be brought back to life on a large scale in a modern society, even for those who might so wish, and thus we face increasing pressure on private care resources. In addition there are more other factors that also lead to greater demand for care services in modern society. More people live longer with disabilities, more people live in single person households, more households consist of single mothers and children. And last but not least, due to the increases in economic welfare and in educational level, for a great part of the population, the normative standards for 'good enough care' increase. To exaggerate a bit, it might be that today for a great part of the population in the Western world 'the ideals of care go to heaven, at the same time as many care practices go to hell' as Hochschild (2003) expresses it. In modern Western societies we therefore face great challenges in combining the aim of greater gender equality in addition to increasing the access to good (enough) care. In this situation we need relevant theoretical discourses that can give input to empirical feminist research on care and thus good arguments for a feminist social policy. And in the recent years we have got some new theoretical contributions in feminist social sciences and ethics that exceed the debate on essentialism and reference of care ethic to the private sphere and therefore might be fruitful for a policy relevant feminist research on care.

Care ethic and political theory

In a thorough analysis of Gilligan's book (1982) Tronto (1993) makes us aware that Gilligan, like most male theorists, defines morality by a process of thinking rather as a set of substantive principles. As many have pointed out, the intellectual skill of solving hypothetical moral dilemmas does not necessarily result in a corresponding skill in acting morally. When we focus on care as a process, place emphasis on care as practice and analyse care ethics from such an angle, it is relatively easy to be aware that the analysis will be incomplete if we do not make care a key topic also of the political discourse. Care ethics must be discussed both on the basis of a moral and political context. In order to do this, we must break three boundaries, which apply in the academic mainstream discourse on morality and politics (Tronto 1993:6-11). Firstly, we must break the boundary, which sees morality and politics as separate spheres. Care can serve both as a moral value and as a basis for how to achieve a good society politically. Secondly, we must break the boundary, which says that moral assessments shall be made from a distanced and uncommitted position, because this boundary means that everything to do with feelings, the real world and political circumstances will be irrelevant or of secondary importance. Thirdly, we must break the boundary between the public and private sector, as has been argued for some time in feminist research. Breaking these boundaries does not necessarily mean that they must be done away with, but that they should be drawn up differently, if women are to be equal participants in public life.

In order to progress in the thinking on new moral boundaries Tronto (1993:105-107) analyses care as a process in four phases: 1) Acknowledge the existence of a need for care that should be met (caring about), 2) assume responsibility for this acknowledged need for care and determine how this should be met (taking care of), 3) the direct work in meeting this need for care (care-giving), 4) the recipient's situation after care has been given (care-receiving). Even if these phases can overlap each other in practice, this division is fruitful in order to identify several aspects of the gender and class-related division of responsibility and labour with respect to care, which also makes the care issue in today's society relevant for further development of political theory. Here are a few important examples: Men's care responsibility for the family has traditionally been limited to 'taking care of' (phase 2), while women have responsibility for providing specific care-giving (phase 3). The division of labour between a doctor and nursing staff can be described in the same way, even if in the health sector we eventually have a hierarchy within phase 2, where also leaders in traditional female professions have (subordinate) places. By including phase 4, we have to realize that the original definition of the need for care was not necessarily correct, that recipients could assess their situation differently to the caregivers. When we define care in this way as practice and process, it is clear that there are many possibilities for conflict between and within the levels. These may be value conflicts or conflicts regarding allocation of scarce resources in the form of time or money. In the real world you will hardly find care processes that can be described as being completely free of such conflicts, if we include all these four phases.

From a purely conceptual point of view, care is both particular and universal. What is construed to be adequate care may vary between cultures over time and between different groups in society. Despite these variations, care is a universal aspect in human existence. All people need care, even if the need requirement varies, not just based on cultural differences, but also on biological differences. A baby cannot survive without care, and disease, disability and ageing mean that the need is greater than it would otherwise be. Therefore, care is not universal with respect to the specific needs in question, but everyone needs some kind of care.

In both the Western world and in many other cultures, direct care giving (phase 3) has always been a job assigned to the lowest groups in the hierarchy; women, slaves, servants. The direct and specific care for children, as well as for the sick and the elderly has nearly always been exclusively delegated to women. In our late-modern society specific care work is still downgraded, unpaid or poorly paid and to an overwhelming extent left to those who have least power in society. A consequence of the imbalanced distribution of care roles and care work is that the relatively most privileged groups can ignore much of the strain care entails, because they never have to face this. Tronto (1993:121) calls this privilege 'privileged irresponsibility'. This concept might be useful in explaining why the ap-

proach to the care problems until now has been so marginal in the political discourse and why the male intellectual elite so easily refers care ethics to the private
sphere. Women belonging to the elite do not immediately assume such a position
of 'privileged irresponsibility'. To several of the pioneers in women's studies it
was the tension between the academic world's definition of reality and family life's
requirement for everyday care that gave the inspiration to theoretical rethinking of
everyday life (Smith 1987). The whole of the growth of feminist research in opposition to the established academic world can perhaps be said to be a result of large
groups of women being given access to the academic world, but without it being
possible in any simple way to hand over the practical care of their own children or
the family in general to other women. This was not an easy matter economically or
ideologically for most women in the Western world who entered the Academia in
the 1970s and who eventually began to make their mark in the academic and political debate. The time of house-maids in middle-class households was mainly over
and other justifiable and financially reasonable child care services for working and
studying mothers was in short supply at the time large groups of women populated
the institutions of higher education. Feminists have argued strongly for several different practical measures to make it easier for women to combine work and motherhood. Many have also argued in favour of the need to change the ideology that
links mother and child so closely together by defining mother's care as being
unique and necessary for a child's development and welfare. This has partly been
done through historical studies to show that mother's love, in the sense of how we
have defined it in our time, is not something 'naturally' given, but is a modern ideology, which has helped keep women at home (Badinter 1981, Haavind 1975). By
highlighting the reality of fathers' increasing care for their children and of the advantages of different types of professional child care from an increasingly younger
age, Western feminism have helped to change the understanding of motherhood on
which family law and much of the welfare legislation have been based. In several
Western countries the basis of the legislation in these areas has also changed 'from
relational to individual motherhood' (Syltevik 1996). It must be said that feminism
in the Scandinavian countries has succeeded to some extent both with respect to
socio-political measures and ideological changes, in that it has become easier for
women in these countries to combine motherhood and paid work. Use of paid care
leave has increased considerably, fathers participate to a greater extent in this leave
(Brandth and Kvande 1996), and the number of places in state-subsidised kinder-
gartens has increased drastically. The gender equality ideal appears to be in strong
evidence among today's families with small children and in the public sector. It is
even acceptable that men in relatively high positions can leave meetings at work,
because they have to pick their children up from kindergarten. On the other hand,
we are far from having realized any gender equality with respect to salary and career or with respect to workload in the home. Many parents of small children also
probably pay a high price in the form of a heavy workload when trying to live up
to today's ideal of gender equality (Syltevik 2000).

If we take a closer look at the changes on the labour market, the trend in the
Nordic countries today, as in the rest of the modern world, is towards demanding
increasingly more of each employee, at least if this person wants to make a career.

The labour organizations have become 'greedier institutions' and market-orientation has also increased in the public sector. Today, when according to the Norwegian gender equality ombudsman, pregnant women appear to be the victim of unlawful discrimination at work and help with the housework is introduced as a perk for women in career jobs, this is perhaps also a sign that Norway is in a trend where greater gender equality can only be achieved by increasing the social differences between women, as several studies have pointed out apply in other Western countries (Anderson 2000). This means that more of the direct care work must be handed over to low-paid women and as in order to achieve managerial positions, women must achieve some of the 'privileged irresponsibility' with respect to care that hither to in the era of the welfare state has mainly been reserved for men. Perhaps this trend today is about to become just as strong as the trend that men are about to give up some of their 'privileged irresponsibility' by using their right to care leave and having responsibility for collecting the children from kindergarten. Both of these development trends will lead to greater gender equality. But the latter trend will also result in greater social differences between women in a way that probably will also reduce the chance of care values gaining a bigger place in the *political* discourse. Regardless of how we might assess today's development trends with respect to distribution of care responsibilities, we need greater political focus on working conditions for those care workers who perform the specific everyday care of our children, the sick, disabled and elderly. We also need political focus on what division of responsibility and labour in care we want to have and what division actually exists between the family and the political authorities.

'The rationality of caring' – a new concept in research on development trends in public care

As already mentioned, Scandinavian research on care has not had much influence in the theoretical debate on the topic. One conceptualization – 'the rationality of caring' – created in the early phase of the empirically based research on care (Wærness 1984), has however to some extent become part of the international feminist discourse (see Gordonetal 1996). This concept was constructed on the basis of a kind of grounded theory approach in an empirical study of public home-helpers, in addition to being inspired by Arlie Hochschild's concept 'the sentient actor' (Hochschild 1975). This concept functioned well in making visible that both rational action, reason and feelings were important for providing good care both in the private and public sphere. This concept was also important in showing that the rationality which dominates in planning and research on public care, overlooks important aspects of what is important knowledge and available courses of action in order to be able to provide good care (Wærness and Gough 1985).

In socio-political planning there is little understanding that the instrumental rationality, which forms the basis of planning and organization, has limited validity when providing care for individual persons. The general knowledge, which is interesting and useful to administrators and politicians, is often of little help to first line care workers. In order to solve the specific problems in the real world of care, we require a way of thinking, which is *contextual* and *descriptive*, rather than *formal* and *abstract.* The concept 'the rationality of caring' suggests that personal knowledge and a certain ability and opportunity to understand what is specific in each situation where help is required, are important prerequisites in order to be able to provide good care. This means that human and moral qualities in public care can only be elicited in situations where there is not a lot of bustle, but where there is enough *quiet* so that those requiring help are confident and sure that the helper sees them as persons with specific needs. Or in other words; that in his or her state of helplessness, a person feels to be in good hands. This also means that each helper must not be too busy. So far I have not seen that Scandinavian economic studies on 'efficiency' in the public sector have taken into consideration this important aspect of care-giving work. No wonder perhaps, since neoclassical economic theory has no room for concepts of intimacy, interdependence and nurturance and there is no concept of value beyond that given by atomistic, individual utility (Nelson 2003:117).

Several empirical studies on public care have been able to confirm the fruitfulness of theorising based on the concept of the rationality of caring as a critical understanding of the type of modernization that the Scandinavian public care services have undergone in recent years (Bungum 1994, Christensen 1998, Gough 1987, Szebehely 1995, Slagsvold 1995). As a 'sensitising concept' (Blumer 1969:147-148) this concept has proved to be useful in showing the negative aspects of this modernization, to which it may be difficult to relate. This may be the explanation why most of the research on planning and public reports in this area ignore the results from the feminist research on care (Wærness 1999). When several researchers, who have worked on the basis of this perspective for a long time, publish a book entitled *Blir omsorgen borte? Eldreomsorgens hverdag i den senmoderne velferdsstat* (Is care disappearing? The real world of care for the elderly in the late-modern welfare state), we cannot expect to arouse any special interest among planners and researchers within the economic discourse, despite the interest from professions working in the field and despite our basis for critique being the following:

> Our critical view is not based on a kind of nostalgic understanding that care for the elderly was better 'before'. It is primarily based on the fact that we, as experienced researchers in this area, have found several examples of good kinds of care practice and relations between caregivers and those needing help in today's care services that we believe are about to be run over or disappear in the modernization process in progress in this sector. We consider that planners and administrators do not pay enough consideration to the distinctive character of care work when they propose changes and reforms in this sector. The fact that we can find home helps and nurses who provide good care, is rather in spite of than due to what the care organization arranges for (Thorsen and Wærness 1999:20).

In economists' analyses of efficiency and productivity in the nursing and care sector we find cause to express certain reservations and doubt regarding the use or value of the efficiency measures used (refer for example to Erlandsen, et al. 1997, Edvardsen et al. 2000). This can be expressed as follows:

One may ask the question whether we are so far removed from data for real nursing and care services that the study has no value. We would argue that the efficiency measures relate after all to variables and factors of great interest to the municipalities (Edvardsen et al. 2000:10).

But even with the reservations regarding the validity of the measures that this study gives voice to in the text, one can conclude in the summary that the calculations tell which municipalities can function as 'teachers' for the inefficient municipalities. Important objections to such measurements of efficiency, which the feminist research on care have made, are usually not discussed in economic studies on efficiency in this sector, if there is any reference at all to the fact that such research exists. Feminist economists argue that the present feminist analysis of neoclassical economics at a basic emotional and motivational level is suppressed because it is feared (Nelson 2003:111). The relation between feminist and economic scientific discourse on public care in Scandinavia does not seem to differ from this general relation between feminism and mainstream economics.

The need for a new paradigm in research on care

As already mentioned feminist inspired research on public care has had quite a significant scope in the Scandinavian countries, without this having any special influence on planning and organization of welfare services. The existing Nordic studies on philosophical and theoretical care thinking, which are based on women's care work in the public sector and in particular, Kari Martinen's historical and philosophical studies in the last few years have however had increasing influence among nurses. A separate book about her care thinking for use in basic nursing training has now been published (Alvsvåg and Gjengedal 2000). Her work has formed a school in Nordic research on nursing and her normative care theory is claimed to have had a great influence on nurses and student nurses (Kirkevoll 2000). In the same way as the empirical research on women within the field of care, this care theory is very critical of the economical and technological rationality that dominates the development in today's public health and care services. This theoretical work is also not in dialogue with the economical discourse and thus has no influence on the planning and organization of these services. The influence on attitudes from this way of thinking, which takes place through education of care workers, can therefore make matters worse: Those working in this sector can experience increasing frustration due to the gap between how care should be according to what they learn as students and how it is practised. And this can also mean that even more of those who have the possibility to do so, seek jobs where they do not have to provide direct care for individuals requiring help.

An increasing gap between demand and supply of public care services during the recent years in Scandinavian countries has partly been filled by immigrant care workers. When elderly Norwegian patients in a nursing home tell a journalist 'that the colour of the hands does not matter when it comes to providing good care', this statement can be taken to support an assumption that important basic elements in giving and receiving care and nursing today are connected to universal values. This may be true, even if there also exist very important cultural differences and we in the Western world today can find different ideals of care, named traditional, post-modern, cold modern and warm modern (Hochschild 2003:213-223).

This basic universalism implies that skilled care workers today may easily cross borders in order to get jobs. In itself this might seem very positive in a globalising world. There are however some very negative distributional effects of this universalism. We can say that there is going on what has been called 'a care drain' (Hochschild 2003) from South to North – a transfer of care workers from the poorer to the richer countries, either we measure poverty in terms of money or in need for care services. This transfer probably also contributes to the continued devaluation of care in the modern world.

A problematic relationship between a dominant economic discourse and other social and humanistic approaches in policy oriented research is a general problem today both on national and international levels of policy and planning. Martha Nussbaum (1998) discusses this as a very serious problem in the field of development economy. She criticizes the dominant economic profession to be extremely self-satisfied and having a tendency to repudiate non-formal and foundational work as irrelevant to its concern. On the other hand, she criticizes philosophers for mainly communicating with their own kind and for often not being able to discuss problems at a high degree of sophistication in a clear and jargon-free language with concrete factual and narrative examples. Nussbaum argues strongly that feminist theorists should involve themselves more in this field, interest themselves more in the facts and people's experiences and communicate more directly with planners, politicians and workers within development economy. The description Nussbaum gives of the problems in development economy has many similarities with the problems I have described in social research on care in the context of a modern welfare state. Today we see a new academic field emerging on the international academic agenda that is of great relevance in relation to these problems. This field, with roots in different academic disciplines, can be named 'feminist ethics of care' (Sevenhuijsen 2002). This ethic of care is inherently characterized by a relational ontology both in the descriptive and the normative respects. This is encapsulated in the idea that individuals can only exist because they are members of various networks of care and responsibility, for good or for bad. The self can only exist through and with others and vice versa. The ethic of care takes the idea of self-in-relationship as the point of entry for thinking about obligations and responsibility. The moral subject in the discourse of care dives in a network of relations and (inter) dependence in which she/he has to find balances between different forms of care: for the self, for others and the relation between these. The ethic of care implies a radically different account between morality and politics than political programs that are based on constructions of individual right holders as the 'basic units' of society. Because it starts from a relational ontology it focuses primarily on the question of what politics could mean for the safeguarding of responsibility and relationship in human practice and interaction. Social policies should accordingly be governed by the responsiveness to the needs of those with whom they are concerned. And the caring attitude should not be confined to private interactions, but should also count as a public virtue, which should enter the considerations of policy-makers. In the feminist care ethics responsibility is crucial for social policy. But instead of deriving responsibilities from rights (a top-down model) the care ethic starts political reasoning from an understanding of interconnection and relationship and therefore from knowledge about daily practices of care and responsibility and the dilemmas implied there. The feminist ethic of care does not argue that care is the only value or the value that should always be given the highest priority in social planning and policy. The argument is rather that care, justice and freedom are three different value domains that have to be balanced in all human activities (Staveren 2001).

The theoretical works in feminist ethic of care so far seem very promising in order to bridge the gap between theoretical and empirical research in this field and to get more theorists involved in the concrete problems in the real world of care in a way that also practicians in health and social services could feel comfortable with. It should also be a responsibility for theorists and empirical researchers in this field to try to break the dominance of the economic discourse in planning and organization of public care services. Though this is not easy, it should not stop us from trying. Care researchers should also try to influence the education of care workers so that they become more aware of how organizational structures create problems with respect to uniting ideals about good care and today's economic efficiency requirement. In the longer term the goal should of course be not only to break the dominance of the economic discourse, but the more ambitious one, to try to develop a genuine cooperation on research across the two discourses, which currently run parallel and have such a different influence on the policies and planning on all political levels in the modern world. The fact that feminist economics is a growing field, which also is closely related to the feminist ethics of care, might be one reason to be somewhat optimistic in this connection.

References

Abel, E. og Nelson, M. (1990): *Circles of Care: Work and Identity in Women's Lives.* New York: State University Press.

Abrahamsen, B. (1986): *Harde yrker i myk sektor.* Oslo: Institutt for Samfunnsforskning.

Alvsvåg, H. og Gjengedal, E. (ed.) (2000): *Omsorgstenkning. En innføring i Kari Martinsens forfatterskap.* Bergen: Fagbokforlaget.

Anderson, B. (2000): *Doing the Dirty Work? The Global Politics of Domestic Labour.* London: Zed Books.

Badinter, E. (1981): *Det naturligste av verden? Om morskjærlighetens historie.* Oslo: Universitetsforlaget.

Baldwin, S. and Twigg, J. (1991): 'Women and Community Care – Reflections on a Debate', in: Maclean, M and Groves, D (eds.): *Women's Issue in Social Policy.* London and New York: Routledge.

Blumer, H. (1969): *Symbolic Interactionism. Perspective and Methods.* Berkeley: University of California Press.

Brandth, B. and Kvande, E. (1996): 'Nye fedre i likestilte familier', in: Brandth, B. and Moxnes, K. (eds.) *Familie for tiden. Stabilitet og forandring*: 161-176. Trondheim: Tano Aschoug.

Bungum, B. (1994): *Effektivisering av omsorg. Kjønnsperspektiv på omstilling av offentlig omsorgsarbeid.* Hovedfagsoppgave ved Institutt for sosiologi og statsvitenskapelige fag. Trondheim: Universitetet i Trondheim.

Chodorow, N. J. (1989): *Feminism and Psychoanalytic Theory.* Cambridge: Polity Press.

Christensen, K. (1998): *Omsorg og arbejd: en sociologisk studie av ændringer i den hjemmebaserede omsorg.* Dr.polit. avhandling. Bergen: Sosiologisk Institutt, Bergen Universitet.

Clement, G. (1996): *Care, Autonomy and Justice. Feminism and the Ethics if Care.* Colorado and Oxford: Westview Press.

Edvardsen, D. m.fl. (2000): *Effektivitet i pleie- og omsorgssektoren.* Rapport 2/2000. Stiftelsen Frischsenteret for samfunnsøkonomisk forskning.

Eliasson, R. (1987): *Forskningsetik och perspektivval.* Stockholm: Studentlitteratur.

Eliasson, R. (1996): 'Efterord', in: Eliasson, R. (ed.): *Omsorgens skiftninger.* Lund: Studentlitteratur.

Eliasson-Lappalainen, R. (1999): 'Etik och moral i äldreomsorgens vardag', in: Christensen, K. and Syltevik, L.J. (eds.): *Omsorgens forvitring? Antologi om velferdspolitiske utfordringer,* 229-240. Bergen: Fagbokforlaget.

Erlandsen, E. m.fl. (1997): *Effektivitet, kvalitet og organisering av pleie og omsorgssektoren i norske kommuner.* SNF-rapport Nr. 91/97.

Faludi, S. (1991): *Backlash.* New York: Crown Publishers.

Finch. J., and Groves, D. (eds.) (1983): *A Labour of Love: Women, Work and Caring.* London: Routledge & Kegan Paul.

Gilligan, C. (1982): *In a Different Voice: Psychological Theory and Women's Development.* Harvard University Press.

Gordon, Gough, R. (1987): *Hemhjälp till gamla.* Stockholm: Arbetslivcentrum.

Gordon, S., Brenner, P. and Noddings (eds.) (1996): *Caregiving. Reading in Knowledge, Practice, Ethics and Politics.* Philadelphia: University of Pennsylvania Press.

Gough, R. (1996): *Personlig assistans: En social bemästringsstrategi.* Göteborg: GIL förlaget.

Griffith, M. (1995): *Feminism and the Self: The Web of Identity.* London: Routledge.

Haavind, H. (1975): *Myten om den gode mor.* Oslo: Pax Forlag.

Habermas, J. (1990): *Moral Consciousness and Communicative Action.* Cambridge: MIT Press.

Hochschild, A.R. (1975): 'The Sociology of Feeling and Emotion: Selected Possibilities'. pp. 280-307, in: Millman, M. and Kanter, R.M. (eds.): *Another Voice.* New York: Anchor Books.

Hochschild, A.R. (1995): 'The Politics of Culture: Traditional, Cold Modern and Warm Modern Ideals of Care', in: *Social Politics: International Studies in Gender, State and Society 2,* no 2: 331-46.

Hochschild, A.R. (2003): *The Commercialization of Intimate life. Notes from Home and World.* Berkeley, University of California Press.

Kirkevoll, M. (2000): 'Utviklingstrekk i Kari Martinsens forfatterskap', in Alvsvåg, H. and Gjengedal, H. (eds.): *Omsorgstenkning. En innføring i Kari Martinsens forfatterskap.* Bergen: Fagbokforlaget.

Martinsen, K. (1989): *Omsorg, sykepleie og medisin.* Bergen: Tano.

Martinsen, K. (1993): *Fra Marx til Løgstrup. Om moral, samfunnskritikk og sanselighet i sykepleien.* Oslo: Tano.

Martinsen, K. (1996): *Fenomenologi og omsorg. Tre dialoger med etterord av Katie Eriksson.* Oslo: Tano Aschehoug.

Martinsen, K. (2000): *Øyet og kallet. Sykepleiefilosofiske betrakninger.* Bergen: Fagbokforlaget.

Morris, J (1991/92): "'Us' and 'them'? Feminist Research, Community Care and Disability', in: *Critical Social Policy,* 11,3.

NAVF's Sekretariat for kvinneforskning 1979: *Lønnet og ulønnet omsorg.* Arbeidsnotat 5, 79.

Nelson, E.A. (2003): 'Once More, with Feeling: Feminist Economics and the Ontological Question', in *Feminist Economics*, 9, 1, March 2003.

Nelson, E. and Noddings, N. (1984): *Caring*. Berkley: University of California Press.

Nussbaum, M.C. (1998): 'Public Philosophy and International Feminism', in *Ethics*, 108, 4: 762-797.

Puka, B. (1990): 'The Liberation of Caring: A different Voice for Gilligan's different Voice'. *Hypatia* 55, 1.

Qureshi, H. and Walker, A. (1989): *The Caring Relationship: Elderly people and their families*. London: Macmillan.

Sevenhuijsen, S.L. (1998): *Citizenship and the Ethics of Care. Feminist Considerations on Justice, Morality and Politics*. London and New York: Routledge.

Sevenhuijsen, S.L. (2002): 'A Third Way? Moralities, Ethics and Families. An approach through Ethic of Care' in Carling, A. (ed): *Analysing Families, Morality and Rationality in Policy and Practice*: 129-144. London and New York: Routledge.

Slagsvold, B. (1995): *Mål eller mening*. Rapport nr. 1. Oslo: Norsk Gerontologisk Institutt.

Slagsvold, B. (1999): 'Kvalitet og kontekst' in Thorsen, K. and Wærness, K. (ed.): *Blir omsorgen borte?*: 105-126. Oslo: ad Notam Gyldendal.

Smith, D.E.(1987): *The Everyday Life as Problematic*. Oxford: Open University Press.

Staveren, I. van, (2001): *The Values of Economics. An Aristotelian View*. London and New York: Routledge.

Syltevik, L.J. (1996): *Fra relasjonelt til individualisert alenemoderskap. En studie av alenemødre som mødre, lønnsarbeidere og klienter i velferdsstaten*. Bergen: Sosiologisk institutt, University of Bergen.

Syltevik, L.J. (2000): *Differensierte familieliv. Familiepraksis i Norge på slutten av 1990-tallet*. Rapport 2/2000. Bergen: Senter for samfunnsforskning, University of Bergen.

Szebehely, M. (1995): *Vardagens organisering. Om vårdbitrâden och gamla i hemtjänsten*. Lund: Arkiv Forlag.

Szebehely, M. (1996): 'Omsorg og omsorgsforskning', in: Eliasson, R. (ed.): *Omsorgens skiftninger*. Lund: Studentlitteratur.

Thorsen, K. and Wærness, K. (1999): 'Eldreomsorg i omforming', in: Thorsen, K. and Wærness, K. (ed.): *Blir omsorgen borte? Eldreomsorgens hverdag i den senmoderne velferdsstaten*, 11-24. Oslo/Bergen: Ad Notam Gyldendal.

Tronto, J.C. (1993): *Moral Boundaries. A Political Argument for an Ethic of Care*. New York: Routledge.

Wærness, K. (1982): *Kvinneperspektiver på sosialpolitikken*. Bergen: Universitetsforlaget.

Wærness, K. (1984): 'The Rationality of Caring', in: Söder, M. (ed.): *Economic and Industrial Democracy*: 185-212. London: Sage Publications. Published also in: Saasson, A.S. (ed.) (1987): *Women and the State*. London: Hutchinson. And in Gordon, S. et.al. (eds.) (1996): *Caregiving* Philadelphia: PENN

Wærness, K. (1996): 'The Rationality of Caring': 231-255, in: Gordon, S., Benner, P. and Noddings, N. (eds.) (1996): *Caregiving*. Philadelphia: PENN.

Wærness, K. (1999): 'Hva er hensikten med sammenliknende studier av effektiviteten i pleie-og omsorgssektoren i norske kommuner?' *Sosialøkonomen*, 1/99.

PART II
DILEMMAS IN THE
NORDIC WELFARE STATE(S) AND
THEIR PROVISION OF CARE

Chapter 2

The Modernization of Power in Norwegian Home Care Services

Karen Christensen

Introduction

Since the 1970s the Norwegian public care services have undergone a process of modernization. In the light of research into Norwegian home help services I will investigate this process as a development that can be broken down into three phases: *traditional care*, followed by *modern services*, followed by *late modern outputs*. In order to present the analysis behind these three phases I will use a model that describes relevant phases and dimensions of power. The more general aim of this chapter is to show the richness of using a power perspective when analysing the modernization of care and the challenges that ensue.

Power and care services

Hannah Arendt (1996) points out two types of power, which she characterises as potential and relational. According to Arendt, power is a basic aspect of all social life. However, a precondition of power is social relations, and this in turn presupposes a public space capable of containing at least two people. Without these requirements, no power can exist. Assuming the existence of such relations and of public space, one can start by drawing attention to potential power, since one can have power without using it. Furthermore, power can be exerted in different ways. Very often we think of power merely negatively, as authority. But it can also be used positively, to strengthen the autonomy of individuals. As I will demonstrate below, this positive power becomes important when facing the challenges in the field of care.

On the basis of the assumption that power only exists within a public space, we can differentiate several levels of power, first and foremost *structural power* and *relational power*. Structural power exists in virtue of social structures, which can be economic, legal, ideological and organizational. A researcher interested specifically in this kind of power will work on a macro-sociological level. In addition, power exists in the everyday interactions between people and in the way these interactions are organized, for example in the way care services for the elderly are organized. Thus we also have to talk about relational power.[1]

Relational power adds something important to structural power in that it is relatively concrete and is directly instantiated by actors and, through their actions, in practice. In other words, relational power manifests itself in interactions between actors and is characterized by the kind of relation those actors actually have at any one time. From this perspective power is always an aspect of interaction, although this does not necessarily imply that it is always actively exerted.

Related to the basic aspect of power as something that is always present, at least in potential, we can distinguish between *explicit* and *implicit power*.[2] Whereas explicit power is exerted in pursuit of explicit purposes, implicit power is exerted in ways that do not involve the direct verbalizations of explicit power; it might be seen, for example, in a casual or off-hand gesture, whether intentional or unintentional. It is therefore necessary to be aware of the existence of implicit power, which is not verbalized and concrete, but which can, for example, be documented by research about practice in the care field. Another writer to have inspired this kind of thinking is Bourdieu (1996), through his discussion of 'symbolic power'. Here as well the concept emphasizes the relation between the individual and her/his environment as something that presupposes not only consciousness but the entire individual – the body as a whole. Indeed, it is by means of the latter that symbolic power operates in concrete interactions. Power is not just about being persuaded; power is also manifested through accepted symbols. The authority we associate with a white uniform is an obvious example of implicit power.

Thus we have structural and relational power, and we have a dimension that expresses the difference between explicit and implicit power. But this is still not sufficient to allow the construction of a model, in other words, a simplified representation of reality. It is important, especially in this context, to introduce an intermediate position that can accommodate reflections, attitudes and value orientations, whether conscious or not. One example of such would be the way we typically think of ageing as something that leads to retirement from public participation in society. One of the ideological sources of this way of thinking lies in patterns of structural power, and at the same time it will play a part in the concrete acts that make up the interactions between caregivers and care recipients. The important

---

[1] In sociology these kind of different perspectives are based on different theoretical traditions. Thus we have (among others) the classical Marxist perspective primarily on a macro-sociological level. This is very much about power in terms of structures, classes, social positions and their related resources. And we have (among others) the modern symbolic interactionistic perspective on a micro-sociological level. This tradition represents an understanding of power by starting with the way people interact with each other and themselves by means of symbols (see for example Ritzer 2000). But we do not have to regard these different perspectives as incompatible. In fact, the model shows that they are compatible.

[2] Related to this is a discussion about power with and without actors. But since this is not essential to an analysis of the development of the care services, I will not bring it into my model.

point about this intermediate position is that it makes it clear that women and men, for example in care relations, are not just victims of structural power, but also and always act individually in response to certain reflections.

On the basis of these ideas about power I have constructed a model to illuminate power in the public care services.[3]

Figure 2.1 Powerspaces

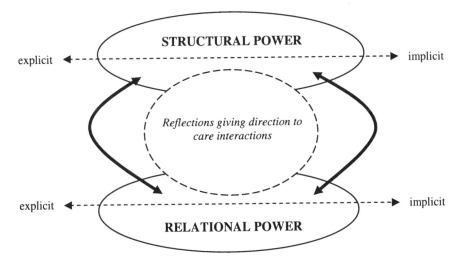

This model illustrates that power occurs within two operational spaces: one of these spaces is defined by structural power, the other by relational power. The intermediate area overlaps with both main spaces, since the mental processes that it encompasses are never completely disconnected from the structural level and are at the same time a very important determining factor in care relations.

On an analytical level there is an important so-called sensitive concept[4] involved in this intermediate position, namely that of the *rationality of caring*, a concept that has been developed empirically by the Norwegian sociologist Kari Wærness (1984). This is based on what is known as 'the sentient actor model' (Hochschild 1975), which regards the actor as both rational and emotional. The rationality of caring implies a critique of the dominant formal rationality,[5] yet it is

---

[3] This model is also inspired by ideas from my ongoing project about *Services for the mentally disabled*, financed by the Research Council of Norway.

[4] In contrast to definitive concepts, which are clearly defined in advance, sensitive concepts are 'open', and merely provide the researcher with a direction in which to look (Blumer 1954). Many classical sociological concepts are sensitive, for example, class, culture and institutions.

[5] To illustrate this with a concrete example from relational care practice, an actor with a formal rationality orientation who performs some (instrumental) washing tasks in the home

also a rival, or at the very least an alternative, to the latter. The concept of the rationality of caring therefore deserves further attention when considering power as something used positively by caregivers as a means of bringing benefits to care recipients. In my own study of home-based care, one particular empirical example of a phenomenon that animates and motivates care-rational actions is conceptualised as *other-orientation* (Christensen 1998a). The term 'other-orientation' refers to a type of dialogue that can arise in care-giving, which aims to strengthen individuality and self-determination in the recipient; for such a dialogue to develop, the caregiver must have a certain level of power and a certain freedom of action (in terms of sufficient time, relative independence in making resolves etc.). This other-orientation could be an example of what has been called *bonding social capital* in research concerning women and volunteer work, a term signifying activities that strengthen close community (Leonard 2000). Core elements of this social capital are trust, strong *social* norms, help freely given (not coerced) and without expectations of return. Because social capital can be realised to different degrees and on different levels of social networks, it is a concept that may serve in the current context to widen my own concept of other-orientation to encompass, not just bonding social capital within the space of relational power, but also, more inclusively, the possibilities of connecting this relational power to structural power in ways that produce network conditions for the strengthening of the community within society. In this perspective, the richness of the rationality of caring concept is that it shows us the kind of (alternative) rationality that underlies this social capital and the various challenges implied by that rationality in different periods.

Modernization of home-based services

In what follows I will use the power model as a tool to review the development of the field of public home help services. This means I will point out aspects of both structural and relational power in the three phases of this development and discuss how power can be used in accordance with the care-rationality.

Roughly speaking, the three phases correspond to the three decades of the 1970s, 1980s and 1990s, although certain characteristics of one phase may well originate in the foregoing phase. Norway founded its welfare state following World War II, since when it has been progressively developed. Home help has its roots in voluntary work organised by women's organizations in Oslo in the 1950s. It took 17 years before the state began to subsidise it, which it did in 1969 (Wærness 1982). Subsequently, home help became increasingly successful, and its activities were expanded. By the 1970s Norway had become a typical Scandinavian welfare state. As such it embodied a high degree of universalism[6] and assumed conside-

---

of an elderly woman will act without regard to individual needs, or the conditions that justify the activity, and without engaging in a dialogue with the recipient. The instrumental act consists in doing just the washing tasks and nothing more.

[6] That means providing services not just to those in low social positions but also to the middle classes.

rable responsibility for the social security of its citizens (Esping-Andersen 1990). In the 1980s this picture began to change. Certain kinds of service were cut back, and ideologies were developed to legitimate the reductions. By the 1990s it had become clear that the welfare state no longer assumed all the responsibilities it had taken on in the 1970s and 1980s. Many of these responsibilities were transferred to the individual (which in practice means also the individual's relatives). The changes also entailed greater involvement of the private sector, which in this context encompasses everything from informal family networks and voluntary organizations, to commercially provided services.

Traditional care

This first phase follows the establishment of publicly organised home-based care. Some early Norwegian care studies describe the characteristics of this phase. These studies (Lie 1987, Ones 1988, Wærness 1982) show that, in the field of home help, relations between caregivers and care recipients were characterised by qualities such as nearness and consideration for the individual recipient. Furthermore, there were few rules for the care work, and although caregivers had no theoretical knowledge, they had considerable experience-based knowledge of care work in general and of housework from their own private homes. A striking feature of the organization of care work during this phase was that employees had few but regular clients. Together with the fact that there were few rules for the work, this meant that it was possible to develop a qualitative nearness to the individual elderly person. The care researcher Marta Szebehely (1995) has identified three ways in which home help work was organised in Sweden. She calls the model that she constructs to account for the above-mentioned characteristics a 'traditional model'. Thus there existed structural organizational conditions for home help in this period, providing opportunities for the development of care-rational power. But there were further structural conditions for care-rational power during this phase, which lay on a higher, macro-level.

From a legal point of view home help work was covered by the Law on Social Care of 1964. But in the practice of caregiving, no attention was given to these legal aspects. Consequently, control and regulation of home help was weak and of marginal consideration.

With the possible exception of the social-political idea that the elderly should have the possibility to live in their own homes as long as possible, there was no dominant national ideology during this phase. This means there was little ideological significance in the work that was actually done during care work. The way this work was carried out therefore depended primarily on the value-orientation of the individual employee. Studies of this phase (Lie 1987:60, Wærness 1982:146) show a general desire to develop personal relations with clients, and the presence of altruistic motives among caregivers.[7] This kind of value-orientation can be under-

---

[7] This altruism is also one of the central elements that leads me to the concept of other-orientation based on data for the late 1980s (Christensen 1998b).

stood in terms of the experience of care and housework that these caregivers had from their own homes.

It is crucial to mention that, especially during this early phase of modernization, the field of caregiving was almost exclusively a woman's world. The majority of both employees and elderly recipients were women, and from a quantitative point of view this is still the case. But from a qualitative point of view, the position of the woman has changed since this early phase. The early phase was dominated by a traditional view of female responsibilities, with women being recruited among experienced housewives. There were no traditions of trade unions and none that focussed on the role of being an employee. In this light, the altruism mentioned above implies that home-helpers sometimes did more for their clients than they were paid for (Wærness 1982:145). In fact it was this interesting aspect of home-helpers' activity that formed the empirical basis for the 'rationality of caring' concept (Wærness 1996). Doing work without getting paid for it was an irrational action when judged by the values of the paid labour market. This also explains the dilemma of these homehelpers, arising from the conflict between traditional feminine values derived from the family sphere and values derived from the labour market (Wærness 1982, Christensen 1998b).

In summing up this early phase of modernization in the field of home help, it is essential to mention that the legal and ideological control of the field was weak and unfocused. This meant that the women who performed this care work tended to let the informal values of family care determine the value orientation of their professional work. Due to this lack of explicit and clear power, the space of relational power was relatively free to foster the rationality of care within the sphere of care interactions. The indispensable condition for this situation was the presence of women with the social capital to act according to this pattern. But it would be wrong to suppose that home care during this phase was idyllic. The negative side of this picture is that the work was poorly paid, often consisting of very small part-time commitments, that it was of low status, protected by very few worker's rights, and lonely, since it consisted exclusively of activities performed within the homes of the elderly without contact to other home help workers. As we shall see, these problematic aspects of the work improved.

Modern services

If we look at the field of home-based care as a form of activity slowly moving from an outside position to one where it was increasingly integrated in the traditional paid labour market, we will see that it closely reflects more general social developments. Max Weber (1994) characterized the modern development of society as a process of bureaucratization. He used this term to highlight the trend towards increased specialization, standardization and formalization with the objective of achieving greater effectiveness, rationality and stability. Applying this analysis of modernization to the welfare state society, the objective becomes especially distinct when the welfare state reaches the limit at which increased use of the public sector no longer seems the best and only way to meet society's welfare requirements. In the field of home-based services this development starts to become clear in the 1980s. Looking at this from the perspectives of, firstly, the services in general, secondly, the caregivers, and finally, the recipients, we identify three important processes: a bureaucratization of the services, a professionalization of the caregivers, and a differentiation of the recipients.

Starting with the institutional frame, we can mention the kind of circumstances that strengthen bureaucratization. Whereas the organization of care work used to be based on the model of just a few regular clients, it is now based on the model of many rotating clients. Szebehely calls the latter 'the assembly line model' (Szebehely 1995). The aim of this development is to divide the work in the home into separate and clearly defined tasks that are allocated to an increasingly diverse group of increasingly different service providers (see below). This change towards separation and standardization in care work reflects broader trends in the industrial sector and is therefore sometimes referred to as tailored work (Eliasson 1992).

During this phase the ideology that encouraged people to remain at home for as long as possible was strengthened, although it seems to coincide with the much clearer value orientation of the so-called ideology of rehabilitation (Christensen and Næss 1999). The official aim of the latter was to change attitudes that regard the elderly as weak and dependent on people with resources. In practice this ideology encourages people to care for themselves, yet many elderly people cannot manage this (see below). Responsibility is therefore passed on to relatives and others close to the elderly who might be able to provide informal care when the welfare state cannot do so. The ideology of rehabilitation raises the question of where to draw the limits within the range of claims for selfcare (Christensen 1990).

From the legal point of view the 1980s were an important decade, primarily for institutional structures. A law passed in 1984 moved responsibility for public care from a higher administrative level to a lower, local level. This law promoted decentralization and coordination. On a higher institutional level, this coordination meant that the municipality had to make it possible for both institutional and home-based care for the elderly to be managed on the same level. On a lower institutional level, the coordination implied an integration of home help and home nursing. The two types of coordination are called the 'big integration' and the 'small integration' (NOU 1986:4). When structural power is made more visible and stronger, changes also occur in relational power. Thus both power spaces became more explicit and more concretely based on the actions of the main actors involved in the process: the welfare state and welfare municipalities, and the local organizations and their representatives. In 1988 additions were made to the law of 1984, which entailed responsibility for nursing homes being passed to the Norwegian municipalities. This was a further step towards major integration.[8] In this context it is also important to mention that the idea of coordination coincided with a reduction in the number of lay-in days in hospitals. Consequently, home-based care came under pressure to relieve the pressure on hospitals.

---

[8] Despite the aim to coordinate, home help is still regulated by the Law on Social Services of 1991, while home nursing is still regulated by the law passed in 1984 concerning municipal health. Thus no unified law was passed during this development.

On the one hand, the professionalization of the services can be seen as a consequence of institutional changes due to higher claims on nursing care, local administration, professionally argued resolves etc. On the other, it is also a consequence of changes in the identity of those who became employees. Professionalization is not just about more formal education. We have to understand it as a much wider concept that covers any change relating to the entire work situation, including how that work is understood. In this view, professionalization implies management on both the structural and the relational levels of power. It is also important to notice that professionalization is most distinct among those with least formal education, especially the home-helpers. For this group, professionalization meant a change of identity from that of housewife to that of employee, whereby the latter was associated with wages, organized labour and a move towards improved knowledge (Christensen 1998b, Lie 1987). But of course, professionalization also involved more formal education. Among other things, the reduction in lay-in days in hospitals and in relief places at various health institutions, and the growing population of very old people, increased the need for elderly nursing (Christensen and Næss 1999). Although the most acute need was for home nurses, there was also a need for home-helpers. In Norway, a new vocational training was established during this phase, which could be pursued either directly after secondary school, or following a certain period of practical experience in the field of care. This was a four-year training that encompassed two years of theory and two years of practice (Høst 1997). The demand for professionalization arose within the space of structural power due to organizational and demographic changes, but it had a significant and direct impact on caregivers and their relations to care recipients. It should also be mentioned that raised levels of formal knowledge among employees helped to improve confidence in elderly care. Viewed in this way, professionalization became a kind of solution to modern bureaucratization and increased efficiency.

For their part, recipients became more differentiated in terms of age, nursing, cultural identity and lifestyle (Christensen and Næss 1999).[9] In other words, whereas some of them were able to meet the modern demand on them not to be mere recipients, most of them were not. It is worth noting that the Norwegian terms for care recipients changed during the 1980s from *clients* and *patients* to *users*. If we see this in association with the ideology of rehabilitation, which became increasingly clear in this phase, the user concept implies the idea of giving more responsibility to the recipients themselves. The demographic changes that occurred during this phase, which resulted in increased numbers of very old, sick, and lonely people, meant that this was a largely unrealistic project (ibid.). Furthermore, there was a reduction in the social capital of daughters and stepdaughters, who were increasingly absorbed into the general labour market in the 1980s (ibid.). In other words, in this phase an increasing discrepancy arose between the dominant ideology about the elderly and the reality of dependence among old people. And here we have the crucial point of the modern phase: from the perspective of care ratio-

---

[9] *Differentiation* is a concept I use analytically, to cover all the various demographic changes and the results of these changes among the elderly.

nality, the first step in cutting the necessary tie between structural and relational power has been taken. There was an increasing discrepancy between, on the one hand, bureaucratization, professionalization and the ideology of rehabilitation, and on the other, the situation and needs of the recipients, such as the need of many old people for regular helpers (Christensen 1998b, Næss and Wærness 1996, Rønning 1995) and the need among caregivers to be able to offer what was really needed (Næss and Wærness 1996:37).

Instead of developing the rich social capital that existed in the traditional phase by providing it with structural conditions, modern bureaucratization and professionalization ignored and destroyed it. The increase in explicit structural power during this phase compared to the traditional phase entailed a corresponding decrease in power among both recipients and caregivers, but especially the latter, although they did acquire more rights on an official level. The possibilities of strengthening care-rational power in the interactions between caregivers and care recipients were obviously reduced (Bungum 1994).

Late modern outputs

The modern model of bureaucracy underwent a final change in the 1980s. Criticism of this model focuses especially on its inflexibility and the constraints it places on employees (Pedersen 2001). In the field of home-based care these tendencies are documented in the research on the modern phase mentioned above. However, this change to a final condition does not mean that the model disappears, but rather that it is supplemented by a new model that focuses on quite different issues. This new model is called New Public Management (Pedersen 2001, Vabø 2001), and it began to affect the field of care in the 1990s.[10] This model encompasses ideas from market economics, which have obvious influence in the field of care in relation to documentation, quality control, competition and user orientation.[11] In what follows I will review some of these changes. The idea of user orientation is here also strengthened by the idea of legal security, with roots in the model of bureaucracy. And because legislation in the field of care was rendered much clearer during this phase, I shall start with these changes, before moving on to other institutional changes. I shall then conclude by mentioning some new characteristics in the situation of care recipients and givers.

One central legal change resulted from the Law on Social Services of 1991. This law resulted in several changes of which I want to mention one: the new requirement for a formal legally based requisition every time a citizen receives a social service (Christensen 2001b, Thorsen 1998). The consequence of this requi-

---

[10] This model has parallels in other fields of late modern working life, for example the industrial (see Olberg 1995).

[11] It is not possible to say precisely how widespread the influence of this model has been, but neither is that my concern here. First and foremost, I wish to highlight an important new structural power that will influence the direction in which care interactions develop in practice during this phase (see the power model).

sition is that municipal practice changed from being flexible and informal to rule-based and formal. The requisition specifies how much help the recipient will receive from the welfare state and for how long. Furthermore, this requisition supplies recipients with information about their opportunities to claim. But if the amount of help given has to be revised, then a new requisition is required. In addition to the legal requisition, many Norwegian municipalities supply a formal deal describing in detail which tasks will be performed by the recipient and which by the caregiver. Thus a contractual relation with significant legal aspects is established with the purpose of strengthening the power of both recipients and givers. But in fact the research (ibid.) shows that, on the structural level, these legal rights are not realised in practice. Accordingly, this implies a certain powerlessness for both recipients, since their needs are not met, and caregivers, since they have no scope to provide individualized services. Both explicit and implicit power (as powerlessness) at the relational level is therefore present in this situation.

The field of care has also become more willing to privatize services. This development began in the modern phase but became much more explicit in the late modern phase. There are several types of privatization, but the most tested one is open competition, where the welfare municipality competes with private agents in offering services on the open market. It is worth noting that there is uncertainty about the consequences this will have for the conditions of the employers (Bogen 2001). This market orientation results in other changes, such as the appearance of newspaper advertisements for independent organizations offering home help and home nursing to the elderly and others. Sometimes these new private services become alternatives to those offered by the welfare state, but in some cases they supplement welfare services, as for example where the latter have been radically cut back.

I must now mention a new procedure whereby services are assigned to citizens. Instead of letting the caregiver and care recipient make an informal deal about the details of the help to be supplied, the new procedure involves a formal clarification of the recipient's specific needs (Vabø 2001). This model, called a 'purchaser-provider model', results in formalization and standardization of the work of assigning services. The principal feature of the model is that assignment of the kind and amount of work to be provided in the individual household are made by employees who do not themselves perform those services. We are dealing here with a new separation of responsibility that goes with authority and responsibility associated with the performance of the work.

Thus we see how both the assignment of help and the help itself have been separated and formalised. However, formalization does not stop there. It continues after the help has been assigned in the form of documentation (all help prochased must be documented) and quality assurance (Christensen 1995). Research on this (Slagsvold 1995) shows that unless this quality assurance is based on concrete situational care relations, there is a tendency to fabricate a kind of 'mock quality'. Many Norwegian municipalities use a computer system called Gerix, where the key idea is that identical needs require identical help. The thinking behind this is a simple input-output model. One condition for this development is the availability of appropriate technology (see Christensen 2001a). Technology makes it possible to achieve constant control at the functional level of the recipient's needs, and to develop what Slagsvold has called a 'standicator measure of quality', in other words, standard measures of quality. But since these standicator measures do not cover concrete care needs, the risk of mock quality is considerable.

When it comes to the caregivers and recipients in this phase, two concepts are relevant: individualization and independent reflection. Both the professionalization of caregivers and the differentiation of recipients in the modern phase are important background factors in the process of personal individualization in late modern society. From the point of view of the employee, these changes increase the importance of worker's rights, own career, of formal work requirements and of formal rules for doing the work in the home.[12] Between being more preoccupied with own career among the care work, this also has to do with a greater desire to retain one's identity.[13] Here I want to underline the care dilemma of this development between on the one hand the female employees' central desire to retain their identity, and on the other, because of these desires at the same time complying with the process of formalization and standardization of the services – thus also reducing the possibilities for care-rationality, which is important to the identity.

The key organizational model here is what Szebehely has called a 'self-regulated small group model' (Szebehely 1995). This model is based on the assembly line model, with the difference that the caregivers and recipients are individualised. They have broader rights, but at the same time both parties are more replaceable and their interaction is greatly reduced. It is no longer important *who* is giving help to *whom*; the services rendered have become independent of both parties – and this amounts to a further step away from care-rational power within the relational space. There may well be a time lag in this late modern process of change among recipients, since there are still many old people who find it easier to show gratitude than to take the initiative to order the services they require from commercial providers. But this will change when the rights-oriented generations (women and men born in the 1940s who were young in the 1960s) replace the grateful generations.

To sum up, in the early part of the modern phase, both caregivers and recipients, and especially the latter, acquired further rights and hence more power. But increasing formalization and standardization made it increasingly apparent that this power remained individual and one sided (for both the giver and the recipient). The double effect of more explicit power and more implicit powerlessness in the relational space becomes still clearer. Thus the structural conditions for care-rational actions are still more reduced.

---

[12] For example, the law concerning the work environment requires the home to be prepared for the rendering of help (it must contain washing equipment etc.).

[13] In a Danish study this is related to a symbolic change from (white) coats to the use of personal clothes; this change has to do, among other things, with a change in femininity (Dahl 2000).

The challenges in the field of care

By means of the power model it has been possible to throw light on the development of home-based care services. During the modern and late modern phases,
these services have developed away from an implicit structural power that accords
considerable freedom to the (also implicit) relational power, towards a more explicit type of structural power that influences relational power. The welfare state
has changed from being an actor that exercised only weak control in the traditional
phase, to one that exercises much greater control in the later phases of modernization. In the modern phase, control and regulation of services have been increased
relative to the early traditional phase. A more explicit ideology is constructed – in
particular, the ideology of rehabilitation – and the services are reorganized. This
forms the basis of the late modern phase. Here we see a clear development towards
a combination of greater explicit power and implicit powerlessness for both parties
in the care relation. The general consequence of this overall development is a
steady weakening of the possibilities for care relational power, although this is
attributable to a variety of reasons. In the traditional phase social capital was available, which could be used as a basis for care-rational power. But there were no
explicit structural conditions for this. Moreover this social capital had a negative
aspect. In the modern phase this negative aspect improved as professionalization
resulted in broader worker's rights. But since this was not accompanied by structural conditions for developing social capital, the care-rational power grew weaker.
In the late modern phase the rights of care recipients also improved, but the discrepancy between structural power and the realities of the care situation for the
elderly became yet more pronounced. Thus the social capital lost both the structural and the relational conditions that would have promoted care-rational power.

   Accordingly, the challenges in the field of care can be focused on two issues.
The first revolves around the relative autonomy of every caregiver in her/his role
as intermediary and interpreter of the rules and laws that regulate the structure of
the welfare state (Lipsky 1980). No matter how strong and explicit the structural
power, there will always be scope for resistance and personal reflection (see the
power model) that can give rise to individual care-rational actions. Power does not
have to be about authority or what amounts to the same: sins of omission (Eliasson
1987). Power can be used positively when it is care-rational. But if this power is to
include more than individual and occasional acts, it has to be given an explicit collective basis in the kind of structural conditions – economic, legal, ideological and
organizational – that strengthen care-rational practice. Until this happens there will
exist important care dilemmas between what is needed in the care relational praxis
and what is possible in the light of structural conditions.

   The second challenge concerns the low status of care work that results from its
concern with the necessities of life. Arendt (1996) has mentioned that a separation
of work from productivity is characteristic of the concept of work throughout history. From the earliest times craftwork (i.e. productive work) has been distinguished from the tasks necessary to maintain bodily existence. The latter constitute
a kind of work that leaves no traces, nothing lasting, and it is therefore easy to
comprehend it as unproductive. Thus the challenge is to overcome the separation

of productivity and work. In the late modern phase the care services adopted the notion of outputs, which allowed them to see their activities from a commodity producing perspective. But if the aim is to strengthen care-rational power, this kind of commodity-like productivity (which can only strengthen mock quality) must be replaced by an understanding of care, not as something that can be reduced to limited standardised outputs, but as one of the mainstays of society, with social capital as one of its foundations. Care work must therefore be restored to its central place in society, which means re-establishing its structural and relational conditions. This would allow social capital to be transformed from mere low-status voluntary work to one of the basic elements in interactions between people in everyday life, and this in turn would strengthen the community. In this respect research on care faces a crucial and significant challenge in the future.

References

Arendt, H. (1996): *Vita activa: det virksomme liv.* Oslo: Pax.

Blumer, H. (1954): 'What is wrong with Social Theory?', in: *American Sociological Review* 19/1.

Bogen, H. (2001): 'Hvilke konsekvenser har konkurranseutsetting for ansatte?', in: *Tidsskrift for Velferdsforskning*, 4/4: 207-221.

Bourdieu, P. (1996): *Symbolsk makt.* Oslo: Pax.

Bungum, B. (1994): *Effektivisering av omsorg. Kjønnsperspektiv på omstilling av offentlig omsorgsarbeid.* En rapport fra LOS-prosjektet 'Mulighetsstrukturer i offentlige og private foretak'. Universitetet i Trondheim: Institutt for Sosiologi og statsvitenskap.

Christensen, K. (1990): 'Et kvindekritisk syn på rehabilitering i ældreomsorgen', in: *Aldring og Eldre* 2/90: 22-25.

Christensen, K. (1995): 'Quality in Home Care and Nursing?' 229-239, in: Evers, Haverinen, Leichsenring, and Wistow (eds.): *Developing Quality in Personal Social Services.* Vienna: Ashgate.

Christensen, K. (1998a): 'Andre-orientering og omsorgsarbejde', in: *Tidsskrift for Velferdsforskning*, 1/2: 82-96. (And in Danish periodical *Social kritik* 63/99).

Christensen, K. (1998b): *Omsorg og arbejde. En sociologisk studie af ændringer i den hjemmebaserede omsorg.* Afhandling. Universitetet i Bergen: Sosiologisk institutt.

Christensen, K. (2001a): 'Computerbrug og omsorgsarbejde?', in: Skånning Nielsen and Lomborg (eds.): *På arbejde i hjemmet*: 55-83. Copenhagen: Gyldendal.
(First published in: Thorsen and Wærness (1999) (eds.): *Blir omsorgen borte? Eldreomsorgens hverdag i den senmoderne velferdsstaten.* Oslo: Ad Notam Gyldendal.)

Christensen, K. (2001b): 'Mellem politikken og folket. De sociale tjenesters græsrodsbureaukrater og deres fordelingspraksis', in: *Tidsskrift for velferdsforskning*, 4/4: 222-238.

Christensen, K. og Næss, S. (1999): *Kunnskapsstatus om de offentlige omsorgstjenestene.* Bergen: Senter for samfunnsforskning (SEFOS).

Dahl, H.M. (2000): *Fra kitler til eget tøj – Diskurser om professionalisme, omsorg og køn.* Ph.D.-thesis. Århus Universitet: Institut for Statskundskab.

Eliasson, R. (1987): *Forskningsetik og perspektivval.* FoU-rapport 7A. Stockholms Socialförvaltning, Stockholm: Forsknings- och utvecklingsbyrån.

Eliasson, R. (1992): 'Omsorg som lönarbete: om taylorisering och professialisering', in: Eliasson (ed.): *Egenheter och allmänheter. En antologi om omsorg och omsorgens villkor*: 131-142. Lund: Arkiv förlag.

Esping-Andersen, G. (1990): *The Three Worlds of Welfare Capitalism*. Cambridge: Polity Press.

Hochschild, A. (1975): 'The Sociology of Feeling and Emotion: Selected possibilities', in: Millman and Kanter (eds.): *Another Voice*. New York: Anchor Books.

Høst, H. (1997): *Konstruksjonen av omsorgsarbeideren*. AHS serie 2/97. Bergen: Arbeidsliv-Historie-Samfunn, Gruppe for flerfaglig arbeidsforskning.

Leonard, R. (2000): 'Older women, community organizations and social capital', in: *Third Sector Review*, 6, 1/2: 43-57.

Lie, B. (1987): *Et yrke tar form. En analyse av hjemmehjelpernes yrkesrolle og yrkesdanning*. Hovedoppgave, Universitetet i Oslo: Institutt for sosiologi.

Lipsky, M. (1980): *Street Level Bureaucracy. Dilemmas of the Individual Public Services*. New York: Russell Sage Foundation.

Norges offentlige utredning, NOU (1986:4): *Samordning i helse- og sosialtjenesten*, Oslo: Universitetsforlaget.

Næss, S. og Wærness, K. (1996): *Bedre omsorg? Kommunal eldreomsorg 1980-95*. Bergen: Senter for samfunnsforskning (SEFOS).

Olberg, D. (1995): 'Endringer i arbeidslivets organisering – en introduksjon', in: Olberg (ed.): *Endringer i arbeidslivets organisering*: 5-28 Oslo: FAFO.

Ones, T. (1988): *Organisering av omsorgsarbeid*. Hovedoppgave i Helse- og sosialpolitikk, Universitetet i Bergen.

Pedersen, A.R. (2001): 'Fortællinger om hjemmeplejens organisering', in: Skånning Nielsen and Lomborg (eds.): *På arbejde i hjemmet*: 84-112. Copenhagen: Gyldendal.

Ritzer, G. (2000): *Sociological Theory*. New York: McGraw Hill.

Rønning, R. (1995): 'Kvalitet i hjemmehjelpstjenestene – en lokal studie', in: *Aldring og Eldre*, 1, 2-7. Oslo: Universitetsforlaget.

Slagsvold, B. (1995): *Om å måle kvalitet i aldersinstitusjoner*. Afhandling. Oslo: Norsk gerontologisk institutt.

Szebehely, M. (1995): *Vardagens organisering. Om vårdbiträden och gamla i Hemtjänsten*. Stockholm: Arkiv.

Thorsen, K. (1998): *Den pressede omsorgen. Kvaliteter i hjemmehjelpstjenesten for eldre i lokal kontekst*. NOVA-rapport 18/98. Oslo: Norsk institutt for forskning om oppvekst, velferd og aldring.

Vabø, M. (2001): '(For)brukerorientering og omsorg', in: Thorsen, Dahle og Vabø: *Makt og avmakt i helse- og omsorgstjenestene*. NOVA-rapport 18/2001. Oslo: Norsk institut for forskning om oppvekst, velferd og aldring.

Weber, M. (1994): *Makt og byråkrati*. Oslo: Gyldendal Norsk Forlag.

Wærness, K. (1982): *Kvinneperspektiver på sosialpolitikken*. Oslo, Bergen, Tromsø: Universitetsforlaget.

Wærness, K. (1984): 'The Rationality of Caring', in: *Economic and Industrial Democracy* 5: 185-211. London: Sage Publications.

Wærness, K. (1996): 'Omsorgsrationalitet. Reflexioner över et begrepps karriär', in: Eliasson (ed.): *Omsorgens skiftninger*: 203-220. Lund: Studentlitteratur.

The most important laws

Law on Social Care from 5.06.64

Law on Nursing Services in Municipality from 19.11.82 (passed in 1984 and revised in 1988)

Law on Social Services from 13.12.91.

Chapter 3

A Changing Ideal of Care in Denmark: A Different Form of Retrenchment?[1]

Hanne Marlene Dahl

Many stories about the recent developments of the European welfare states are told. One hegemonic story is about the (need for) retrenchment of the welfare state (Ferrera and Rhodes, 2000; OECD, 1981), and another concerns 'modernization' (Pierson, 2001b). In opposition to these two stories, a feminist counter discourse on the emerging care deficit has arisen; care is threatened because of the decline of informal, family based care and the (supposed) withdrawal of the welfare state (Boje and Leira, 2000; Hochschild, 1995; Knijn and Kremer, 1997; Saraceno, 1997).

General stories often have a wide appeal and heuristic (and polemical) value, but often lack scientific accuracy. The Danish case on elderly case questions these three stories, since there is no significant change on the quantitative level, but instead a qualitative, paradigmatic shift in the politico-administrative discourse on care. The ideal of care is substantively rewritten in the beginning of the 1980s focussing upon the cost containment and the engineering of an active life for the recipient. This change involves a different kind of retrenchment than usually described in the literature on welfare state reform, since it contains an ambiguous twist with both a qualitative retrenchment and an extension of the states disciplinary power in elderly care.

My argument is both theoretical and empirical, since a Danish case study is used to question the simplicity of the three stories mentioned above. The development in the discourses of the Danish welfare state can theoretically be analysed from various perspectives.[2] My interpretation is based upon that of Foucault due to his understanding of the subtle forms of power emanating from the state and inspired by a feminist research tradition that has tried to make care (informal and formal) visible on the scientific agenda, a tradition that has remained

---

[1] I wish to thank Bente Marianne Olsen, John Andersen and Thomas Boje for valuable comments to earlier drafts of this contribution.

[2] The two most relevant, and opposing, perspectives are those of the responsive state which increasingly grants more rights to the citizen (a view developed by Jürgen Habermas) and the disciplining state which restrains its subjects through an invisible cage, the view propounded by Michel Foucault.

critical towards welfare state services, their aims and organization (Dahl, 1997; Leira, 1992; Tronto, 1993; Wærness, 1982; Ungerson, 1987).

This paper concerns elderly care services understood through the lenses of the discourses prevalent in the field. Understanding the discursive development provides a background to understanding the development of elderly policy. I understand a discursive threat as a threat present in a discourse that might be implemented. I have identified three discursive threats: *the splitting up of care and an internal marketization, the tyranny of transformation* and *the will of the pleasant* in some of the competing discourses that I have identified elsewhere (Dahl, 2000a): governance and budgetary discourse, a leadership and development discourse and a discourse on care.

The paper is divided into five parts. Firstly, I will clarify my theoretical framework, method and describe a discursive, paradigmatic change. Secondly, I will make a brief presentation of the Danish case and the development of paid, professional home-helpers employed by the welfare state. Thirdly, I will briefly expand upon my thesis of a different form of retrenchment, this leads into the fourth part which is a description of the discourses in the field, the different elements of retrenchment, its ambiguous character as well as the potentially threatening character of the rewritten discourses if they are translated into policy. Fifthly, I relate the three discourses to the general tales in my conclusion.

Politics of need construction and a paradigmatic change

When we speak about 'something', we simultaneously bring 'it' into speech and existence. It becomes visible as a social and linguistic entity, since it enters language and becomes a phenomenon (Andersen, 1997). Theoretically, I am inspired by the French historian Michel Foucault (1978) especially his later works (1993, 1996) as well as by the American philosopher Nancy Fraser (1990).

Like Fraser, I believe that it is necessary to move from a focus upon needs to focussing on *discourses on needs*. I understand a discourse as a horizon of intelligibility and possibility, i.e. as defining a limit for what can be considered meaningful and what can be seen as possible.[3] Needs are only speakable within a discourse which implies an analytical attention to the *politics of need construction*.[4] Some needs may attain priority, whereas others may become marginal and even

---

[3] The British-South African political theorist Aletta Norval inspires this definition of a discourse (1996) and like her, I believe that discourses contain various degrees of material and linguistic elements, and discursive effects are the effects of a discourse at a given time on the future development of this discourse.

[4] I basically agree with Fraser's important redirection of our analytical attention, but I do so from a different epistemological stance that tempts me to modify her 'politics of need interpretation' to a 'politics of need construction'. Due to my vague realism I neither speak of representation nor translation of needs, but the construction of needs. Needs are in my understanding not 'out there' to be represented, since the world and our minds co-constitute reality (Visker, 1995).

silenced. When analysing needs-talk, it is necessary to investigate the ideals of care (Dahl, 2000a).[5] An ideal of care is the *leitmotiv* in a discourse on care (and needs) and it brings together the image of the recipient, the culturally and politically recognised needs and their provision.

My focus is upon how the *images of the recipients of care change*[6] wherefore I have investigated the political-administrative discourse and its changes. This is a Top-down perspective where I analyse the discourses used by politicians, civil servants, experts and representatives from major interest groups to describe (and regulate) social and political reality. The discourse analysis is based on written and publicly available texts such as commission reports, memorandums, reports, legislation and internal reviews (Dahl, 2000a). The material analysed includes all relevant material in a study covering the period 1943-95 (Dahl, 2000a), but in this chapter my focus is upon the most recent period from 1980 to 1995. In the material, various voices compete to define social reality, i.e. to become hegemonic in this political-administrative discourse and articulate the needs of the recipient and their provision.[7] I focus upon discourses about needs, which frames the elaboration of policies. The threats that I will describe in detail are discursive, and they *may or may not* be transferred into concrete welfare policies.[8] Discursive effects are only visible in a longer time span, but a study of discourses will allow us to get a glimpse of potential future(s).

Change is potentially immanent in every reproduction of a discourse by subjects, but some changes are more profound than others. As a researcher of policy change Peter Hall argues that we can analytically distinguish between three levels of change: first, second and third order change (1993). The first order and second order concern minor changes of a paradigm. A first order change is an incrementalist change often undertaken by officials due to a review of policy and concerns the change of settings for the policy instruments. A second order change involves an alteration of the instruments themselves. A third order change is more profound since it changes the policy paradigm substantively into a different paradigm. This involves a change of instrument settings, the instruments themselves and a radical alteration of the hierarchy of goals behind policy. Hall describes the radical change from Keynesian fiscal policies to monetarist modes of macroeconomic regulation policies as a third order change in Britain in 1976-79.

---

[5] I another article I argue in favour of a particular feminist ideal of care (Dahl, 2000b).

[6] I have discussed the changing images of the caregiver from a gender perspective elsewhere (Dahl, 2001).

[7] The unveiling of these struggles takes place from a particular perspective and position, and my constructivism implies that I cannot use reality 'out there' as a standard of validity. Instead my analytical strategy acts as one standard of validity (Dahl, 2000b) where I hope to avoid relativism. My discourse analysis is influenced by the notion of 'critique' developed by Foucault and interpreted by Judith Butler (Visker, 1995; Butler, in press). Critique as a practice aims at identifying the rationalities at work in discourses and intends to destabilize them.

[8] The discourses investigated can be seen as framing policies at the national level that direct its policies at the municipalities. The municipality, however, retains some autonomy in regard to implementation.

The goal of reducing inflation replaced the former policy goal of low unemployment (Hall, 1993: 279).

I believe that these three orders can be transferred to the terrain of discourses. I will argue that the change in the ideal of care is so profound that it constitutes a new paradigm and in more technical terms refers to a dislocation of the discourse and the ideal of care.[9] The leitmotiv changes for example from relieving distress to engineering growth in the recipient and towards a closer attention to optimization of resources. This change of paradigm can simultaneously be considered as a novel form of retrenchment where the theoretical concept of retrenchment usually understood as a 'cut back, scale down, or curtail welfare state benefits' (Green-Pedersen, 2001) needs to be redefined. I will redefine retrenchment as a subtle change that does not necessarily entail financial cuts, but involves a withdrawal of the articulated obligations of the state (rewritten and reduced) and/or a discursive attention to cost containment. The ambiguous character of this discursive retrenchment refers to the simultaneous extension in its regulation of the subject, i.e. the recipient of care.

In order to understand the discursive changes taking place in the beginning of the 1980s, it is necessary to give a brief introduction to the Danish case, and the development on the caregivers side, i.e. the creation of professional home-helpers paid and employed by the welfare state.

The professional home-helpers

The Nordic countries are known for the extensive rights they grant to recipients of care (Knijn and Kremer, 1997; Saraceno, 1997). Rights for elderly people in Denmark have increasingly been codified in legislation (Lov om Social Service, 1997; Lov om retssikkerhed og administration på det sociale område, 1997). According to these laws, elderly people with permanent or temporary limited physical or cognitive skills have a right to receive help in their own home, and approximately 20% of those above retirement age receive such aid, which is carried out by home-helpers (Daatland and Szebehely, 1997). The home-helpers are qualified through one to two years of education in particular social- and health schools. Training first became obligatory in 1974, at which time only four weeks of training were required.

However, such training has not always been required. The concept 'home-helper' was introduced into national legislation in 1958[10] and it was a response to policies enacted by municipalities that were employing women who had the experience of being a housewife but did not have any formal training in relation to the provision of care for elderly people in their own homes. From the 1960s and onwards, the home-helpers have gradually been inscribed into a discourse of

---

[9] A dislocation of a discourse is defined as a destabilization of a discourse where an existing discourse is dissolved or radically rearticulated (Torfing, 1999: 301).

[10] With the law: 'Lov om ændring i lov om folkeforsikring'.

professionalization.[11] A discourse that has stressed the work done by home-helpers as being complex, having a particular scientific knowledge base and has continuously tried to gain recognition for other types of knowledge as well. There has been a move from describing the home-helpers as 'good housewives' within a complementarily, gendered discourse to a more androgynous, professional discourse in the late 1960's stressing pre-emptive measures as the core task for home-helpers.[12]

In short, the professionalization of the Danish home-helpers contains a novel, and different route to another form of professionalization (Dahl, 2000a).[13] The creation of a profession has not been a continuous story of progression, since there have been several backlashes during the process (Dahl, 2000a). In general, the story of the Danish home-helpers has been a successful one, since formerly suppressed values, qualifications and knowledge bases have been *partly* recognized within the political-administrative field.[14] I will now expand upon my thesis and elaborate upon the differences in relation to other stories about the welfare state, i.e. that of retrenchment and modernization.

A discursive retrenchment with an ambiguous twist

The general tale of exogenous and endogenous pressures leading to a retrenchment and modernization of the European welfare state has been prevalent within welfare state research (Ferrera and Rhodes, 2000). The research tradition, however, seems to have regained its composure and retreated from its previous, rather grand, statements. Here, in contrast, more specific arguments are put forward based on

---

[11] I define a discourse of professionalization as analytically different from a process of commodification (Dahl, 2000a). However, a process of professionalization requires a previous or a contemporary process of commodification. Professionalization in a Weberian understanding of the concept requires a monopoly as well such as seen among doctors, lawyers and nurses. Such a closure of access (monopoly) has so far not been the case for home-helpers.

[12] By an androgynous discourse I refer to a discourse where explicit gender references disappear and an ideal of (supposedly) gender neutrality pervades the text (Dahl, 2000a).

[13] Some sociologists of professions would argue that the gradual inscription into a discourse of professionalism constitutes a semi-professionalization. In line with Anne Witz (1992) I would argue that the notion of 'semi-professionalization' contains a male bias, since it normatively builds on particular male (elitist) experiences at a particular point in history. This alternative form has been described by Stina Johansson as '... a female, a subordinate and a mass profession' (1995, my translation).

[14] For the negative aspects of this development, please consult my articles (Dahl, 2001; 2002). In these articles I outline the negative aspects of the seemingly positive story. One negative aspect is the increased regulation of home-helpers Self including their emotions, i.e. the disciplinary regime they become subject to. Another aspect is the overrepresentation of home-helpers in the statistics concerning job related accidents compared to other groups as well as the problems in gaining acknowledgement of these accidents in the Board of Industrial Injury.

particular case studies. In the case of the Scandinavian welfare states, it has been argued that they have not experienced any significant retrenchment, although cost containment strategies of a particular kind have been applied (Andersen, 2000; Ferrera and Rhodes, 2000; Kuhnle, 2000; Pierson, 2001a, 2001b). The Norwegian political scientist Stein Kuhnle argues that Denmark has not seen a retrenchment of its policy towards the elderly, since the share of elderly services and transfers of the social expenditures *en toto* remained at 48.3% between 1990 and 1995. Similarly, Scandinavian researchers have argued that Danish elderly care has experienced a curb on public expenditures from 1980-90. Expenditures (resources) for elderly services have fallen by three percentage points when taking into account inflation and the increase in the number of elderly people (Daatland and Szebehely, 1997). This minor reduction does not constitute a significant change.

In addition, on the qualitative level, Kuhnle argues that the basic values of the Nordic welfare system such as universalism, comprehensiveness, redistribution and employment outlook have 'stood the test' (2000). In line with this view, Christoffer Green-Pedersen argues that retrenchment is more rhetoric than reality in the Danish case, since commodification and contracting out have not been implemented in policy to any significant degree (2002). Only a few municipalities have in fact contracted out elderly services such as meals on wheels, home help, and nursing homes. The exceptions seem to prove the rule.

Agreeing with the scientific consensus on the stability of elderly policies on the quantitative level I will nevertheless argue that there has occurred a qualitative, paradigmatic change in the ideal of care.[15] This change involves as mentioned previously three discursive tendencies: the splitting up of care and an internal marketization, the tyranny of transformation, and the will of the pleasant all of which mark a change in the ideal of care and therefore introduce a new 'leitmotiv' concerning elderly care. The change identified is, among others, due to incorporated elements of New Public Management (NPM) that have become dominant in the public sectors of the Western World. NPM can generally be characterised as a rising body of managerial thought dominated by ideas about marketization, 'doing more with less' and an idea of a management of change (Ashburner, Ferlie, Fitzgerald and Pettigrew, 1996). Others describe it as a change in culture, ideologies and practices that underpin the 'emergent political settlement' (Clarke and Newman, 1997). New Public Management and the policy change towards a service-management outlook provide us with parts of the (policy) story about the development of Danish elderly care. NPM must be identified as embodying a particular, discursive retrenchment and not just interpreted as a neutral strategy of modernization. This I will show later.

Modernization and retrenchment are not the only stories to be told about the discursive field, since the story also contains an ambiguous twist. A discursive

---

[15] A similar argument about about change of policy has been advanced by the former Danish Social Democratic Minister of Social Affairs Bent Rold Andersen. He argues that elderly policy in Denmark went astray in the beginning of the 1980s (1999) and identifies a change in the form of a retrenchment from a model based on 'being together' to a service-management outlook governing elderly service.

force extends its discipline to the elderly and pictures a particular version of the good life as one of change. This image becomes the norm and consequently functions as a moral prerogative in the discursive field as I will show later. I will now elaborate upon my thesis and consider the three discourses and their discursive effects in turn. Now I will turn my attention to the first discourse, that of a budgetary and governance discourse.

The splitting up of care and an internal marketization

In the discursive field, various discourses compete about the power to define reality. One of the dominant discourses is the 'Governance and budgetary discourse'. It has existed in various versions in the field since its genesis in 1943. The discourse articulates the political problem as an insufficient utilization of resources, and its constructs the political and administrative solution as improved productivity and an adjustment of the political aims within the sector. The most frequent words applied within this horizon are planning, efficiency, assessment process, budgetary awareness, rate of coverage, and optimization of resources, the sliding of standards, de-composition and functions.[16] The cost-containment/rationalization strategy is obvious and exposes similar features with NPM and its dictum of 'doing more with less'.

In this discourse a splitting up of care occurs, since a discursive reification enters the field through a new language and a changed image of care. There is a discursive focus upon 'functions' in care and a de-composition of care. Care is divided into codified functions in a rather technical vein: it is de-composed into what is seen, as its constituting parts. Care is split up into the most visible tasks as in an assembly line production. This discursive tendency brings the process of Taylorization to my mind as a form of scientific management, where work procedures are designed and planned scientifically in order to improve productivity and efficiency (Taylor, 1947). The de-composition implies that some parts of care become nearly invisible or only reluctantly can be described within such a discourse. In my understanding, needs related to the alleviation or reduction of sufferings cannot easily be included in the discourses. They cannot be fit into a scheme where tasks must be easily identifiable and possible to deal with in a political and administrative logic. Fraser describes such logic as that of articulating needs into 'administrable needs' (1990). An example being that needs for rehabilitation is more easily translated into a political-administrative discourse than needs related to the suffering and/or the vulnerable subject.

---

[16] For this analysis the material has consisted of the following: Vejledning om bedre ressourceanvendelse i ældresektoren, 1980; Visitation på ældreområdet, 1981; Personaleforbruget på ældreområdet 1981-1984 og 1985, 1985; Rammer for fremtidens bistands-, pleje- og omsorgsuddannelser, 1989; Rapport om udviklingen i hjemmehjælpen, 1991; Rapport fra arbejdsgruppen om minimumsrettigheder og kriterier for evt. Ankeadgang for tildeling af hjemmehjælp, 1994.

The governance and budgetary discourse increasingly focuses upon the commodity status of care, i.e. that care contains some commodities that can be produced in various contexts, commercial as well as non-commercial. One of the articulated options aimed at improving efficiency is contracting-out understood in the sense that other private or public agencies (than the home-helper) can produce some of the tasks. However, contracting-out is only an option for certain parts of care in the horizon, since it constructs a division between tending and service.[17] Tending is articulated as caring including emotional and cognitive needs, which is articulated as a task for state employees due to what is constructed as the fragility of the subject.[18] Tending is articulated both as urgent and as necessary needs. In contrast, services are neither constructed as urgent needs nor related to the fragility of the elderly person. Services are still perceived as a state responsibility, but not necessarily produced within the welfare state. The division concerns the responsibility and the exercise of care (its 'production' to use the terminology of the discourse). Service, the non- personal, is articulated as domestic chores. The division is simultaneously related to a hierarchy of needs where the most personal tending needs are given priority compared to domestic needs like cleaning, shopping and cooking.

On the face of it, these discursive tendencies might not seem that troubling. However, several troubling discursive effects for the recipients of care might become more real within a short space of time. Firstly, the discursive de-composition of care destroys the former, discursive unity of care, and reduces the responsibility towards the recipient. Specifically, the distinction between tending and service creates the possibility for some, and not other, tasks to be legitimately (in political terms) contracted-out to firms, semi-public firms or other public agencies. The danger at this moment is not the possibility of contracting-out *per se* to private firms, although this might have a disciplining effect upon the home-helpers, but instead the new ethos introduced by a new language that internally values cost containment. The ideas deriving from NPM are not neutral instruments, but might change the way home-helpers think and act.

Secondly, and more hypothetically, it is possible to argue that the more agents involved in the provision of care, the more time used for co-ordination and less time for the fragile elderly. Thirdly, the de-composition of care into functions also implies a retrenchment in another way, since a potential silencing of less tangible (and less administrable) needs might occur. And finally from the perspective of the

---

[17] This interpretation is based on the following text: Budgetanalyse for hjemmehjælp, 1995. When de-constructing the division between tending and service it becomes apparent that it contains a paradox. The division is applied in two different ways that are contradictory: as a generally applicable distinction, and as a more flexible division. In the latter use, the concrete caring needs of the recipient define what in such a particular case is considered to be tending and what is considered a service (Dahl, 2000a). I presume the ambiguity is due to the contradictory aims articulated on the discursive field, namely those of self-determination of the recipient and efficiency in care produced by firms or self-governing units.

[18] The division is constructed as an understanding of the limits between the personal understood as that concerning the body and the non-personal (Andersen, 1996).

professional home-helpers, the splitting up of care and the increased codification is negative, since it might result in a de-professionalization removing autonomy from the home-helpers. There is yet another dominant discourse that simultaneously overlaps with and questions the governance and budgetary discourse. I will now describe the ambiguous character of this discourse of leadership and development.

The tyranny of transformation

A new discourse enters the field in the middle of the 1970's, namely a leadership and developmental discourse. It is a discourse, which attempts to engineer change and within its own logic, it identifies change with development. Development becomes a self-referential term, since it does not demand to be substantiated. 'Development is preferable, because development is preferable' seems to be the argument. There occurs a valorization of change. In a British context, similar ideological developments have aptly been paraphrased as a 'tyranny of transformation' within the language of NPM (Clarke and Newman, 1997).

Later when the discourse on leadership and development becomes more articulated, it questions the definition of the main political problem as that of insufficient utilization of available resources, and instead argues in favour of the problem as constituted by an insufficient leadership and the lack of professional knowledge. By this rewriting of the political problem, it questions the governance and budgetary discourse. The aim of development becomes so pervasive, that recipients of care, the elderly, also are understood as in need of development. The key words become restructuring, development and education (Omlægning og fornyelse af indsatsen for ældre, 1983). The vocabulary introduces two groups of concepts. One group of concepts are transferred from the market to the state by analogy. The other group of concepts refers to a new understanding of leadership. I will now explain the new concepts transferred from (the ideal of) the market.

New concepts like contract, offer, options, supplier, service and agreement enter the vocabulary. These market concepts are applied in respect to two relations, i.e. that between the state and the recipient, and the relation between the state and the private firm. Recipients have obligations and rights, i.e. obligations to fulfil their part of the agreement with the state and rights encompassed in the agreement.

The other group refers to a novel notion of leadership. Leadership becomes leadership of oneself, and engineered through the commitment of the employees. Or rather they are no longer considered as employees, but instead as a fellow worker/a colleague. New concepts like communication, personal development, partnership, equality, co-operation, collective home help, users and colleagues enter the political and administrative discourse.[19, 20]

---

[19] The texts used for these analyses are: Hjemmehjælp til gamle mennesker, 1982; Hjemmehjælp I bevægelse, 1986; Ny hjemmehjælp faser i en overgang, 1986; Rammer for fremtidens bistands-, pleje- og omsorgsuddannelser, 1989.

[20] Leadership becomes closely related to the development of the professional's knowledge and personal abilities of the fellow worker and to the development of the recipient of care.

The past is re-articulated, and so is the client/user/citizen/recipient. S/he is articulated as being capable of change and self-determination. Compared to the recipient in the governance and budgetary discourse, the recipient is constructed as more capable and autonomous. However, being an autonomous subject (recipient) is not an option, but instead an obligation in the discourse. This rewriting silences elements of dependency and the wishes of the elderly. Any elderly person is supposed to develop in a 'reciprocal developing co-operation' with her/his home-helper (Dahl, 2000a).

The focus upon development might direct attention towards the more developing and professional tasks and away from the continuous, necessary tasks like for example the emissions of the body and cleaning.[21] Put more generally, the discourse on leadership and development is threatening paid care in several ways. The discourse implies a disciplinary effect upon the elderly person since s/he is expected continuously to develop. Involuntarily s/he becomes an object in a disciplinary regime, where mere existence for the elderly is deemed insufficient.

Granted the discourse will result in an increased focus upon improved, formal qualifications, this might imply an increased discontinuity in the care for the recipients. When home-helpers attend courses, another person must care for the sick, handicapped or elderly person. The discourse relies upon self-management to a larger extent than previously. This is probably good for some active, healthy and self-reliant elderly, but bad for others such as more fragile people. Without the tools for such self-management this could result in frustrations and experiences of inadequacy for some elderly people.

The discursive articulation implies an ambiguous development. One discursive threat is a retrenchment caused by the silencing of the fragile elderly person and his/her needs. Another threat becomes the extension of the regulation of the recipient, since a new ideal of the 'good' recipient is generated. An ideal embodied by a capable and self-reliant elderly person that can develop reciprocally with his/her home-helper. From my Foucauldian inspired position, the articulation can alternatively be interpreted as a coercion of the elderly into a tyranny of transformation and development.[22] The development of this discourse is less clear-cut and less tangible compared to the potential effects of the budgetary and

---

The construction of a need for an improved professional knowledge stems from the (new) articulation between the field and gerontology. This requires a partial re-construction of the past in which imagery the home-helpers (of the past) become identified with cleaning. When speaking of development the discourse refers to professional knowledge and personal aspects. Focusing increasingly upon personal aspects implies an extension of the area of the regulation, since commitment and emotions become tools for management.

[21] This might in turn be beneficial for the caregivers. An increased focus upon the developmental tasks might become a vehicle for a further process of professionalization of the home-helpers/health and social helpers and the health and social assistants. Such a process might provide more recognition of their work than it is often portrayed in the media.

[22] According to another interpretation, i.e. from a Habermasian point of view, this development is responsive to the resources of the elderly, since they are rewritten into responsible partners in the process of mutual development.

governance discourse. The third discourse also implies some threats that embody a more contradictory development.

A will to the pleasant

Needs are formed by the welfare state as well as by social and cultural factors (Fraser, 1990; Knijn and Kremer, 1997). When analysing the ideals of care in the period 1943-95 for elderly care, it becomes evident that a shift in needs articulation has occurred towards more intimate and positive needs. The displacement involves three interrelated tendencies: a discursive movement away from the domestic chores as mentioned previously, a will to the pleasant[23] and finally a turn towards the Self of the recipient.

The discursive movement away from the domestic chores towards tending can be identified in the articulated needs in various historical periods. In the period 1943-54, needs were articulated as understanding and housework. However, in the period 1980-95 needs were, among others, constructed as personal tending, personal needs, safety, respect and growth. The new words point towards the individual and her/his more specific needs, and away from housework as a need for the elderly. As mentioned earlier this historical development is reflected in the valorization of tending as opposed to services as evident in the governance and budgetary discourse.

The will to the pleasant becomes increasingly visible in the material. It is a textual movement away from the negative and unpleasant towards the pleasant and positive. It can be identified simultaneously in the articulation of the aims of care and caring needs. In the periods 1943-54 and 1954-68 the aims of care were to relieve distress and to relieve loneliness. Whereas in the periods 1968-72, 1972-80 and 1980-95 the political aims were to create well being, create growth and enable life-realization. Well being and life-realization are more positively associated in our contemporary discourses than to relieve distress and loneliness.

Similarly, when the construction of needs are considered. The discursive construction of needs have increasingly been defined as concerning growth and the quality of life in contrast to earlier constructions as concerned with counteracting decay and providing pretty simple services. The textual move towards the more positive aspects of ageing is simultaneously a move towards more diffuse, abstract needs and intervening measures. A term such as 'quality of life' cannot be considered an easily 'administerable need'. The move towards intervening measures can be identified in the high priority affiliated with pre-emptive measures. Pre-emptive measures presuppose a surveillance of the behaviour of the clients/citizens/recipients (Schmidt and Kristensen, 1988). Such surveillance implies a clinical view that relies upon a standard of the (clinically) normal, and an attention to any

---

[23] The 'will to the pleasant' is a pun upon words, or rather, a pun upon Foucault's 'a will to knowledge'. I owe thanks to my former student Niels Buus for his creativity when brainstorming on an adequate term for this transformation.

deviation from the norm. An increased focus upon pre-emption is also a re-direction towards the Self and even the smallest aberrations.

A more general discursive tendency towards the Self can be identified in an increased discursive attention towards care of the self and self-determination.[24] The Self is articulated as active and self-determining, and not exclusively as a recipient.

It is difficult to determine the potential effects of the above-mentioned discursive developments. The present valorization of the more intimate needs presents a danger, since it delimits caring needs and silences some needs which for some recipients are experienced as important. How is one to feel comfortable and having quality in life if one's apartment is dirty? The focus upon pre-emptive measures is like a double-edged sword. Good when it discovers diseases at an early stage, but some its effects are negative due to the surveillance included. Finally, what about the effects of care on the self? Is it wishful thinking for some groups of elderly? And in that case, what are the discursive effects? Installing a bad conscience? Or is it rather to be understood as a withdrawal of the welfare state and as an educational project, where citizens are expected to care about themselves and monitor their condition and needs? It is in fact a truly ambiguous development.

Conclusions

The general tale of retrenchment and modernization cannot be applied without great caution to the Danish case. Quantitatively only minor adjustments seem to have taken place. However, analysing the construction of needs and the development of discourses in the field reveals a different picture of an ambiguous retrenchment involving a discursive retrenchment and extension. A paradigmatic shift has occurred in the discursive field. The ideal of care was increasingly formed by three discursive tendencies: a splitting up of care and marketization internally, a tyranny of transformation and a will to the pleasant. The shift is represented with the change from relieving distress to engineering development in the elderly person and also seen in the increased focus upon cost containment in the politico-administrative discourse.

These three discursive tendencies might be framing policies now and in the future. The splitting up of care into functions could imply 'administerable needs' becoming prioritised and the dilution of the responsibility towards the recipient. Parallel to this division of tasks the recipients of care are re-written, since they increasingly become associated with self-determination, self-management and care of oneself. Finally, there has been a discursive turn to needs concerning growth, pre-emptive measures and tending: a will to the pleasant. Needs that do not easily

---

[24] The word 'care of the self' is a radical concept, since it signifies a basic re-orientation in care from a Greek to a Roman perception of care (Vejledning om skole- og praktikuddan-nelser i de grundlæggende social- og sundhedsuddannelser, nr. 223, 1990; Foucault, 1996). Care is no longer exclusively articulated as based upon a relationship (the Greek notion), but instead as including a need directed towards oneself (the Roman notion): a need for care of oneself.

lend themselves to the logic of 'administerable needs'. However, it is not yet possible to determine the concrete effects of such a re-writing upon policies and the concrete discourses applied by home-helpers. We can only speculate upon their potential effects.

The threats present in the budgetary and governance discourse as well as the leadership and development discourse are related to NPM and its focus upon efficiency and engineering change. The third discursive threat implied in the will to the pleasant involves a rather different articulation of caring needs, since there is an increasing focus upon intimate and pleasant needs as opposed to more tedious and negatively associated needs such as relieving distress and loneliness. It implies a redirection of the fulfilment of needs towards the self of the recipient. The will to the pleasant and the two other discourses are threatening care in a different way than the advocates of a care cap presume. The feminist adherents to a thesis of a care gap have premised their diagnosis upon an image of a golden past and a retrenchment of the welfare state. Retrenchment understood as a withdrawal of obligations, i.e. of rolling back the state in relation to eligibility and level of services. However, the will to the pleasant, the splitting up of care and the tendency towards an internal marketization, and the tyranny of transformation are threatening care from *within,* and not from the outside of the welfare state. Managerialism and intimization jeopardize care from within and not from exogenous pressures to retrench.

The new paradigm involves a change in the language of power, and the way it is possible to think and talk about care. Some needs become prioritised whereas others become silenced. Codification, restructuring, and a presupposed need for better leadership are articulated as the cure for the diagnosed ills of publicly provided elderly care. This shift in paradigm has not only potentially negative effects for the recipients of care, but for the caregivers as well. The increased codification and splitting up of care could imply a de-professionalization of home-helpers, since they might not be able to retain their present degrees of autonomy. The splitting up of care becomes tantamount to a Taylorization. On the other hand, the leadership and development discourse might pull the home-helpers in a different direction, that of an increased professionalization. The leadership and developmental discourse has previously functioned as a condition of possibility for such a process, and might enable a further professionalization of home-helpers.

References

Andersen, B. Rold (1999): *Ældrepolitik på afveje.* Copenhagen: Fremad.

Andersen, J. Goul (2000): 'Welfare Crisis and Beyond', in: Kuhnle, S (ed.): *Survival of the European Welfare State,* London: Routledge.

Andersen, N. Åkerstrøm (1996): *Udlicitering – Når det private bliver politisk.* Copenhagen: Nyt fra samfundsvidenskaberne.

Andersen, N. Åkerstrøm (1997): *Udlicitering – strategi og historie.* Copenhagen: Nyt fra samfundsvidenskaberne.

Ashburner, L., Ferlie, E., Fitzgerald, L. and Pettigrew, A. (1996): *The New Public Management in Action*. Oxford: Oxford University Press.

Boje, T. and Leira, A. (2000): 'Introduction', in: Boje and Leira: *Gender, Welfare State and the Market*, London: Routledge.

Budgetanalyse om hjemmehjælp, 1995. Copenhagen: Finansministeriet.

Butler, J. (in press): 'What is Critique? An Essay on Foucault's Virtue'.

Clarke, J. and Newman, J. (1997): *The Managerial State*. London: Sage.

Daatland, S.O. and Szebehely, M. (1997): 'Tjenestene og utviklingen I sammenheng', in: Daatland, S.O. (ed.): *De siste årene*. Oslo: Norsk Insitutt for forskning om oppvekst, velferd og aldring.

Dahl, H.M. (1997): 'Mellem kærlighed og arbejde – Omsorgsteori: Traditioner og centrale temaer', in: *Kvinder, Køn og Forskning* 6, 2: 56-65.

Dahl, H.M. (2000a): *Fra kitler til eget tøj – Diskurser om professionalisme, omsorg og køn*. Århus: Politica.

Dahl, H.M. (2000b): 'A Perceptive and Reflective State?', in: *The European Journal of Women's Studies*, 7, 4: 475-494.

Dahl, H.M. (2001): 'Empowerment og disempowerment? To historier om hjemmehjælperfeltet', in: *Kvinder, Køn og Forskning*, 10, 2: 58-68.

Dahl, H.M. (2002): 'En køn retfærdighed? Et spørgsmål om status og lighed med hjemmehjælpen som case', in: Borchorst, A.: *Kønsmagt i forandring*. Copenhagen: Hans Reitzel.

Ferrera and Rhodes (2000): 'Recasting European Welfare States: Introduction', in: *West European Politics*, 23, 2: 1-10.

Foucault, M. (1978): *The History of Sexuality*. London: Penguin.

Foucault, M. (1993): *Diskursens Ordning*. Stockholm: Brutus Östlings Forlag.

Foucault, M. (1996): 'The Ethics in the Concern of the Self as a Practice of Freedom', in: Lotringer, S (ed.): *Foucault live*. New York: Semiotext(e).

Fraser, N. (1990): 'Struggle over Needs: Outline of a Socialist-Feminist Critical Theory of Late-Capitalist Political Culture' in: Gordon, L. (ed.): *Women, the State and Welfare*. Madison: University of Wisconsin Press: 199-225.

Green-Pedersen, C. (2001): 'Welfare-State Retrenchment in Denmark and the Netherlands 1982-88. The Role of Party Competition and Party Consensus', in: *Comparative Political Studies*, 34, 9: 963-985.

Green-Pedersen, C. (2002): 'Markedsreformer af velfærdsservice i Danmark og Sverige: Hvad er der sket, og hvad er forklaringen?', in: *Samfundsøkonomen*, 3: 20-25.

Hall, P. (1993): 'Policy Paradigms, Social Learning, and the State', *Comparative Politics*, 25, 3: 275-296.

Hjemmehjælp til gamle mennesker (1982). Copenhagen: Socialstyrelsen.

Hjemmehjælp i bevægelse (1986). Copenhagen: Socialstyrelsen.

Hochschild, A.R. (1995): 'The Culture of Politics: Traditional, Postmodern, Cold-modern, and Warm-modern ideals of Care', in: *Social Politics*, 2, 3: 331-346.

Johansson, S. (1995): 'Introduktion', in: *Sjukhus och hem som arbetsplats*, Stockholm: Bonniers & Universitetsforlaget.

Knijn, T. and Kremer, M. (1997): 'Gender and the Caring Dimension of the Welfare States: Toward Inclusive Citizenship', in: *Social Politics*, 4: 3: 328-361.

Kuhnle, S. (2000): 'The Scandinavian Welfare State in the 1990s: Challenged but Viable', *West European Politics*, 23, 2: 209-228.

Leira, A. (1992): *Welfare States and Working Mothers*. Cambridge: Cambridge University Press.

'Lov om social Service' (1997) (no. 454 af den 10. juni 1997).

'Lov om retssikkerhed og administration på det sociale område' (1997) (nr. 453 af den 10. juni 1997).

'Lov om ændring i lov om folkeforsikring' (Lov nr. 100 af 18. april), 1958.

Norval, Aletta (1996): *Deconstructing Apartheid Discourse*. London: Verso.

Ny hjemmehjælp: faser i en overgang (1986). Copenhagen: Socialstyrelsen.

OECD (1981): *The Welfare State in Crisis*. Paris: OECD.

Omlægning og fornyelse af indsatsen for ældre (1983) Vejledning. Copenhagen: Socialstyrelsen.

'Personaleforbruget på ældreområdet' (1981-1984, 1985). Copenhagen: Socialstyrelsen.

Pierson, P. (2001a): 'Introduction', in: Pierson, P (ed.): *The New Politics of the Welfare State*. Oxford: Oxford University Press.

Pierson, P. (2001b): 'Coping with Permanent Austerity', in: Pierson, P. (ed.): *The New Politics of the Welfare State*. Oxford: Oxford University Press.

Rammer for fremtidens bistands-, pleje- og omsorgsuddannelser (1989), Betænkning no. 1180. Copenhagen: Undervisningsministeriet.

Rapport om udviklingen i hjemmehjælpen (1991). Copenhagen: Socialministeriet.

Rapport fra arbejdsgruppen om minimumsrettigheder og kriterier for evt. ankeadgang for tildeling af hjemmehjælp (1994). Copenhagen: Socialmininisteriet.

Saraceno, C. (1997): *Family, Market and Community*. Paris: OECD (Social Policy Studies no. 21).

Schmidt, L.H. and Kristensen, J.E. (1986): 'Den forebyggende tanke', in: *Social Kritik* 1, 1: 56-59.

Taylor, F.W. (1947): *The Principles of Scientific Management*. New York: Harper & Brothers Publishers.

Torfing, J. (1999): *New Theories of Discourse*. Oxford: Blackwell.

Tronto, J.C. (1993): *Moral Boundaries*. New York: Routledge.

Ungerson, C. (1987): *The Personal is Political*. London: Tavistock.

Vejledning om bedre ressourceanvendelsen i ældresektoren (1980). Copenhagen: Socialstyrelsen.

Vejledning om skole- og praktikuddannelser i de grundlæggende social- og sundhedsuddannelser, nr. 223, 1990.

Visitation på ældreområdet (1981). Copenhagen: Socialstyrelsen.

Visker, R. (1995): *Michel Foucault – Genealogy as Critique*. London: Verso.

Witz, A. (1992): *Professions and Patriarchy*. London: Routledge.

Wærness, K. (1982): *Kvinneperspektiver på socialpolitiken*. Oslo: Universitetsforlaget.

Chapter 4

The Changing Terms of Welfare Service Work: Finnish Home Care in Transition

Sirpa Wrede and
Lea Henriksson

Introduction

In the Nordic countries, the professional groups that provide welfare services are traditionally dependent on the public sector. As the Nordic welfare states invested in building comprehensive health and social care, the welfare state and the occupations became engaged in a particularly close relationship (Brante 1990, Bertilsson 1990, Erichsen 1995, Konttinen 1991, Riska 1993). For welfare service professionals, the welfare state determined the terms of employment and set the limits for professional autonomy.

The Nordic welfare state has been particularly important for women, as those campaigning for women's rights have tended to view women's dependency on the state as less problematic than their traditional dependency on a male breadwinner, the family, community, charity or employer. Women's private dependency on men as providers became replaced by a dependency on the universalist welfare state (Holter 1984, Dahlerup 1987, Hernes 1987). Women have not only been linked to welfare policies as service users. As service professionals, a significant part of the female labour force has been employed by the public sector to provide the welfare services on which primarily women have depended.

The Nordic welfare states sponsored and shaped professional projects of women-dominated professional groups when these were in line with welfare policy (Milton 2001, Wrede 2001, Evertsson 2002). The policies result from political campaigns and the ideologies shaping welfare policies are constitutive for the ways the state regulates gendered relations in welfare service work. When it comes to the regulation of women's work as professionals, the universalist Nordic welfare states were a site of gendered relations and practices that constructed the division of labour and made room for women's interests and agency (Waerness 1984, Julkunen 1991, Rantalaiho and Heiskanen 1997, Mósesdóttir 2001).

Welfare policies structure services and thus shape professional jurisdictions that might otherwise not even exist (Evertsson 2000). This chapter focuses on welfare service work in the Finnish welfare state that is a particular case even among the Nordic countries. In Finnish feminist research, the notion of the 'women's welfare state' has been used to refer to the complex ways women's professional and political projects have been linked to the state formation (Anttonen et al. 1994). In Finland also women-dominated professional groups at the lower levels of professional hierarchies have had successful collective mobility projects linked to the expansion of welfare services (Simonen 1990, Satka 1995, Henriksson 1998, 1999). How has the retrenchment of the welfare state in the 1990s changed this linkage of women as professional care workers?

In this chapter we examine the position of women-dominated professional groups in home care, one of the welfare services provided by the Finnish welfare state. Our focus is on professional projects as collective mobility projects (Larson 1977). Previous literature has claimed that women's professional projects fail because of the way patriarchal relations are institutionalized in the state (Witz 1992). The position of women's professional projects in the context of the Nordic welfare states challenge the taken-for-granted assumptions on the gendered terms of professional projects. Here we examine these more closely.

Home care is an interesting case for our study because it transcends traditional institutional boundaries within the welfare state system. The old home care model in Finland consisted of two separate types of municipal services, home help organised by the social sector and home nursing for which the health sector was responsible. Many different groups of care workers, including different levels of nursing professionals, social care professionals and, to some extent, untrained service workers, provided the services. The ongoing transformation results from the retrenchment policies carried out in the name of the New Public Management (NPM) and the economic recession in the 1990s. NPM as the new ideology of the Finnish welfare state implies that the public resources are limited and need to be carefully rationed. Since the 1990s, particularly economic players in Finland define the relevant political context for public policy in global terms and they no longer vest the national policy frame with the broad mandate it held during the heyday of the Finnish welfare state (Kantola and Kautto 2002). The adopted politics of retrenchment emphasizes the responsibility of the individual for his or her personal welfare. Market logic has become applied to all types of service production. Even though privatization and marketization have not become broad scale trends in the Finnish welfare system, many new types of service producers have emerged. As a result, a cultural shift is occurring, even though municipalities still remain major players in the organization of welfare services (Julkunen 2001, 2003).

The politics of retrenchment has transformed home care from a welfare service into a service mosaic. Our argument is that this institutional restructuring, in turn, leads to a reconfiguration of welfare service occupations. This process of gendered segmentation results in divisions between service workers employed by the different service producers. The universalist welfare state in Finland contributed to the emergence of new ideas concerning the roles professionals play in society that can be termed 'democratic professionalism' (Hugman 1991). As the structure of the welfare services in the universalist welfare state reflected the progressive ideologies underlying it, it empowered both users and members of the professional groups providing them. Through the transformation of the institutional matrix for welfare services, the politics of retrenchment creates a basis for a return to traditional professionalism that is divisive, conservative and individualistic. This style of professionalism that tends to deny the needs of its workers has consequences for gender equality in professional work. It enforces rigid hierarchical divisions of labour and ignores the private lives of professionals (Davies 1995).

The welfare service work framework

Our concept of welfare service work is a development of the interactionist tradition in sociology of work and occupations (e.g., Davies 1979, 1995, 2002, Stacey 1984, Abbott 1988, Dingwall et al. 1988). A particular opening is the concept of health work that Celia Davies (1979) linked to an 'institutional matrix'. Her view offers a fruitful starting point for the analysis of professional projects in the context of the restructuring of the welfare state.

In this study we examine the institutional matrix of home care. We argue that for understanding how welfare service work is organized, it is important to recognise the institutional and occupational dimensions of the matrix that shapes it. Institutional logics include, for instance, the gendered politics of defining the boundaries of welfare services with the dichotomous concepts of informal and formal, paid and unpaid, public and private, social care and health care. Similarly gendered occupational logics include, for instance, distinctions between caring and curing, auxiliary and autonomous, professional and semi- or non-professional. The gendered consequences of these historical, social and cultural divisions were alleviated by the universalist welfare state. The politics of retrenchment revitalizes these divisions by strengthening gendered, ethnic and class inequalities among service workers.

By conceptualising the object of our study, home care, as a welfare service, we emphasise that access to and availability of the service are regulated by policy. The formation of a welfare service, like home care, is a historically and institutionally situated process that is culturally embedded and associated with state tradition (Chamberlayne et al. 1999, Freeman 1999). In Finland the welfare services traditionally constituted a municipally provided complex that is subjected to several types of policies rooted in different policy areas. In the recent restructuring a welfare-mosaic where services are produced by multiple producers has emerged. In this process, home care as a welfare service has become narrower and less equitable.

The analysis builds on an ongoing study of the formation and transformations of home care in Finland (Henriksson and Wrede 2000, Burau et al. 2004).[1] In the

---

[1] The analysis relies on documentary analysis of policy documents, reports and other similar materials. We have also conducted reviews of professional journals for health professionals, i.e. nurses, public health nurses and practical nurses.

next section we examine how home care has been redefined in the 1990s. Secondly, we examine the emergence of integrated home care. Thirdly, we study the recent policies that fragment the formerly uniform service into a welfare mosaic. The fourth section considers how the ideology of flexibility is transforming the required competences and the employment opportunities available for professionals. The analysis pays attention to the point of view of the different nursing professionals that are involved in home care, i.e., nurses, public health nurses and practical nurses. In the final section, we reflect on the fate of 'women-friendliness' in the restructured welfare state. We recognize the polarization of the welfare service labour market and consider its gendered consequences.

Home care as a welfare service in Finland

The roots of modern home care in Finland are in the welfare policies of the 1940s. During that decade, the activities of public health nurses, employed by the municipality, and deaconesses employed by the parishes were first outlined in public policy. Also homemaking was becoming redefined as a municipal, rather than voluntary, service. This did not mean the dominance of the public sector. Before the expansion of the welfare services in the 1970s, multiple producers, including local parishes, municipalities and voluntary organizations, provided services. Even though the state did grant financial aid for the provision of home nursing services, the aid was limited and there was no shared policy for the level of services. For the elderly, a major part of the limited services provided was temporary ambulatory care termed home nursing. Two occupations were central for home nursing services: ambulatory nurses employed by the municipalities and deaconesses employed by the parishes (Sinkkonen 1967, Tallberg 1984). The practice of nurse-trained deaconesses had a religious orientation, whereas the ambulatory nurses were secular, lower grade nurses.

The introduction of municipal homemaking during the 1940s was a rapid development, as municipalities were encouraged to establish a new service. The work of the new professionals was defined as a social welfare service, primarily directed at families with children and belonging to the jurisdiction of the municipal social boards. In 1950, the organization of municipal homemaking became regulated through law. However, it remained voluntary for the municipalities to decide whether to hire homemakers. The services were expanded to the elderly in the late 1960s, when the Finnish welfare state adopted a more universalist orientation.

The expansion of home care to the elderly was organized through the creation of a new lower grade occupation, the home helps. However, they also were regulated municipal service workers. Unlike homemakers who were trained in a young age, home helps generally entered the occupation in adulthood, as many of them were former housewives (Simonen 1990). Their education was much shorter than that of homemakers, reflecting their different occupational profiles. Homemakers were expected to provide a more comprehensive type of social care, whereas the home helps were considered to replace non-qualified informal care.

Nevertheless, the creation of the municipal home help broadened the scope of social services provided at homes. The new services benefited the group of elderly that primarily needed assistance in housekeeping. The elderly in need of long-term care generally became institutionalized. The increase in residential care was related to structural change in health care. When local health centres providing primary care were established in the early 1970s, home nursing became defined as one of the tasks of the health centre. Home nursing was not emphasised in the new scheme and, consequently, nursing care organised in ambulatory fashion diminished substantially (Ohtonen et al. 1983). It is safe to say that home care was not perceived as a core service in elderly care. Instead, publicly organized institutional care for the elderly increased rapidly. So-called municipal homes provided care for the elderly in need of continuous but basic care. Health centre hospitals provided more medical-oriented long-term care (Vauhkonen 1978).

Starting from the late 1970s, there were efforts to develop home care and de-institutionalise the care for the elderly. This was in line with the more individual orientation in welfare policy, including that applied in elderly care (Paasivaara 2002). Concerning home nursing, these aims became interwoven with the larger health reform that was implemented in the late 1980s. The 'population responsibility principle' was at that time promoted as a new policy to be implemented in the primary health centres.

The new policy entailed family-oriented primary care provided by a health care team. The core professionals of the team were doctors and public health nurses who were to service a certain population 'from baby to grandpa'. Prior to the new integrated primary care, home nursing was organized separately with personnel consisting mainly of nurses and practical nurses (Koponen 1997). Along the lines of population responsibility, the new policy was to make the planning and organization of home nursing a part of the multifarious activities of the public health nurse. Many public health nurses did not perceive this work as 'theirs', but practical nurses and nurses who continued to practice in home nursing care still feared a loss of autonomy resulting from the involvement of the new group (Koponen and Perttilä 1993).

In the late 1980s, the population responsibility principle was not yet extended to social care. However, a more transformative policy shift was gaining momentum. The reorganization of the National Board of Welfare and Health into the National Research and Development Centre for Welfare (Stakes) in 1993 marks a turning point after which the reforms of the welfare system became outlined according to the principles of the New Public Management (NPM) (e.g., Stakes 1993). The steering role of Stakes is defined as provision of information and consulting to the municipalities, but it does not have a mandate to regulate municipal policy. In the spirit of the NPM, policymaking of the mid 1990s aimed at restructuring the role of the public sector in home care, aiming at the creation of a home care mosaic. Somewhat more tacitly, the reforms have aimed at limiting the responsibility of the public sector for home care. It is to these changes we now will turn.

The emergence of integrated home care

In Finland, as elsewhere, the early 1990s was a period of severe economic problems that gave impetus to the cuts in spending on welfare services (Julkunen and Nätti 1997, Julkunen 2001, 2003, Eräsaari 2002).[2] As a result, the previously 'safe' public sector labour market became insecure and unstable (Kauhanen 2002). However, the restructuring of the public sector did neither originate with the recession, nor with the temporary political shift that left the socialist parties in opposition. Rather, the implementation of NPM resulted from a broader ideological shift in welfare state thinking (Kovalainen 1999, Julkunen 2001). The restructuring and subsequent merge of the central agencies that steer welfare policies and the redefinition of the role of state steering are signs of the weakening of the role of the central state in the implementation of welfare policy.

Despite the breakthrough of the NPM, there was no explicit challenge to universalism as a principle in welfare policy. For instance, national policymakers continued to use the concept of population responsibility in policy rhetoric, but in a different guise. The concept became redefined to include the notion that social care and primary health care were to be provided in an integrated, effective fashion. The ideal of multi-professionalism implied the creation of inter-sector teams. Central aims were to lower institutional barriers and bridge different organizational and occupational cultures (e.g., Stakes 1993).

In elderly care, a reform termed integrated home care was initiated in the mid 1990s. In the policy rhetoric, the individual client became the basis for defining continuity of care. At the same time, the responsibility of the individual for the cost of care increased. Fees for public services became more strongly linked to the client's income (Ministry of Social Affairs and Health 2002a). Additionally, municipalities carried out cuts to their services so that potential clients with 'light needs' are increasingly left without access to publicly provided services (Vaarama et al. 2001).

In accordance with the new policy goals, many municipalities have merged home nursing with the home help services. For instance, in 1999, three out of the five largest cities had created integrated home care (Kumpulainen 1999, 3). This does not, however, mean a uniform service structure. The country is divided into 446 municipalities all of which devise their own policies and practices and are thus able to decide the institutional arrangements and composition of care teams. In the next section, we will consider the policymaking that continues to reshape municipal home care, but we will begin by discussing the policy developments that have redefined its role as a welfare service.

---

[2] The Finnish problems were made particularly severe by the temporary collapse of Finland's trade. The fall of the Soviet Union, Finland's number one trading partner in the 1980s, was reflected, among other things, in a massive unemployment in the 1990s. Unemployment, in turn, created a crisis for the public economy. At its highest level, unemployment in Finland was 16.6% in 1994. In 2002, unemployment was still 9.1% (Statistics Finland 2003).

New policies, new practices

The critique of traditional institutional care occupied a central place in the rhetoric of the Finnish elderly policy since the late 1970s. The criticism was rooted in the ideology of the universalist welfare state and its emphasis on taking individual needs into consideration in care (Anttonen and Sipilä 1996, 2000, Tedre 1998, Paasivaara 2002). The new goal for elderly policy was to enable independent living even when care needs increased. It was expressed in the new policies of the 1990s examined below.

Firstly, there were efforts to reduce the demand for municipally provided care by encouraging informal care. In 1993, economic compensation and other support to family caregivers were included in the Social Welfare Act. At a time of high unemployment, informal care was expected to be an option for some of the unemployed, particularly women, to earn a small income for the family care they provide. Informal care was to be promoted by arranging training and work guidance for family carers, who also were to be arranged regular free time from their commitment (Ministry of Social Affairs and Health 1994, 11). The system was later complemented so that family caregivers who receive support from a municipality accumulate their work pension with this income. The informal carers were expected to be able, with the help of supporting services, to provide care for persons in need of both social and medical care.

Secondly, there were policies that aimed at restructuring the publicly provided elderly care by creating new service alternatives that would support the dismantling of traditional service forms. The municipalities were encouraged with economic incentives to shift the emphasis in care from traditional institutional settings to service housing (Nissinen and Santalo 2001).[3] The rapid increase in service housing created a pressure in the municipal economy. Traditional home care suffered, even though the official policy afforded it a central role in elderly care. Table 3.1 gives an overview of the changes in services for the elderly in Finland during the 1990s.

---

[3] Service housing (*palveluasuminen*) refers to different types of housing services to the elderly. It does not necessarily imply actual delivery of services. It is common to talk about three levels of housing services that are either light, medium or intensified service. About one half of service housing units provide intensive, 24-hour care (Nissinen and Santalo 2001, 15).

Table 3.1
Profile of elderly care service in Finland, 1988-1999

Clients % of all 75 + *)	1988	1995	1999	Change 1988-1999 %
Home help %	46.2	28.8	25.4	-45.0
Support services	36.1	32.6	31.2	-13.6
Benefit to family carers	4.2	3.8	4.0	-4.8
% of elderly living in service housing	2.1	4.6	6.0	185.7
Long-term residential care % of the elderly	10.5	7.0	7.8	-25.7
Long-term care at primary care hospitals	4.1	4.0	4.0	-2.4
Long-term care at special care hospitals	3.0	0.3	0.2	-93.3
Long-term residential care in total	17.0	12.0	12.0	-29.4

*) Figures for the elderly over 75 years of age have been calculated from population-level figures for clients over 65 years of age. Source: Vaarama et al. 2001.

The creation of service housing has blurred the boundaries between home care and residential care, as the new service is categorized as home care. Furthermore, resources, including one third of home care personnel, have been shifted from home care to service housing (Vaarama et al. 2001, 27-28).

The third trend has to do with changes in the orientation of municipal home care. As municipalities struggle to respond to the demand to cater to 'heavy service needs', new expectations are placed on home care. Increasingly often, those who receive publicly provided home care are more aptly described as patients than as clients. One expression of the cultural change is 'intensified home care'. The 24-hour service that many municipalities have introduced as a part of their home care arrangements includes taking care of patients with special care needs like terminal care. Another trend that contributes to the medicalization of municipal home care is related to de-institutionalization of medical care. In recent years, municipalities and inter-municipal associations have sought to organize a new form of care according to the principle of 'hospital at home' (e.g., Tehy 2000 a, b, c, Suomen Lääkärilehti 2001). Such medical services are intended for elderly patients as well as other groups of patients. As people with more and more severe medical problems are to be treated at their homes, elements of specialized medical care are transferred to the home. This type of care is provided in connection to hospitals with continuous involvement of physicians.

This last trend, the intensification of municipal home care towards medical care, has particular consequences for its occupational structure. The culture of home care and its division of labour are changing, as medically oriented care requires personnel with qualifications to provide nursing care. Apart from the fact that medical needs are becoming increasingly important criteria for access to municipal home care, the new orientation challenges the composition of the professional teams providing home care. The extent and form of medicalization of home care varies at the local level. In the traditional model, there are separate organizations for home help and for home nursing. In integrated home care the teams include professionals from both the social sector and the health centre and some of them may have the new trans-sector practical nurse competence. In some municipalities, usually in those that have integrated home care, there are separate units for intensive home care that include doctors. The units providing hospital-level care in an ambulatory fashion are typically at place only in bigger cities.

The changes of the institutional environment and the related transformation of occupational cultures in home care result from the policy of welfare service retrenchment (Julkunen 2001). It emphasizes individual responsibility and promotes the creation of a welfare mosaic. While the structural change in home care does reflect the new ideology of the NPM, the rapid decline in the provision of home care also bears witness to the difficulty of controlling the effects of cuts in welfare policy. At the same time, all the former ideals shaping elderly care policy have not disappeared. During the 1990s, the humanistic rhetoric of the universal welfare state blended with the neo-liberal ideas. In fact, the redefinition of the role of the public sector is often justified by the need to make space for the autonomy of the individual. The co-existence of diverse values concerning elderly care creates a complex setting for its personnel. In the next section, we will examine the implications of the transformation of home care for the reconfiguration of its occupational qualifications and consider the conditions of the welfare service labour market.

Flexible qualifications and flexible workers in the restructured home care

In the universal welfare state home care was primarily a public sector service and its occupational structure reflected this situation. Home care occupations were divided into health and social care occupations. The NPM inspired reforms have sought to overcome this divide in order to achieve flexibility in care. In 1993, a new, shared basic degree for both health care and social care sectors was created when eleven social and health care vocational curricula were integrated into one. In addition to a shared set of basic studies, all students specialize in some field of

care, such as nursing or elderly care. This curriculum leads to a 'vocational qualification in social and health care' for practical nurses.[4] The Centre for Medico-
Legal Affairs registers these professionals as health care professionals. The registration authorises them to perform health care tasks but they also provide social
care. The development of the new practical nurse curriculum has continued with
several modifications. From the point of view of home care the most important
measure is that in the late 1990s, a new speciality in the care of the elderly was
introduced into the curriculum. This reflects the efforts of the policymakers to give
elderly care a higher profile as a professional field. The central actors in the educational reforms are the Ministry of Education and the National Board of Education
together with the polytechnics and the Finnish Association for Municipalities
(Ministry of Social Affairs and Health 2001a).

The creation of the new occupation merged the previously separate educational
paths for homemakers and practical nurses, leaving the two occupational orientations – that still continue to exist in the municipal service structure – without institutional backing. Professionals with old credentials are often encouraged to acquire
the new qualification, but at the same time, the new curriculum has been subjected
to severe criticism and particularly hospitals have been unwilling to employ personnel with the new degree.

The rhetoric of the reform was to enable a broader potential field of practice
for the health and social care professionals at the lowest level of occupational hierarchies. Another goal was to create an easily employable and movable service
worker (Tiilikkala 1995). However, the occupational roles of the new 'practical
nurses' have remained unclear, and many of them report being confined in the traditional role as an assistant. For many practical nurses the occupation has become
only one educational step, as it qualifies for further study (Rintala and Elovainio
1997, Ministry of Social Affairs and Health 2001b).

The second new occupation for elderly care was created at the turn of the 21st
century. The new qualification can be attained in the polytechnics, where a specialised curriculum in the management of elderly care has been created. At present the
new qualification is still rather invisible in public discussion, but the first of the
professionals have already received their qualifications. The term used is geronomi
(~geronomer, building on the word gerontology). The geronomers are not registered health care professionals (Ministry of Social Affairs and Health 2001b). Their
tasks can include, for instance, co-ordination and planning of home care of the elderly in the municipalities, a task that previously was performed separately in the
two sectors of home care. Their competence is to cover the care for the elderly in
both health and social care and they are to be considered as managerial experts in
the domain (Finnish National Board of Education 2002).

It is fair to assume that in the long run, the new curricula tailored for integrated
home care will reshape and challenge occupational as well as institutional boundaries in home care. The professional associations representing nurses feel threa-

---

[4] The occupational term used in Finnish is *lähihoitaja*, meaning the carer who is near or
close to the person cared for. However, the term is generally translated into English using
the term 'practical nurse'.

tened by the policy shift and the related educational reforms. They argue for respecting occupational boundaries (Tehy 2000b, 2002). The loudest reaction against trans-sector home care and its new occupational orientations comes from public health nurses. Apparently, the association representing public health nurses fears that in a fully integrated home care the professional position of public health nurses will be challenged and they will be forced to accept managers lacking their professional qualifications. Furthermore, the claims public health nurses make on elderly care can be explained by their need to defend their position in the labour market. The association representing public health nurses has a professional project of its own in elderly care. In its professionalist rhetoric, elderly care is linked to their traditional professional competence, health promotion. The argument is that the elderly need to be supported to acquire an active role as senior citizens rather than as aged and infirm patients (Terveydenhoitaja 2001a,b,c). The association does, however, acknowledge the problems facing their role in primary care as preventive health care has a marginal role in current health policy.

An additional pressure on all home care occupations comes from the segmentation of the labour market in home care. In the home care mosaic, inequality is increasing, also within the public sector labour market. In the 1990s, major cuts were made in the public spending on municipal services. In the resulting situation, the municipalities have sought to control their costs with new employer practices. One trend is the increased reliance on personnel lacking basic degrees (Vaarama et al. 2001). The trade unions representing health care professionals have drawn attention to the fact that the number of untrained staff is rising (Tehy 2000b, Super 2001). However, the overriding concern for the professional organizations has been the major loss of permanent fulltime jobs in the municipal labour market. Additionally, they have criticized the use of temporary employment as a strategy to control costs and promote flexibility of labour force. The professional associations note with satisfaction that also many leading politicians criticize the municipalities as employers (Super 2000, Terveydenhoitaja 2001d), but despite the vocal criticism and public concern, the structural changes in the welfare service labour market remain unmitigated. The problems of the welfare service labour market have led to a segmented labour force, shaped by a competition for jobs between different groups of professionals. Additionally, the public sector labour force is divided into permanent and temporary workers, with very different positions in both the labour market and the work place (cf., Theobald 2002). Aside from the municipal labour market, a private labour market for home care employees has emerged.

In the near future, a large proportion of the labour force that provides welfare services will retire (Ailasmaa 2000). Recruitment is already emerging as a general policy concern (eg., Suomen Kuntaliitto 2003). Even the Government has recognised that the problems of the public sector as an employer may lead to a recruitment crisis for the welfare services. This was, for instance, one of the reasons listed for the establishment of a 'national health project' to 'secure the future of the Finnish health system' (Ministry of Social Affairs and Health 2002a, b). The task force argues that the problems of the health system come from within: its organization is fragmented, it lacks central steering and the cuts have been too severe. The project is an indication of a renewed willingness among the policymakers at the national level to restrict municipal autonomy. However, these sentiments have not led to an institutional reorientation of welfare policy, nor have the effects of the politics of retrenchment in the 1990s yet become overturned.

Conclusions

This chapter has examined the present dilemmas shaping the position of home care workers. Our aim was to understand the ongoing social and cultural transformation of welfare service work in Finland. Due to the changes in the welfare state labour market, many of the welfare service workers that previously were aptly described as welfare-state professionals can no longer be identified with this term. How does this restructuring affect the welfare state occupations?

Three policy strategies have redefined home care as a welfare service. First, overall retrenchment of services has been sought in publicly provided home care. The cuts have been achieved applying both the 'cheese slicer' techniques of cutting costs evenly from all services and the more transformative pruning techniques directed at services that are not considered as basic services. Cuts in public spending on municipal welfare services have resulted in an increase of temporary employment and use of purchased services. Municipalities have used these means to shift the economic risk in welfare service production to other service producers.

The increased reliance on purchased services is an expression of the second strategy, marketization of care that lacks tradition in Finland. The new care entrepreneurs are mostly former public sector employees who have founded small firms (Kovalainen 1999, 2002, Kovalainen and Österberg 2000). The third strategy in public policy that reflects the new policy on home care is the partial refamilization of home care that is occurring, when informal care in part is expected to cover areas that municipal care previously provided for. The concept of the paid family caregiver supports the new expectation, possibly an obligation, for family members, most often mothers, wives or daughters, to take over the responsibility for the care of their family members. This is promoted through benefits given to informal carers. Together, the three neo-liberal policy strategies of retrenchment, marketization and refamilization support the rise of the subsidiary principle in the way publicly provided home care is produced in municipalities, despite the fact that universalism survives at the level of national policy rhetoric.

For the home care that municipalities provide directly, the 1990s imply implementation of lean production thinking that emphasises flexibility. This is expressed in the creation of integrated home care as a new trans-sector field of municipal policy. Together with the above-described transformation of the institutional matrix of home care, the creation of integrated home care has reshaped home care as an occupational field.

We have here identified three central consequences for the occupational structure in home care. First, the implementation of the policies for integrating municipal home care services has challenged the task-based division of labour in home care that has served to define boundaries between different types of caring expertise. The new managerial logic seeks to restructure the provision of home care so that the care personnel 'flexibly' provide all the service needs of a client. For the health care personnel, this means doing tasks they previously only have wanted to supervise. For social care personnel, the effect of the new principle is more problematic as they lack formal qualifications for health care tasks. Secondly, the role of public health nurses is downplayed in planning and direct supervision of home care. For instance, the cutting of the health promotion activities has narrowed down their professional competence and left them in a nursing role. Third, the role of doctors is emphasized in municipally provided home care, as ambulatory units providing medical care are created.

Together, the three features of integrated home care have supported the introduction of the new trans-sector qualifications. Concerning care professionals, the overall emphasis is on flexibility. Together with the increased medical influence in work settings, the logic of traditional hospital organization appears to be breaking ground in municipal home care.

The new welfare service matrix creates winners and losers. The new integrated home care offers opportunities for new professional projects built around management and for developing a new medical specialty, the home care doctor. By contrast, the personnel that traditionally worked relatively autonomously in home care, now works within doctor-led teams. The group that appears to have lost most in the restructuring are the short-trained home helps whose former work falls under the category 'light service needs'. This means that the production of these services in the public sector diminishes. Often their former tasks and jobs are taken over by other groups, as a result of the new work models.

Our study indicates that the emergence of a welfare mosaic in home care results in the reconfiguration of home care personnel. For the care professionals that represent the different women-dominated groups in home care, new ways of organising home care work create vulnerable employment. The labour market position of welfare service workers may improve in future, when the demographic situation most likely will create a shortage of workforce. More worrisome, because of the depth of the cultural change that is occurring is the impoverishment of welfare service work. Home care is becoming a professional field in the traditional sense: divided and hierarchical according to the logic of medical dominance.

The earlier room for professionalism of women-dominated groups was combined and supported by regulated terms of employment, a safe position in the labour market and a clear division of labour. Women-friendliness did not mean that all were treated equal, or that all groups had shared interests. There were efforts from the more powerful groups to control and limit the work of other groups, reflecting the occupational structure in home care that emerged through divergent policies at different times and for different reasons. However, the universalism of the welfare policy and the overall challenge to class-based social divisions embedded in it formed a powerful counterforce to the social inequalities. It resulted in a development towards democratic professionalism.

The state's commitment to directly provided public services and democratic professionalism created organizational shelters for the autonomous work of different groups of care professionals. In the name of flexibility, such organizational shelters have now been dismantled. A new type of gendered segmentation has emerged in home care. Some groups of care professionals are now facing market conditions; others find themselves in other forms of vulnerable employment. Furthermore, medical dominance, a form of division of labour within which doctors have sovereign positions, appears to be regaining in home care. The ongoing reconfiguration of the occupational structure in home care threatens all care professionals as the values that enabled democratic professionalism no longer direct welfare policy.

The universalist welfare state made room for collective mobility projects for care workers. Now that room is narrowed down and, for instance, the role of the trade unions representing women-dominated professional groups has been weakened as previous policy networks have been dismantled (Wrede 2001). By way of contrast, however, the medical profession is able to defend its central role in the welfare system also in the context of the welfare-mix, as the unified profession is confronted with fragmented policy networks that favour medical solutions (Lehto 2003). The present situation of Finnish home care workers bears witness to the shared dilemmas concerning care workers in the institutional context of a neoliberal welfare-mix.

Acknowledgement

This research is funded through the project 'Service Professions in Transition. Encounters in Finnish Home Nursing' (Academy of Finland project number 50453) and through a research grant from the Jenny and Antti Wihuri Foundation.

References

Abbott, A. (1988): *The System of Professions.* An Essay on the Division of Expert Labor. Chicago: The University of Chicago Press.

Ailasmaa, R. (2000): *Sosiaali- ja terveydenhuollon henkilöstö kuntasektorilla.* (Social and health care personnel in the municipal sector) Tilastoraportti 10. Helsinki: Stakes.

Anttonen, A., Henriksson, L. and Nätkin, R. (eds.) (1994): *Naisten hyvinvointivaltio.* (Women's Welfare State). Tampere: Vastapaino.

Anttonen, A. and Sipilä, J. (1996): 'European Social Care Services: Is it possible to identify models?', in: *Journal of European Social Policy* 6(2): 87-100.

Anttonen, A. and Sipilä, J. (2000): *Suomalaista sosiaalipolitiikkaa.* (Finnish Social Policy) Tampere: Vastapaino.

Aro, S. and Liukko, M. (eds.) (1993): *VPK Väestövastuisen perusterveydenhuollon kokeilut 1989-1992. Mikä muuttui?* (Demonstration projects in population responsibility for primary care 1989-1992. What changed?): 91-104. Raportteja 105. Helsinki: Stakes.

Brante, T. (1990): 'Professional Types as a Strategy of Analysis', in: Burrage, Michael and Torstendahl, Rolf (eds.): *Professions in Theory and History: Rethinking the Study of Professions*: 75-93. London: Sage.

Burau, V., Henriksson, L. and Wrede, S. (2004): 'Doing comparison on professional groups: towards a context-sensitive analysis', in: *Knowledge, Work and Society* no. 2 (May 2004) (in print).

Chamberlayne, P., Cooper, A., Freeman, R. and Rustin, M. (1999): *Welfare and Culture in Europe. Towards a New Paradigm in Social Policy*. London and Philadelphia: Jessica Kingsley Publishers.

Dahlerup, D. (1987): 'Confusing Concepts – Confusing Reality: A Theoretical Discussion of the Patriarchal State', in Showstack Sassoon, A. (ed.): *Women and the State*: 93-127. London: Hutchinson.

Davies, C. (1979): 'Comparative occupational roles in health care', in: *Social Science and Medicine* 13A: 515-521.

Davies, C. (1995): *Gender and the professional predicament of nursing*. Buckingham: Open University Press.

Davies, C. (2002): 'What about the girl next door? Gender and the politics of professional self-regulation', in: Bendelow, G., Carpenter, M., Vautier, C. and Williams, S. (eds.): *Gender, Health and Healing*: 91-106. London and New York: Routledge.

Dingwall, R., Rafferty, A., and Webster, C. (1988): *An introduction to the social history of nursing*. London: Routledge.

Erichsen, V. (1995): 'Health care reform in Norway: The end of the "profession state"'?, in: *Journal of Health Politics, Policy and Law* 20(3): 719-737.

Eräsaari, L. (2002): *Julkinen tila ja valtion yhtiöittäminen*. (Public space and corporatization of the state) Helsinki: Gaudeamus.

Evertsson, L. (2000): 'The Swedish welfare state and the emergence of female welfare state occupations', in: *Gender, Work and Organization* 7(4): 230-241.

Evertsson, L. (2002): *Välfärdspolitik och kvinnoyrken. Organization, välfärdsstat och professionaliseringens villkor*, Umeå Universitet: Akademiska avhandlingar vid Sociologiska institutionen, No 25.

Finnish National Board of Education (2002): *http://www.oph.fi/koulutusoppaat/amkopinnot/alasosi.htm*; Guides on education, document retrieved 11.6.2002.

Freeman, R. (1999): 'Institutions, States and Cultures: Health Policy and Politics in Europe', in: Clasen, J (ed.): *Comparative Social Policy. Concepts, Theories and Methods*: 80-94. Oxford and London: Blackwell Publishers.

Henriksson, L. (1998): *Naisten terveystyö ja ammatillistumisen politiikka* (Women's health work and the politics of professionalization). Tutkimuksia 88. Helsinki: Stakes.

Henriksson, L. (1999): 'Sisterhood's Ordeals: Shared Interests and Divided Loyalties', in: *Finnish Wartime Nursing'*. DYNAMIS 19: 305-327.

Henriksson, L. and Wrede, S. (2000): 'Service Professions in Transition. Encounters in Finnish Home Nursing', in: *Research plan for the Academy of Finland* (unpublished). Tampere and Turku: University of Tampere and Åbo Akademi University.

Hernes, H. (1987): *Welfare State and Women Power*. Oslo: Norwegian University Press.

Holter, H. (1984): 'Caring as Women's Work in the Welfare State', in: Holter, H. (ed.): *Patriarchy in a Welfare State*: 67-87. Oslo: Universitetsforlaget.

Hugman, R. (1991): *Power in Caring Professions*. London: Macmillan.

Julkunen, R. (1990): 'Women in the Welfare State', in: Manninen, M. and Setälä, P. (eds): *The Lady with the Bow. The Story of Finnish Women*: 140-160. Keuruu: Otava Publishers.

Julkunen, R. (1991): 'Hoiva ja professionalismi' (Care work and professionalism), in: *Sosiologia* 28(2): 75-83.

Julkunen, R. (2001): *Suunnanmuutos*. (The Change) Tampere: Vastapaino.

Julkunen, R. (2003): 'Suunnanmuutosta lukemassa' (Reading the Change), in: Saari, J. (ed.): *Instituutiot ja sosiaalipolitiikka. Johdatus instituutionaalisen muutoksen tutkimukseen*: 71-92. (Institutions and Social Policy. Introduction to the Study of Institutional Change) Helsinki: Sosiaali- ja terveysturvan keskusliitto ry.

Julkunen, R. and Nätti, J. (1997): *Työn jakaminen: moraali, talous ja politiikka.* (Diving Work: moral, economy and policy). Tampere: Vastapaino.

Kantola A. and Kautto, M. (2002): *Hyvinvoinnin valinnat. Suomen malli 2000-luvulla.* (The Choices of Welfare. The Finnish Model in the 2000's. Helsinki: Edita.

Kauhanen, M. (2002): *Määräaikaiset työsuhteet ja toimeentulon riskit.* (Temporary employment contracts and the risks of inadequate income). Sosiaali- ja terveysturvan tutkimuksia 69. Helsinki: KELA.

Konttinen, E. (1991): *Perinteisesti moderniin. Professioiden yhteiskunnallinen synty Suomessa.* (Traditionally Towards Modernity. The Birth of the Professions in Finland) Tampere: Vastapaino.

Koponen, P. (1997): *Public Health Nursing in Primary Care Based on the Population Responsibility Principle.* Acta Universitatis Tamperensis 581. Tampere: University of Tampere.

Koponen, P. and Perttilä, K. (1993): *Laaja-alaisuus vai erikoistuminen terveydenhoitajien työssä – Väestövastuu 'vauvasta vaariin'?* (Extensive service role or specialization in the work of public health nurse – Population responsibility 'from baby to grandpa'?).

Kovalainen, A. (1999): 'The Welfare State, Gender System and Public Sector Employment in Finland', in: Christensen, J. and Kovalainen A. (eds.): *Working Europe. Reshaping European Employment Systems.* Aldershot: Ashgate.

Kovalainen, A. (2002): 'Luottamus, lama ja hyvinvointipalvelujen muutokset'. (Trust, recession and changes in welfare services), in: Ilmonen,. K, Kovalainen, A. and Siisiäinen, M. (eds.): *Lama ja luottamus.* (Recession and trust) Forskningsrapporter 55. Svenska handelshögskolan. Helsinki: Hanken.

Kovalainen, A. and Österberg, J. (2000): 'Sosiaalinen pääoma, luottamus ja julkisen sektorin restrukturaatio'. (Social capital, trust and restructuring of the public sector), in: Ilmonen, K. (ed.): *Sosiaalinen pääoma ja luottamus.* (Social capital and trust). Jyväskylä: SoPhi.

Kumpulainen, A. (1999): *Viiden suurimman kaupungin vanhuspalvelujen palvelutaso- ja kustannusvertailu 1998.* (Comparison of standard and cost of care in services for the elderly in five biggest cities). Sosiaaliviraston julkaisusarja SuSe 17. Helsinki: Helsingin Kaupunki.

Larson, M.S. (1977): *The Rise of Professionalism. A Sociological Analysis.* Berkeley: University of California Press.

Lehto, J. (2003): 'Terveydenhuoltojärjestelmän muutos ja muuttumattomuus'. (Change and constancy in the health care system), in: Saari, J. (ed.): *Instituutiot ja sosiaalipolitiikka. Johdatus institutionaalisen muutoksen tutkimukseen.* (Institutions and social policy. Introduction to the study of insitutional change): 126-140. Helsinki: Sosiaali- ja terveysturvan keskusliitto ry.

Milton, L. (2001): *Folkhemmets barnmorskor. Den svenska barnmodskaekårens professionalisering under mellan – och efterkrigstiden* (Midwives in the Folkhem. Professionalization of Swedish midwifery during the inter-war and post-war period). Acta Universitatis Upsaliensis. Uppsala: Studia Historica Upsalienska 196.

Ministry of Social Affairs and Health (1994): *Finland's targets and policies for municipal social welfare and health care.* (National plan for organizing social welfare and health care services in 1994 and 1997). Bureau of International Affairs. Helsinki: Ministry of Social Affairs and Health.

Ministry of Social Affairs and Health (2001a): *Sosiaali- ja terveydenhuollon työvoimatarpeen ennakointitoimikunnan mietintö.* (State Committee Report on the need for labour) *Komiteanmietintö* 2001:7. Helsinki: Ministry of Social Affairs and Health.

Ministry of Social Affairs and Health (2001b): *Terveydenhuollon ammatinharjoittamista ja ammattihenkilölainsäädäntöä koskeva selvitys.* (State Committee Report on health care personnel and legislation concerning health care professionals) Nojonen, K. Työryh-mämuistioita 2001:4. *http://www.stm.fi/suomi/eho/julkaisut/nojosenselvitys/luku5.htm* Document retrieved 11.6.2002.

Ministry of Social Affairs and Health (2002a): *Kansallinen projekti terveydenhuollon tulevaisuuden turvaamiseksi. Terveydenhuollon rahoitus, rahoituksen taso ja vakaus, rahoituskanavat ja voimavarojen kohdentaminen, valtionosuusjärjestelmä, kuntalaskutus, asiakasmaksupolitiikka, valtion ohjausjärjestelmien kehittäminen.* (National project to secure the future of health care. Health care funding) Helsinki: STM 125:03.

Ministry of Social Affairs and Health (2002b): *Kansallinen projekti terveydenhuollon tulevaisuuden turvaamiseksi. Työvoiman tarve ja keskinäinen työnjako. Työolosuhteiden ja täydennyskoulutuksen järjestäminen.* (National project to secure the future of health care. Need for and division of labour) Helsinki: STM 125:02.

Mósesdóttir, L. (2001): *The Interplay Between Gender, Markets and the State in Sweden, Germany and the United States.* Burlington: Ashgate.

National Board of Welfare and Health (1991): *VPK Väestövastuisen perusterveydenhuollon kokeilut.* (PRPC. Demonstration projects in population responsibility for primary care) Liukko, M. et al. Helsinki: Lääkintöhallitus.

National Board of Welfare and Health (1992): *VPK Väestövastuisen perusterveydenhuollon kokeilut.* (PRPC. Demonstration projects in population responsibility for primary care). Aro, S. (ed.) Helsinki: Sosiaali- ja terveyshallitus.

Nissinen, K. and Santalo, M. (2001): 'Vanhuspalvelut puntarissa'. (Elderly care in focus) *www.vtt.fi/rte/fm/projects/vanhuspalvelu.pdf* Document retrieved 30.4.2002.

Ohtonen, J., Koski, P. and Vinni, K. (1983): *Katsaus Suomen terveydenhuoltojärjestelmän kehitykseen.* (Review of the development of the Finnish health care) Official Statistics of Finland. Special Social Studies SVT XXXII: 96. Helsinki: Ministry of Social Affairs and Health Research Department.

Paasivaara, L. (2002): *Tavoitteet ja tosiasiallinen toiminta. Suomalaisen vanhusten hoitotyön muotoutuminen monitasotarkastelussa 1930-luvulta 2000-luvulle.* (Aims and the real action. The shaping of Finnish elderly care within a multilayered framework). Oulu: University of Oulu.

Rantalaiho, L. and Heiskanen, T. (eds.) (1997): *Gendered Practices in Working Life.* London: Macmillan.

Rintala, T. and Elovainio, M. (1997): *Lähihoitajan työ ja ammatti-identiteetti* (Work and Professional Identity of Practical Nurses). Tutkimuksia 86. Helsinki: Stakes.

Riska, E. (1993): 'The medical profession in the Nordic countries', in: Hafferty F. and McKinlay, J. (eds.): *The Changing Medical Profession: An International Perspective*: 150-161. New York: Oxford University Press.

Satka, M. (1995): *Making Social Citizenship. Conceptual Practices from the Finnish Poor Law to Professional Social Work.* University of Jyväskylä: Publications of Social and Political Sciences and Philosophy.

Simonen, L. (1990): *Contradictions of the Welfare State, Women and Caring. Municipal Homemaking in Finland.* Tampere: Acta Universitatis Tamperensis ser A vol 295.

Sinkkonen, S (1967): 'Diakonissan rooli'. (The role of the deaconess). *Sosiologia* (5)1: 13-19.

Stacey, M. (1984): 'Who are the health workers? Patients and other unpaid workers in health care', in: *Economic and Industrial Democracy* Special Issue on the Public Sector 2, 157-184.

Stakes (1993): *Alueellinen väestövastuu terveyskeskuksissa: toiminta ja kustannukset.* (Regional population responsibility in health centres: operations and costs) Mäkelä, M. et al. Helsinki: Stakes.

Statistics Finland (2003): Web service 'Finland in Figures'. Section Labour Market/- *Unemploymenthttp://www.tilastokeskus.fi/tk/tp/tasku/taskue_tyoelama.html Unemployment. Retrieved* 25.2.2003.

Suomen Kuntaliitto (2003) Kuntatyö 2010: Kunta kilpailukykyiseksi työnantajaksi. [Municipal work 2010. The municipality as a competitive employer.] *www.kuntaliitto.fi/kuntatyo2010/tietopaketti.htm* Retrieved 06.06.03.

Suomen Lääkärilehti (2001): *Tehostetussa kotihoidossa lääkäritkin tekevät kotikäyntejä.* (Intensified home care sends doctors to homevisits) S. Lääkärilehti 56(48): 4966-69.

Super (2000): 'Super peruspalveluministeri Biaudeta tapaamassa: Hoidon tsaosta ei saa tinkiä'. (No room for compromise in the standard of care). *Super* 47(2): 23.

Super (2001): 'Virkamuutokset riittävät jo'. (No more changes in employment contracts). *Super* 48(1): 15.

Tallberg, M. (1984): 'Den ambulerande sjuksköterskan på landsdygden i början av 1900-talet – en pionjär i hälsovården'. Hippokrates. Helsingfors: Finlands Medicinhistoriska Sällskap: 126-137.

Tedre, S. (1998): *Hoivan sanattomat sopimukset.* (The Unspoken Contracts in Social Care. A Case Study of Paid Workers in Finnish Municipal Home Help Services for the Elderly) University of Joensuu: Publications in *Social Sciences* No 40.

Tehy (2000a): 'Kotisairaala ihmisläheisempi vaihtoehto'. (Home hospital, a more humane alternative), in: *Tehy* 19 (8): 32-34.

Tehy (2000b): 'Tehyltä kannanotto kotisairaanhoidon järjestämiseen'. (Tehy's opinion of the organization of home care), in: *Tehy* 19(9), 34-35.

Tehy (2000c): 'Sairaala ilman yhtään vuodepaikkaa'. (Hospital without hospital beds), in: *Tehy* 19(17): 24-25.

Tehy (2002): 'Täysillä vaikuttamaan'. (We need to influence), in: *Tehy* 21(2): 15.

Terveydenhoitaja (2001a): Terveydenhoitajapäivien kannanotto. (Opinion of public health nurses). Terveydenhoitaja 34(2): 13.

Terveydenhoitaja (2001b): 'Terveydenhoitajia tarvitaan yhä enem-män'. (Public health nurses are needed more than ever), in: *Terveydenhoitaja* 34(4-5): 5.

Terveydenhoitaja (2001c): 'Ikäihmisten terveyden edistämisessä tarvitaan terveydenhoitajaa'. (Public health nurses needed for health promotion among the elderly), in: *Terveydenhoitaja* 34(8): 5.

Terveydenhoitaja (2001d): 'Kuntasektorin taloudellinen tilanne on nopeasti paranemassa'. (Municipal finances improving fast), in: *Terveydenhoitaja* 34(7): 24-25.

Theobald, H. (2002): 'Care for the elderly. Welfare system, professionalization and the question of inequality'. Paper presented at the 5th conference of the ESA 'Visions and Divisions: Challenges to European Sociology'. Helsinki, August 28 – September 1.

Tiilikkala, L. (1995): *Työelämän edustajien näkemyksiä lähihoitajakoulutuksesta.* (Practical nurse training as seen in working life). Moniste 41,1995. Helsinki: Opetushallitus.

Vaarama, M., Luomahaara, J., Peiponen, A. and Voutilainen, P. (2001): *Koko kunta ikääntyneiden asialle.* (The elderly – the responsibility of the entire municipality), Raportteja 259. Helsinki: Stakes.

Vauhkonen, O. (1978): 'Yleiskatsaus Suomen lääkintälaitoksen ja terveydenhuollon kehitysvaiheisiin'. (Overview of the development of the Finnish health care system), in: Vauhkonen, O, Laurinkari, J and Bäckman, G: *Suomalaista terveyspolitiikkaa* (Finnish Health Policy): 2-122. Porvoo: WSOY.

Waerness, K. (1984): 'The Rationality of Caring', in: *Economic and Industrial Democracy* 5(2): 185-211.

Witz, A. (1992): *Professions and Patriarchy.* London: Routledge.

Wrede, S. (2001): *Decentering care for mothers.* The politics of midwifery and the design of Finnish maternity services. Åbo: Åbo Akademi University Press.

Chapter 5

Care as Employment and Welfare Provision – Child Care and Elder Care in Sweden at the Dawn of the 21st Century

Marta Szebehely

The 1990s was a turbulent decade in the field of welfare services in Sweden, as it was in many other parts of the western world. The economic crisis that struck the country in the beginning of the decade brought about an increase in unemployment from 1.7 to 8.3 per cent and a three-year negative growth rate (1990-1993) of gross domestic product (GDP). Far-reaching cuts in almost every social policy programme followed. The post-WWII expansion of health-care, education and social care services was turned into cuts in both public financial resources and the number of employees. Parallel to the tightening of resources, substantial organizational changes were made with market-orientation as a common feature (Palme et al. 2003).[1]

Welfare services such as child care, schools, medical care, elder care and other social services are important for most people's everyday life. This is true not only for all those who use these services in different phases in life. Well-functioning welfare services are also an important resource for people who are not in immediate need of these services, but for whom it can be seen as an insurance for possible future needs. Knowing that there are well-functioning health care services if I become ill and reliable community care for me when I get old and frail affects my welfare today, even if I do not need any of these services at present.

The welfare services have in common that they are created in the relationship between the person providing the service and the person receiving it (for example, teacher – pupil, nurse – patient). Therefore, the welfare services' resource

---

[1] This chapter is based in part on work carried out by the Swedish Welfare Commission. The Commission, which was appointed by the Swedish government to compile a concise review of the development of people's welfare in Sweden during the 1990s, was active between 1999 and 2001 and produced 14 volumes containing contributions from a large number of Swedish researchers. The Commission's conclusions are summarized in Palme et al. 2002 and 2003.

allotment, design and organization affect not only the welfare of those in need of the services, it also affects the labour force – mainly women – who are professionally engaged in providing welfare services.

Who is to provide welfare services has never been a matter of course. The history of the welfare services in Sweden has been characterized – not least during the 1990s – by the drawing of new boundaries. The role of the local governments (municipalities, county councils) as the provider of welfare services has been called into question during this period more than ever before, whereas the importance of the family, the market and the voluntary sector has instead been stressed. Especially when it comes to the social care services (care of children, disabled and elderly people), there has been a crucial realignment of the boundary between paid and un-paid labour – in practice mainly between work performed within and that performed outside the family. Hence, social care services can also be regarded as important resources for the close kin of persons who are in need of constant or temporary care. To administrate daily life and find a balance among the varying needs of the family members is a task that, given the traditional gendered division of labour, to a great extent tends to become the responsibility of women. Accordingly, sufficient and high quality child care and services for disabled and elderly people is of great importance for women's freedom of action and for their possibility to combine caring tasks with gainful employment – or, in the words of Anneli Anttonen, women's prospects of being 'working mothers and daughters' (1990, p.18).

Welfare services are created for the purpose of strengthening citizens' freedom of action and, in the long run, their welfare. Welfare services are evaluated fundamentally in terms of their degree of accessibility and quality. To put it simply: Are the services available when we need them and are they good enough?

In an international comparison Swedish (and Scandinavian) welfare services are often characterized by the existence of *good accessibility to high quality state-financed and publicly produced services offered to and utilised by all social groups* (see, for example, Sipilä 1997).[2] The aim of this chapter is to discuss to what extent this image of a universalistic welfare model holds true of Sweden at the end of the 20th century. The chapter is focused on child care and the care of elderly people and the following questions are discussed: How was accessibility and quality of the services affected during the 1990s? Are the services still being publicly financed and publicly provided? Are the same services being used by all social classes including the better-off? And what are the similarities and differences in the development of child care and the care of elderly people?

---

[2] Also, characteristic for Sweden is the fact that the 289 municipalities responsible for providing social care services have a high degree of independence, including the right to decide on the scope and quality of their services and to levy taxes. Due to the relative autonomy of the local authorities in all the Scandinavian countries, the concept 'welfare municipality' (rather than welfare state) has been used by Scandinavian researchers to point at the large local variations (see e.g. Kröger 1997, Wærness 1998, Trydegård 2000).

Child care – both increased universalism and resource cut-backs

For quite some time, Swedish child care policy has had a dual objective: on one hand, to make it easier for parents to combine parenthood and gainful employment or studies; and, on the other, to stimulate children's development through pedagogical interventions and to work towards equalising the conditions under which children from different groups in society are raised.[3] The concept *educare* is sometimes used to underline that child-care policy in Sweden consists of both education and care. To make it possible for both parents to work, child care has been dominated by full-time rather than part-time care ever since the late 1970s.[4]

The development of child care in the 1990s can be described in terms of both volume *expansion* and a *tightening* of resources. The expansion was brought about by changes in legislation in 1995: the scope of public responsibility was broadened when the municipalities became obliged to provide child care facilities without undue delay for all children between one and twelve years of age whose parents were either working or studying, or where the child had special needs. So, despite these legislative changes, the right to state-subsidized child care was not universal in the same way as, for example, the right to education at the compulsory school level; rather, the right to child care was linked to the parents' employment situation or to their continuing their education. However, new legislative measures effective from July 1, 2001 guarantee unemployed parents child care for at least three hours a day. From 2002 this law applies as well to parents staying at home with a younger sibling. The limitation of the number of hours implies, however, that, despite this latest change in the child welfare legislation, the conditions for child care do not apply equally to all children.

There was an increase in the number of children in some form of child care (pre-school daycare centres, registered child-minding homes or after-school care) from 532,000 to 730,000 between 1990 and 2002. The percentage among 1-2-year-olds in child care rose from 44 to 65 per cent, among 3-6-year-olds from 64 to 89 per cent and among 7-9-year-olds from 49 to 72 per cent (Bergquist and Nyberg 2001, p. 252 and own calculations from NAE 2003b, pp. 14-17).[5] Child care has accordingly moved towards *increased universalism* during the 1990s; the new legislation has given more parents the right to child care and the expansion of child care encompasses a greater percentage of children. This substantial expansion has

---

[3] This section is based in part on Christina Bergquist and Anita Nyberg's contribution to the Welfare Commission; see also Bergquist and Nyberg 2002.

[4] Swedish pre-school daycare centres are generally open between 8-12 hours a day and children to parents who are gainfully employed or studying spend an average of 32 hours a week in daycare (NAE 2003a, p. 21).

[5] Although the levels may vary, the trend is the same in all the other Scandinavian countries as well as in most other European countries: the number of children in state-subsidised childcare increased during the 1990s (Daly and Lewis 2000; Leira 2002). Among the Scandinavian countries the percentage of 3-5-year-olds in childcare in the year 2000 was the highest in Denmark (92 per cent) and the lowest in Finland (67 per cent) (Nososco 2002, p. 59).

also led to *decreased differentiation* in terms of *access* to child care of different social groups: in 1982, 44 per cent of the working parents affiliated with the Swedish Trade Union Confederation (LO) had their children in state-subsidized child care compared with 79 per cent of the parents with university degrees who were members of the Swedish Confederation of Professional Associations (SACO). By 1995 the percentage among LO-affiliated parents had increased to 63 per cent, while the share among SACO-affiliated parents rose only slightly (82 per cent) (LO 1996).

During the 1990s there also occurred an institutional shift *within* state-subsidized child care towards an increase of *privately managed child care*, above all in the pre-school daycare centres where the share of children in privately managed daycare centres increased from 5 to 17 per cent between 1990 and 2002 (Palme et al 2003, p. 50 and NAE 2003a, p. 19). Within all the forms of child care (i.e. pre-school daycare centres, registered child-minding homes and after-school care), the share of privately employed personnel rose from four to nearly ten per cent between 1993 and 2000, see Figure 5.1.

Figure 5.1

Personnel employed in the private sector of state-subsidized child care

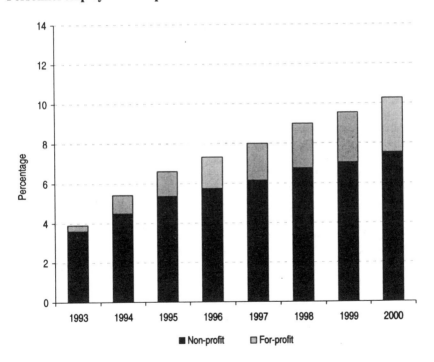

Source: Trydegård 2001, Figure 2.

Within the privately managed state-subsidized child care sector, non-profit enterprises dominate the scene, most of them organised as parent co-operatives. There was an increase, however, also in the number of for-profit firms during the 1990s (Trydegård 2001). More often than other social groups, well-educated and in other ways affluent parents choose privately managed child care, whereas for example children whose parents were born outside Sweden are clearly underrepresented in privately managed tax-subsidized child care. In 1999, three per cent of the parents with compulsory schooling had their children in privately managed tax-subsidized child care, while the corresponding percentage among well-educated parents (with at least three years of university education) was 18 per cent (NAE 2000). The expansion of the privately managed child care sector indicates that there is a trend towards *increased differentiation* in terms of *type* of child care. This unequal distribution contradicts the ambition to make child care 'a meeting-place for children with different ethnical, cultural and social backgrounds' (Government Bill 1999/ 2000:129, p. 8).

Looking at the financing of state-subsidized child care, there has been a shift in the 1990s towards *increased privatization*. Child care fees rose during the decade and parents' contributions to the total resources for child care increased from 10 per cent at the beginning of the decade to 18 per cent up to year 2001 (NAE 2002, p. 23). This trend was broken at the beginning of 2002 by the introduction of a national maximum fee reform in child care. The reform set the maximum parental fee for child care at SEK 1,140 per month (about 125 Euro) for pre-school children, but not to exceed three per cent of household's income (the fee is reduced for the family's second and third child in pre-school and is free of charge for the family's fourth child). The reform has led to lower fees for a majority of parents, on average a decrease of SEK 1,000 per month for a dual earner family with moderate incomes (NAE 2003c, p. 57). Thus, the reform constitutes a *'deprivatization'* of the financing of child care.

When measured by the amount of tax money reserved for child care, there was unquestionably a *diluting of resources* during the 1990s. Despite cut-backs in governmental funding, the total funds reserved for child care was roughly the same in 2001 as in 1990, some SEK 40 billion, due to the increase in parental fees (Palme et al. 2003, p. 50 and NAE 2002, p. 21). However, this sum was distributed among 35 per cent more children in 2001 than in 1990, which has meant a substantial *staff reduction*. Between the years 1990 and 2002, the size of children's groups increased from 13.8 to 17.4 in the pre-school daycare centres and from 17.8 to 34.1 in after-school care, while the number of children per full-time employed staff member rose from 4.4 to 5.3 in the daycare centres and from 8.3 to 18.4 in after-school care (NAE 2003c, pp. 32-34). The staff-child ratio was about 17 per cent lower in daycare centres in 2002 compared with 1990; in after-school care the staff density was 55 per cent lower, see Figure 5.2.[6]

---

[6] These figures are national averages; the differences among the municipalities are large and increasing (Bergmark 2001).

Figure 5.2
Staff-child ratio in child care 1990-2002 (index, 1990=100)

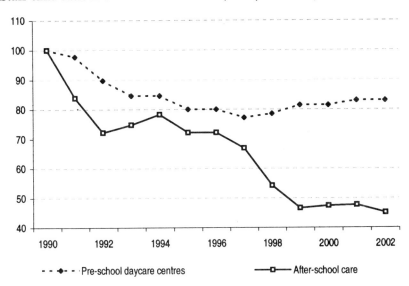

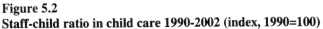

Source: Own calculations from Palme et al. 2003, p. 50 and NAE 2003c, p. 34.

The diluting of resources, the reduction of staff density and the enlarged children's groups can be seen as indirect indicators of lower quality standards in child care. According to the Swedish National Agency for Education, which supervises child care services (and the school sector), it is not possible to arrive at a more comprehensive estimation of the direct consequences of these changes for children. However, the Agency reports serious concern for the large child groups and the low staff-child ratio in after-school care and notes that this has hit vulnerable children the most. A large number of after-school professionals report an unsatisfying psycho-social environment in their centres, a situation that is not only problematic for the children but might also affect the staff's own health (NAE 2003 d).

During the last decade, arduous working conditions and work-related problems and absences from work increased among child care workers and other welfare staff more than in most other occupational groups. The stressful working environment for welfare workers at the start of the decade worsened, and the differences between the welfare services and other occupational groups grew (Tegsjö, Hedin and Eklund 2000). Among child care and school staff, the number of personnel who claim that they have too much to do has increased more than among other professional groups, as has the percentage of those who suffer from anxiety and insomnia because of their deep concern about their work situation (Bäckman 2001).

Care of elderly people – decreased universalism with a focus on the frailest

Whereas increased accessibility and the dilution of resources has characterized Swedish child care throughout the 1990s, the tendency within elder care has been towards *reduced accessibility* and a *concentration of resources* on a small group of persons with extensive help needs.[7]

According to the national plan of action for elder care adopted by the Swedish parliament in 1998 (Government Bill 1997/98:113), the fundamental principles that have been in effect for the last few decades remain unchanged: elderly people should be able to grow old in security with sustained independence and with access to good health-care and social services. The plan of action also states that the care of older persons is to be state-financed and accessible according to need, not according to purchasing power. Despite the unchanged goals, the 1990s was a turbulent period for elder care services.

New directives and new forms of management and operation (New Public Management) have emerged on a broad front within the elder care sector, and the breakthrough of organizational models fashioned after the market has been more pronounced in this sector than in any other welfare service (Palme et al. 2003). More than half of the Swedish municipalities have now implemented a form of purchaser/provider model by which the responsibility for granting care services for elderly people is separated from the responsibility for providing the service. In many instances this has been connected to the introduction of result units and performance-based financing systems. Out-sourced care, that is state-subsidized and state-regulated care carried out by actors other than the municipalities, quadrupled during the decade, but this figure is still low in comparison with countries outside Scandinavia (Rostgaard and Lehto 2001; Palme et al. 2003). In contrast to child care, tax-subsidized private care for older people is provided mainly by for-profit firms, and while the percentage employed in non-profit deliverers of privately managed elder care rose from just under two to three per cent between 1993 and 2000, the percentage employed in joint-stock companies and other for-profit organizations rose from under one to nearly 10%; see Figure 5.3.

---

[7] This section is based mainly on the author's contribution to the Welfare Commission.

Figure 5.3
Personnel employed in the private sector of state-subsidized care of elderly people

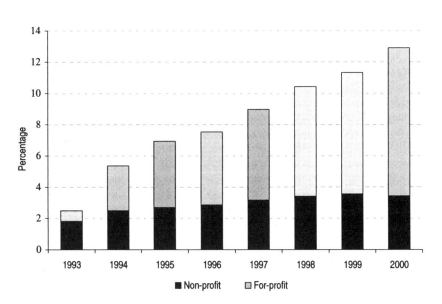

Source: Trydegård 2001, Figure 17.

A growing proportion of elder care is being carried out by large for-profit companies; in 1999 the four largest private actors controlled half of the contracted business for care of elderly people (NBHW 1999).[8] Both the increased emphasis on out-sourced elder care and market-inspired organizational changes in the public care sector have occurred rapidly and without any credible national follow-up of the possible consequences for the welfare of the people concerned or for the staff's working environment (Palme et al. 2003). As recent as April 2003, the Swedish government commissioned the National Board of Health and Welfare to evaluate the consequences of the competitive tendering on the quality of care for elderly people.

---

[8] Some of the largest firms on the Swedish market in 2002 belong to multinational groups of companies (ISS, Capio, Attendo Senior Care). What this means for the quality of care and working conditions for care staff is not known, but it is interesting to note that, in 2002, on the home page of one of the actors (ISS CarePartner), the first item on the list of the company's objectives is to be 'profitable and a market leader'. This is a prevailing ambition among business enterprises, but what happens if such ambitions clash with the socio-political and ethical objective to provide good care according to need?

The financial situation of elder care during the first part of the 1990s was characterized by cut-backs and the increase of public funds did not keep pace with the rising number of elderly people. During the latter part of the decade, however, there was a substantial increase in resources, even when the greater number of elderly people is taken into account. However, the care of elderly people cannot be separated from health- and medical care. Elderly people generally have a greater need for medical care, and changes in the medical care sector affect the need for elder care in the municipalities. The increased resources allotted to the municipalities for elder care must therefore be regarded in light of the substantial decrease of personnel in the medical care sector during the 1990s. The number of hospital beds was nearly halved at the same time as the length of treatment was substantially reduced, especially for older patients (Palme et al. 2003). Elderly people in great need of care were previously often cared for within the medical care system, but today they consume an increasing share of the municipal resources for elder care. As a consequence, municipal care is being concentrated more and more to a smaller number of elderly people who have extensive care needs. Those with a lesser need of assistance (mostly help with domestic work such as cleaning, laundry and shopping) are being excluded more and more from the municipality's area of responsibility.

A characteristic of elder care in Sweden (and the other Scandinavian countries) has been the great emphasis given to municipal home care, a form of assistance that has been available to and highly regarded by all classes in society (Szebehely 1998). The number of home care recipients reached its highest level in the late 1970s, but since then has declined by some 100,000 at the same time as the number of citizens over 80 years of age has increased by some 200,000. Despite the policy emphasis on home-based care, in practice there has been a shift towards institutional care since 1980, see Figure 5.4.

Figure 5.4
Care for elderly people in Sweden 1960-2000. Number of persons receiving home care and living in special housing (institutions and service flats), respectively, and the number of persons in the population 80 years and older

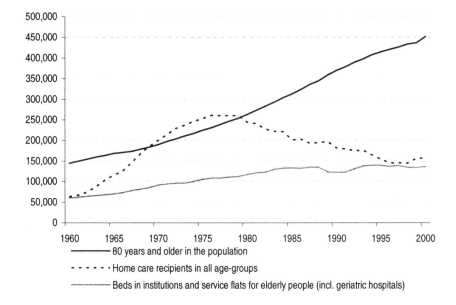

- 80 years and older in the population

- - - - - - Home care recipients in all age-groups

─────── Beds in institutions and service flats for elderly people (incl. geriatric hospitals)

Source: Szebehely 1999; Ministry of Health and Social Affairs 2002.

During the last decades, the services have become more and more targeted towards the oldest age-group, but also this group has seen a substantial decrease in services: Between 1980 and 2000 the percentage of elderly people (80+) receiving home care declined from 34 to 21 per cent, while the percentage accommodated in so-called special housing for elderly (nursing homes, old people's home, service flats etc.) declined from 28 to 22 per cent) (Ministry of Health and Social Affairs 2002, p. 41).[9]

---

[9] In the early 1980s, home-based care services were far more extensive in Scandinavia than in the rest of Europe; in all the Scandinavian countries one of six elderly persons (65+) were receiving public home care. Since then, home care has declined both in Sweden and in Finland, whereas the percentage receiving home care has increased in Denmark and is almost unchanged in Norway (Szebehely 2003). In the year 2000, home care was three times more common in Denmark than in Sweden (25 per cent of persons 65 and over compared with 8 per cent; Nososco 2002, p. 135). Also, the extent of institutional care differs between the Scandinavian countries, although not as much: between 12 per cent in Norway and 7 per cent in Finland (ibid., p. 134).

While tax-subsidized home care declined in the 1990s, there has been an increase in *informal forms of assistance*, that is, in assistance provided by the spouse or other closely related persons within or outside the elderly person's own household (Sundström, Johansson and Hassing 2002). The increase in assistance purchased on the *private market* (primarily laundry and cleaning services) has been even more extensive (Palme et al. 2003, p. 39). These shifts, which can be described as an *informalization* and a *marketization* of community care, are, from a social class perspective, unevenly distributed: elderly persons with a higher educational background tend to turn to the private market for home help assistance, whereas among elderly people with a low educational background there has been an increase in care provided by their relatives, see Figure 5.5.

Figure 5.5
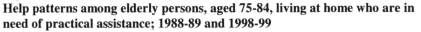
Help patterns among elderly persons, aged 75-84, living at home who are in need of practical assistance; 1988-89 and 1998-99

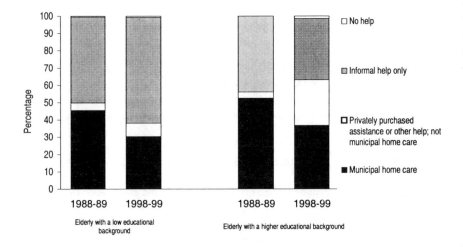

Source: Own analysis of Swedish Surveys of Living Conditions, Statistics Sweden; see Palme et al. 2003, p. 48.

Thus, the cut-backs in municipal home care contribute to a *dualization* of care for older people. From a welfare perspective, it is important to take note of the consequences of these shifts for both help recipients and help providers. The decrease in municipal assistance should be seen inrelation to research findings that show that elderly people in the Scandinavian countries prefer to receive assistance from the public sector rather than the assistance provided by either relatives or the market sector. This is especially true of women (see for example Daatland 1990; Andersson 1996, Svallfors 1999). It should also be noted that the relatives who now bear a greater part of the responsibility for care are usually female, primarily elderly spouses and middle-aged daughters. The decrease in municipal home care has therefore directly affected the everyday life and welfare of women more than it has of men.

The shift from state-subsidized elder care to care by family members and relatives and by privately purchased help is partly a result of new restrictions in the allotment of assistance, but also (and probably more so) of higher fees and changes in the content and organization of home care. The *stricter help allotment* is not a result of legislative measures, but rather of the implementation of increasingly stringent municipal guidelines (Thorslund, Bergmark and Parker 1997). Persons in need of help with household chores such as cleaning, laundry and shopping are in some municipalities routinely turned down, and in many places the civil servants who decide on the applicant's need of municipal help have been instructed to examine more closely if there are not any relatives who could provide the help (NBHW 2003a). Although the Social Services Act, which regulates municipal home care, guarantees by law that every person has the right to have his/her help needs individually assessed, such local guidelines have the effect of reducing demand. For this reason, there are few formal rejections of applications for assistance, and it is even more rare for elderly people to appeal a negative decision.[10]

The raising of user fees has led to a shift towards increased private financing of elder care in a manner similar to what has occurred in child care. However, in many municipalities the fees are used as instruments of control rather than as a source of income. By raising the fees, primarily for person with modest help needs, the municipalities have attempted to reduce some of the demand for public assistance. This trend may have been broken recently. On July 1st, 2002 a fee-reform for elder care came into effect that is expected to reduce the fees for approximately half of today's help recipients. According to this reform, a single person shall have at least SEK 4,162 (approx. 460 Euro) per month (housing costs exempted) after the fee for elder care is paid, and no one will have pay more than SEK 1,544 (170 Euro) per month for care (NBHW 2003b). Studies conducted prior to the max-fee-reform show that it was not unusual for elderly people – especially women with low pensions – to forgo public assistance for financial reasons; in the late 1990s approximately every sixth person over 75 years of age in need of help refused home care because the fees were too high. It has, therefore, been a matter of concern that close kin of elderly persons having limited financial resources are now forced to bear a more substantial part of the responsibility for care (NBHW 2001).

According to an initial evaluation of the new max-fee-reform, the proportion of home care recipients exempted from fees because of low income rose from 14 per cent before the reform to 34 per cent; the study also shows, however, that when implementing the reform many municipalities have raised the minimum fee,

---

[10] According to one calculation, one per cent of homecare applications in 2001were rejected in full or in part, and of this one per cent only every 20th decision was appealed (NBHW 2002).

resulting in increased costs for an unknown number of home care recipients (NBHW 2003b). Whether the max-fee-reform actually has increased the accessibility of the services is therefore too early to conclude.

To what extent care is a resource for elderly people in need of assistance and for their family and relatives depends not only on *access* to care, but also to a great extent on the *quality* of the care. Among the *changes in content and organizational structure* that have most likely had an impact on the quality of care and, consequently, on the demand for home care are a decline in staff continuity, fewer hours of assistance in relation to actual need and a thinning out of domestic support (Eliasson-Lappalainen and Motevasel 1997; Szebehely 2000). Criticism of these conditions seems to have escalated also among the home care recipients themselves; according to a comprehensive user study conducted in Stockholm, the percentage of persons who are of the opinion that the home care they receive is insufficient increased from 26 to 42 per cent between 1995 and 1998, and the percentage reporting receiving supplementary help from close kin increased from 30 to 41 per cent (Fried 1998).

According to the National Board of Health and Welfare (NBHW 2001), several problems still remain, despite an increase of resources in recent years. One problem is the lack of co-ordination between institutional medical care, primary care and municipal care, which leads to serious problems for the increasing number of elderly people with extensive medical and social needs who are being cared for in their own homes. Here a paradox can be noted: the group of elderly people upon whom Swedish home service resources are concentrated today is the very group which home-based care has the least possibility of helping satisfactorily; rather, the home-help organization is more suited to meeting the needs of the unprioritised group of elderly people, that is, those who are in need of assistance with *caring for the home* rather than *caring for the body*.

Another problem that the National Board of Health and Welfare has highlighted concerns staff recruitment, a serious problem in a majority of the Swedish municipalities. A part of the problem has to do with the introduction of new efficiency measures, reorganizations and the opening up of care to competition, all of which have had negative consequences for 'the possibilities of recruiting, training and keeping staff and, ultimately, the possibility to offer elderly people good and reliable care' (NBHW 2001, p. 9). The combination of an increased care load and a shortage of time for carrying out the caring tasks has most likely been of significance for the increased occurrence of physical discomfort, tiredness, exhaustion and long-term sick leaves among care staff noted during the 1990s (Bäckman 2001). These conditions have most likely had negative consequences for personal welfare, both directly for the staff and indirectly for the recipients, not least through the increase in staff turnover.

The care of children and elderly people during the 1990s – similarities and differences

During the last decade, in both child care and elder care, the ideal image of the universal Scandinavian welfare regime has become more remote, even though certain trends to the contrary have also been noted. A common tendency that constitutes a departure from the universal model is *privatization* in various forms:

- Increased fees for service users have led to a shift in the boundary between the private and the public share of the financial resources towards a gradual *privatization of* financing.[1]
- The increased presence of private providers of state-subsidized care has led to a shift towards *privatization of service provision*.
- At the same time, the services still provided by the public sector have been affected by market-inspired organizational models, which can be seen as a *privatization of the work organization*.

Still another common trend in child care and elder care seems to be a *deterioration of the psycho-social working environment*, and there are also similar indications of a *quality deterioration* – a reduction of the staff-client ratio, which is most clearly evident within the child care sector, but is also noticeable within the elder care and medical care sectors, and has led to reductions in the number of care hours allotted to elderly people in relation to the extent of the help needed (Sundström and Malmberg 1996).

When it comes to accessibility, however, there are striking differences between the two care sectors:

- *Child care has (through legislative changes)* moved towards *increased universalism* and comprises an increasing percentage of the children.
- *Care of elderly persons has (without any legislative changes)* moved towards – *decreased universalism* and comprises a decreasing percentage of elderly people.[12]

---

[11] Cf. Lehto, Moss and Rostgaard (1999), p. 114, describe the fee increases in the care sector in the Nordic countries as 'a slow privatization of service funding'. The 'max-fee' reforms that have been implemented within child care and elder care should be regarded as a trend in the opposite direction.

[12] Sweden and Finland share similar experiences of a decreased universalism in the care of older people (cf. Kautto (2000), p. 70): 'Home help has traditionally been the form of service distinguishing the Nordic countries from the rest of Europe, but with the radical reductions in absolute number of services and consequent push for more family- or market-based care, Sweden and Finland seem to have moved further from an idealised "caring state".' See also Kröger, Anttonen and Sipilä (2003) who describe childcare and elder care in Finland in terms of weak and strong universalism, respectively, and find that these differences have been reinforced in recent years.

The decrease of state-subsidised care for older people has been accompanied by an increase in the care provided by family and relatives and in the purchasing of services on the private market – a *dual privatization of elder care* in the form of *informalization* and *marketization*, which has no correspondence in the child care sector. There has rather been a *deprivatization* in that the boundary has shifted in the opposite direction; the expansion of state-subsidised child care has led to a decrease of both unpaid parental care and the utilization of privately financed nannies (Szebehely 1998).[13]

Equally distributed welfare or dualized welfare services?

In conclusion, I would like to draw attention to the tendency towards *dualization in the care of children and elderly people* that has arisen during the last decade and which has led to a pronounced move away from the ideal image of the Scandinavian care model. I would here like to highlight some of the options that I believe the Swedish welfare politics are facing today.

In the child care sector, there is a tendency for parents with better resources to choose private providers of tax-subsidized child care, whereas parents with fewer resources are becoming even more dominant within municipal child care. This trend is in contradiction to the expressed socio-political objective that child care should be a meeting place for children with different social and ethnic backgrounds. In elder care, the issue is whether there should continue to be a state-subsidized care utilized by elderly people from all social classes, or if the need for care should be a question for the market to solve for people who can afford it and become the responsibility of close kin for those who cannot. An essential aspect of the Scandinavian care model is that it should not be 'the wallet that rules'. Thus, a central issue for both the child care and the elder care sectors is how citizens react to the possibility for affluent persons who can afford private insurance coverage and surcharges to obtain greater access to or a higher quality of state-subsidised welfare services; for example, in child care by paying an extra fee to ensure a higher staff-child ratio in pre-school than the 'basic supply', or in elder care by purchasing private insurance coverage to guarantee that one will be given priority should the need for institutional care arise.

Although these and a whole range of similar options are based on value judgements, we must be aware that the absence of conscious decisions can also lead us on a course from which it may be difficult or even impossible to turn back (Palme et al. 2002). If public welfare services are not given sufficient resources, they cannot live up to the citizens' demand for accessibility and quality. Thus, confidence in the system is undermined, as it does not offer sufficient assurance that future needs will be met. If the quality of child care and elder care is regarded

---

[13] Since this trend means a shift both from informal care and services purchased within the informal economy, I have in another context characterized the shift as a *formalization* of child care (Szebehely 1998).

as insufficient, the wealthier groups in the population will most likely look for other solutions or will argue for the right to pay surcharges in order to 'top up' the public supply. Such a flight from the public system could, in future, reduce their will to continue to contribute with their taxes, which will consequently limit the possibility of financing future welfare services.[14]

Adequate resources and sufficient organizational conditions are decisive factors also for preventing welfare service staff from being disproportionately affected by negative working conditions. Improved working conditions for this highly female-dominated group, which was the loser when it comes to the working environment in the 1990s, is not just a question of justice, it is also most likely a prerequisite for future staff recruitment. In addition, it is a necessary condition for the existence of high quality welfare services in the future. Hence, how the welfare services are financed and organized is a question that affects the everyday welfare of most citizens, but until there is a radical change in the gendered division of labour, it is a question of particular importance for women.

It is crucial to note that the examples of a departure from the universal welfare model discussed in this chapter are not a result of altered political objectives or legislative revisions. They are examples of changes in practice rather than in policy. A body of legislation that has the ambition of universality is not enough to spread welfare services universally in practice. The services offered also have to be regarded as suitable and sufficient by a large part of the population. If not, there is a risk that a creeping selectivization will undermine the strong popular support for the Scandinavian welfare model.

References

Andersson, L. (1996): 'Visible and invisible informal care – Swedish elder care at the crossroads', in Minichiello, V. et al. (eds.): *Sociology of Aging. International Perspectives*. International Sociological Association, Melbourne: Thoth.

Anttonen, A. (1990): 'The Feminization of the Scandinavian Welfare State', in Simonen, L. (ed.): *Finnish Debates on Women's Studies*. University of Tampere: Research Institute for Social Science.

Bergmark, Å. (2001): 'Den lokala välfärdsstaten? Decentraliseringstrender under 1990-talet', in Szebehely, M. (ed.): *Välfärdstjänster i omvandling*. Research Volume from the Welfare Commission. SOU 2001:52. Stockholm: Fritzes.

Bergqvist, C. and Nyberg, A. (2001): 'Den svenska barnomsorgsmodellen – kontinuitet och förändring under 1990-talet', in: Szebehely, M. (ed.): *Välfärdstjänster i omvandling*. Research Volume from the Welfare Commission. SOU 2001:52. Stockholm: Fritzes.

Bergqvist, C. and Nyberg, A. (2002): 'Welfare state restructuring and childcare in Sweden', in: Michel, S. and Mahon, R. (eds.): *Child Care Policy at the Crossroads. Gender and Welfare State Restructuring*. London: Routledge.

---

[14] Studies show that there is still strong *support* for state-financed and provided welfare services in Sweden, whereas *confidence* in the society's ability to guarantee pensions, medical care and elder care for future needs seems to be declining (Svallfors 1999, 2001).

Bäckman O. (2001): 'Med välfärdsstaten som arbetsgivare', in: Szebehely, M. (ed.) *Välfärdstjänster i omvandling*. Research Volume from the Welfare Commission. SOU 2001:52. Stockholm: Fritzes.

Daatland S.O. (1990): 'What are families for? On family solidarity and preference for help', *Ageing and Society*, 10 (1): 1-15.

Daly, M. and Lewis, J. (2000): 'The concept of social care and the analysis of contemporary welfare states', *British Journal of Sociology*, 51 (2): 281-298.

Eliasson-Lappalainen, R. and Motevasel, I. (1997): 'Ethics of care and social policy', *Scandinavian Journal of Social Welfare*, 6 (3): 189-196.

Fried, R. (1998): *Hemtjänsten i Stockholm 1998*. Stockholms stad: Stadsledningskontoret.

Government Bill 1997/98: 113. *Nationell handlingsplan för äldrepolitiken*.

Government Bill 1999/2000: 129. *Maxtaxa och allmän förskola m.m.*

Kautto M. (2000): *Two of a Kind? Economic crisis, policy responses and well-being during the 1990s in Sweden and Finland*. Report from the Welfare Commission. SOU 2000: 83. Stockholm: Fritzes.

Kröger, T. (1997): 'Local government in Scandinavia: autonomous or integrated into the welfare state?', in: Sipilä, J. (ed): *Social Care Services: The Key to the Scandinavian Welfare Model*. Aldershot: Avebury.

Kröger, T., Anttonen, A. and Sipilä, J. (2003): 'Social Care in Finland: Stronger and Weaker Forms of Universalism', in: Anttonen A., Baldock J. and Sipilä, J .(eds.), *The Young, the Old and the State: Social Care Systems in Five Industrial Nations*. Cheltenham: Edward Elgar.

Lehto, J., Moss, N. and Rostgaard, T .(1999): 'Universal public social care and social services?', in: Kautto, M. et al. (eds.): *Nordic Social Policy. Changing Welfare States*. London: Routledge.

Leira, A. (2002): *Working parents and the welfare state: family change and policy reform in Scandinavia*. Cambridge: Cambridge University Press.

LO (1996): *Barnomsorg, förvärvsarbete och jämställdhet*. Stockholm: LO.

Ministry of Health and Social Affairs (2002): *Välfärdsfakta Social. Juni 2002*. Stockholm: Socialdepartementet.

NAE (2000): *Tillgång och efterfrågan på barnomsorg. Enkät till föräldrar med barn i åldern 1–12 år*. Stockholm: National Agency for Education.

NAE (2002): *Beskrivande data om barnomsorg, skola och vuxenutbildning 2002*. Rapport nr 218. Stockholm: National Agency for Education.

NAE (2003a): *Barnomsorg, skola och vuxenutbildning. Jämförelsetal för huvudmän. Del 1*. Rapport nr 229. Stockholm: National Agency for Education.

NAE (2003b): *Barnomsorg, skola och vuxenutbildning i siffror. Del 2*. Stockholm: National Agency for Education.

NAE (2003c): *Uppföljning av reformen maxtaxa, allmän förskola m.m.* Stockholm: National Agency for Education.

NAE (2003d): *Gruppstorlekar och personaltäthet i förskola, förskoleklass och fritidshem*. Stockholm: National Agency for Education.

NBHW (1999): *Konkurrensutsättning och entreprenader inom äldreomsorgen*. Äldreuppdraget 99:6. Stockholm: National Board of Health and Welfare.

NBHW (2001): *Nationell handlingsplan för äldrepolitiken*. Lägesrapport 2001. Stockholm: National Board of Health and Welfare.

NBHW (2002): *Nationell handlingsplan för äldrepolitiken*. Slutrapport 2002. Stockholm: National Board of Health and Welfare.

NBHW (2003a): *Ekonomisk prövning av rätten till äldre- och handikappomsorg*. Stockholm: National Board of Health and Welfare.

NBHW (2003b:) *Avgiftsenkät november 2002*. Stockholm: National Board of Health and Welfare.

Nososco (2002): *Social protection in the Nordic countries 2000*. Copenhagen: Nordic Social Statistical Committee.

Palme, J. et al. (2002): 'Welfare Trends in Sweden: Balancing the Books for the 1990s', in *Journal of European Social Policy*, 12 (4): 329-346.

Palme, J. et al. (2003): 'A Welfare Balance Sheet for the 1990s. Final Report of the Swedish Welfare Commission', in *Scandinavian Journal of Public Health*, Supplement 60, August.

Rostgaard, T. and Lehto, J. (2001): 'Health and social care systems: How different is the Nordic model?', in: Kautto M. et al. (eds.): *Nordic Welfare States in the European Context*. London: Routledge.

Sipilä, J. (ed.) (1997): *Social Care Services: The Key to the Scandinavian Welfare Model*. Aldershot: Avebury.

SOU 2001:79: *Välfärdsbokslut för 1990-talet*. Final Report from the Welfare Commission. Stockholm: Fritzes.

Sundström, G. and Malmberg, B. (1996): 'The long Arm of the Welfare State shortened. Home help in Sweden', in: *Scandinavian Journal of Social Welfare*, 5: 69-75.

Sundström, G., Johansson L. and Hassing L. (2002): 'The Shifting Balance of Long-Term Care in Sweden', in: *Gerontologist*, 42 (3): 350-356.

Svallfors, S. (1999): 'The middle class and welfare state retrenchment: Attitudes to Swedish welfare policies', in: Svallfors S. and Taylor-Gooby P. (eds.): *The end of the welfare state? Responses to state retrenchment*. London and New York: Routledge.

Svallfors, S. (2001): 'Kan man lita på välfärdsstaten? Risk, tilltro och betalningsvilja i den svenska välfärdsopinionen 1997–2000', in: Fritzell, J. and Palme, J. (eds.): *Välfärdens finansiering och fördelning*. Research Volume from the Welfare Commission. SOU 2001: 57. Stockholm: Fritzes.

Szebehely, M. (1998): 'Changing Divisions of Carework. Caring for Children and Frail Elderly People in Sweden', in: Lewis, J. (ed.): *Gender, Social Care and Welfare State Restructuring in Europe*. Aldershot: Ashgate.

Szebehely, M. (1999): *Caring for Frail Older Persons in Scandinavia: the impact of moving borders between traditional institutions and care at home*. Unpublished report for the OECD, Social Policy Studies. Paris: OECD.

Szebehely, M. (2000): 'Äldreomsorg i förändring – knappare resurser och nya organizationsformer', in: Szebehely, M. (ed.): *Välfärd, vård och omsorg*. Research Volume from the Welfare Commission. SOU 2000: 38. Stockholm: Fritzes.

Szebehely, M. (2003) (ed.): *Hemhjälp i Norden. Illustrationer och reflektioner*. Lund: Studentlitteratur.

Tegsjö, B., Hedin, G. and Eklund, I. (2000): *Kartläggning av magra organizationer*. Stockholm: Rådet för arbetslivsforskning.

Thorslund, M., Bergmark, Å. and Parker, M. (1997): 'Difficult Decisions on Care and Services for Elderly People', *Scandinavian Journal of Social Welfare*, 6: 197-206.

Trydegård, G.-B. (2000): *Tradition, change and variation. Past and present trends in public old-age care*. Stockholm University, Department of Social Work (Diss.).

Trydegård, G.-B. (2001): 'Välfärdstjänster till salu – privatisering och alternativa driftformer under 1990-talet', in: Szebehely M. (ed.): *Välfärdstjänster i omvandling*. Research Volume from the Welfare Commission. SOU 2001:52. Stockholm: Fritzes.

Wærness, K. (1998): 'The Changing 'Welfare Mix' in Childcare and Care for the Frail Elderly in Norway', in: Lewis, J. (ed.): *Gender, Social Care and Welfare State Restructuring in Europe*. Aldershot: Ashgate.

PART III
DILEMMAS IN PROFESSIONS AND USERS IN PUBLIC HEALTH

Chapter 6

Dirty Work in a Norwegian Health Context (The Case of Norway)

Rannveig Dahle

The modern health sector is not a naturally given domain, it is constituted through a cultural an historic process. And in one sense or another, all work in this domain has to do with people's bodies. Bodies give the work its corporeal or somatic dimension, besides that it is always relational and contextual and loaded with symbolic meanings. In order to do the work properly, health personnel need to go beyond all bounds of decency in dealing with human bodies, and they often have to 'breach' normal rules of intimate physical contact. For instance, one needs to get access to parts of the body that in other circumstances would be considered to be strictly private and/or sexualized.

In this chapter I shall discuss some aspects of the health care providers work with peoples' bodies, sometimes labelled 'dirty work'. I examine how this work is socially structured and gendered, how it is understood, interpreted and ranked in different medical contexts.[1] The notion 'dirty work' itself needs to be explored and also such things as theoretical and practical tasks will be challenged. I start by looking at certain attributes of the body in its increasingly privatized and ambiguous contemporary state. The fact that the body has become an even more private domain is assumed to affect the ways in which health care providers pick up practical skills, regarding both caring and treatment. This again is reflected in ambiguous teaching contexts. In the next section I examine a particularly intimate aspect of medical treatment, that related to bowel incontinence, to illuminate the case. Finally I discuss some implications of the different and gendered symbolic meanings of practical and theoretical knowledge in health care work.

---

[1] The study of male nurses constitute a smaller part of a larger study 'Smell – Dampness and Embarrassment' (1998-2000). The study was funded by the Norwegian Research Council.

The body

The body became one of the key sociological topics of the 1990s. For a considerable period of time the circumstance that all social action has a bodily element was almost ignored. There was a fear of being imprisoned within biological determinism, hence the body had been abandoned (Annandale 1998). It can be argued, however, that the body has never been totally absent from social theory, more 'absent-present', as Chris Shilling (1993) aptly expressed it. Now that the body once more is on the agenda of the social sciences, it is being approached from new directions, especially the identity management angle. For people of today, the body is an instrument of self-presentation, the raw material of not just one but many, partly diverse, even antagonistic identities. We now take for granted our virtually unimpeded right of ownership to our own body. Norwegian psychiatrist Skårderud (1994) states that instrumentally speaking, the body has moved dramatically from production to presentation. This again has an impact upon the construction of selves and modern identities.

But despite all this new freedom, widened sense of ownership and increased opportunities, our relation to the body is probably deeply ambivalent. The body is a source of pleasure, desire, knowledge and experience, but also of discontent, embarrassment and shame. On the one hand, all taboos and rules regulating intimacy seem to have been transcended. On the other, the body has never been so private as it is today. In our culture for instance, toilet functions are highly privatized, which could be interpreted as a sign of our exclusive and sacred right to our own body, privacy and 'insides' (Sørhaug 1994). There is also a deep contempt for ageing bodies with strict taboos associated with picturing older people in sexually explicit positions. Visual depictions of older women enjoying their sexuality tend to provoke disgust. The way advertisers depict menstruation and sanitary towels illustrates the paradoxical moment in our view of the body. In the spirit of the new openness on bodies, the fantastic absorptive properties of new sanitary towels are presented. But the fluid we see is blue, not red. Everything is effectively absorbed, leaving the woman to feel assured that her menstruation remains known only to her – satisfying the ultimate goal of concealing a bodily fluid. In an age characterized by sweeping change, uncertainty and a strong emphasis on the creation and formation of the individual, the body becomes a defence against the accompanying uncertainty (Johansson 1999). The body's interface with the outside world works to shield the body and protect us from inner chaos.

Both mounting privatization and public exposure of the body may be accompanied by a sense of shame. It is probably a sign of the times that increasing numbers of people report feeling ashamed of their bodies (Davies 1997). Few among us, and virtually no women, have bodies that compare favourably with the image of the beautiful and successful. Our bodies are either too fat, our faces too wrinkled, our legs too thick, and so on. Not unexpectedly, women top the statistics of the most bodily disenchanted.

Doing research on the body, therefore, is both complex and multifarious (Davies 1997). Theories have often been applied in a post-modern critique aimed at shattering dichotomies such as body/soul, nature/nurture, emotions/rationality etc. There is a danger that the theories are over-intellectual, exotic and, remote from the body. According to Kathy Davies, bodies are not simply abstractions, they are embedded in the immediacies of everyday, lived experience. 'Embodied theory requires interaction between theories of the body and analysis of the particularities of embodied experiences and practices. It needs to explicitly tackle the relationship between the symbolic and the material, between representations of the body and as experience or social practice in concrete social, cultural and historical contexts' (1997:15).

Despite the renewal and revitalization of interest in the body, relatively little attention has been paid to the relations involved in the work on actual bodies, or to the relations between the providers, i.e. the relational aspects in concrete and symbolic medical contexts. A vital, but almost unnoticed aspect of the body's invisibility is that it has become inaccessible even to the researcher (Lawler 1991). That has resulted in that the body is almost invisible in research on care and may contribute to explain why we know so little about the power and significance of 'dirty work'. We need an approach that focuses on the way in which health sector work related to the body is organized and performed and also the implications of that mode of organization. One may assume that our sense of privacy and ambivalence with regard to our own body impacts on the way we relate to the bodies of others, i.e. the patients.

Dirty work

What then is dirt? Anthropologist Mary Douglas (1966) argues that from a cultural point of view dirt is simply disorder, it is matter on the wrong place. There is no such thing as absolute dirt: it only exists in the eyes of the beholder (1966:4). Furthermore there are hardly any ideas of dirt and disorder that do not have a bodily reference, Douglas states. She explores the relationship between conceptions and interpretations of the body on the micro level and structures and social processes on the macro level. From quite a different angle the psychoanalyst Lawrence Kubie (1937) launched the thesis that all human beings, conscious or unconscious, have inherited conceptions of bodily secretions as dirty and disgusting. The body could be seen as a dirty fabric against a backcloth of clean and organised surroundings, he maintained.

In the health sector there's a lot of 'dirty work' that needs doing, both literally and figuratively or symbolically. Hence dirty work may serve as a perspective from which to examine social structures, organization, gendering processes and working relations. Basically, dirty work generally bestows little status or esteem on those who do it, and often few formal qualifications are required. Sociologist Everet Hughes (1984) asserts that the work turns dirty when it contradicts in some way the heroic aspect of our moral views and people develop strategies to compensate perceived loss of honour. Hughes adds that one intriguing aspect of dirty work is its embeddedness in precisely the type of activity that gives a profession its charisma. Therefore, the role played by dirty work in the drama of working relationships, has to be ascertained empirically.

Sociologist and former nurse Jocalyn Lawler (1991) found a deep sense of ambivalence to intimate body work among nurses and many tried to conceal the dirtier aspects of the work such as dealing with waste products. Lawler assumes that the increasingly privatized body might give rise to a sense of embarrassment and shame in both the patient and the nurse. Hence, the low status jobs labelled 'dirty' are made invisible and tabooed. Nursing work takes place in a normatively regulated space, where both written and unwritten rules set out what may and may not be done. These rules are not easy to learn, possibly because they articulate cultural codes aimed at protecting the dignity of both parties.

Learning to work with others' bodies

Despite ambivalence we tend to assume that the attitude of health care providers toward the patient's body and dirty work, will be open-minded and unprejudiced simply because they are professionals. This assumption, however, is certainly more complex than is immediately apparent and needs to be explored on many levels, both individual and educational. One male nurse recounted how his first experiences with caring work led made him lose his appetite and spoiled his sex life for a while (Dahle and Isaksen 2002). His intense emotional reactions might have had an impact upon his later relationship to caring work, despite an ability to adjust. As a teacher in physiotherapy Sudman (1998) observed that students try to avoid touching the patient body, preferring to use instrumental treatment methods such as exercises and mechanical equipment rather than massage. This represents a change compared to when she herself was a student. If her observation holds true, the embarrassment of touching the patient body may be changing physiotherapy as a medical discipline, turning it into a more instrumental field of work (Dahle 1992).[2]

What is often overlooked is that much of the work performed by doctors also requires close and intimate contact with the patient's body. Their symbolic role may protect their status but it can not fully protect students from problems arising in practical training situations. Gynaecological examinations are illustrative. Here the doctor needs to deal with the female body's most intimate, personal and sexualized areas. The examination takes place within a strictly professional and normatively regulated context to avoid any hint of sexualization or of crossing into forbidden territory. Parsons (1951) discussed the scene as a mode of regulating nakedness. The code prescribed that the medical doctor (at that time always a man) should never stay alone while performing the gynaecological examination. A nurse would always be on hand. She had a double function, both to assist the doctor and to act as a guarantor that the professional relationship did not develop into a private and sexualized one.

---

[2] An interesting point is emerging popularity of massage during the last ten to fifteen years. This work often located in the intersection between health care and well-being.

Practical training in gynaecology is recognised as a sensitive area for students (Annfeldt 1998), and patients are therefore given a full anaesthetic in teaching contexts. Interestingly, the justification for such an arrangement is said to be consideration for the patients, not the students. But it of course also protects the students from feelings of embarrassment on their first encounter with the intimate parts of the female body. That said, realizing this could have an adverse effect on the illusion of impersonality in professional dealings with patients' bodies, and challenge the heroic aspects of work.

Gendered division of dirty work

As a domain constituted by cultural and historic processes (Ekeland 2001), there are many negotiable division lines and different layers of categorization. There are differences in status and power, tasks are hierarchically ordered by gender and class, and given unequal value. In this domain caring and nursing are viewed as practical, hands-on jobs, they are culturally encoded as 'feminine' and the work is devalued (Wærness 1984). Medical treatment, on the contrary, is considered theoretical and abstract, and has been, and is partly still encoded as 'masculine' and highly respected.[3]

Sociologist Lise Widding Isaksen (2002) argues that the degree of physical intimacy defines the status of a job and that there is a correlation between the degree of bodily intimacy required by a job and that job's low social status. In this hierarchial system, tasks entailing close contact with bodily secretions, or waste products, are ranked at the bottom. Increasing the distance to the patient's body is likely to affect both individual and occupational status positively, irrespective of gender. Requirements for more theoretical qualifications in the nursing and caring professions seem to be accompanied by a move away from practical caring work, despite the opposite being the intention (Wærness 1984). Even management of nursing tasks means less time is spent tending to patients' bodies and is therefore rewarded with higher status (Dahle and Iversen 2001).

There is empirical evidence that male nurses avoid taking on caring tasks (Isaksen 2002, Rasmussen 2002). This is itself a process that reshapes the gendered nature of the work. In Norway, only five per cent of the nursing profession are men. Hence the political ambition to increase the number of men in caring professions has been a failure. In our study we found that male nurses tend to cluster within a few specialities, such as leadership and management, psychiatric wards and acute medicine, including intensive care wards (Dahle and Isaksen 2002). As we explored these statistical figures we discovered that those specialities are constituted around properties inscribed in a cultural notion of masculinity. In

---

[3] We should of course take the feminization of medical work into account in future analysis. The new gender composition is likely to blur the gendered and gendering division lines, but this is not yet the case on this level. My argument is that up to this point in history, women doctors' are to some extent protected and given more or less the same snob value as male medical doctors.

our culture men are seen as having 'natural' capacities for leadership, they have physical strength, a capacity that was needed historically when nurses in psychiatric wards cared for violent patients, and finally men are assumed to have a 'natural' attraction for technology. Maybe unconsciously, they select specialities within an overall female universe that offer structural, social and cultural conditions for shaping and reshaping male identities and which also help them avoid intimate body[4] work and low status.

Less accounted for is that although much of the work of doctors is practical, concrete and intimately related to the patient's body, it is nevertheless conceived as non-bodily. Feminist scholars argue that the use of technology comes *between* the body being treated and the dispenser of that treatment, thereby creating a distance to the body. That in itself will affect our conceptions of medical work (Kvande 1998). This assumption I will challenge in the next section.

The doctors' dirty work

Medical treatment is concerned with diagnosing and, preferably, rectifying the malady or dysfunction. Put differently, medical treatment is the health service's production unit and nursing and care its reproductive unit aimed at meeting the patient's immediate needs, needs that can be either situational or permanent.

As already pointed to, the treatment/caring split is not simply a dichotomy. Neither medicine as a system nor doctors as individuals remain indifferent to the bodily organs requiring intervention. In a Norwegian study of the medical status of a range of diseases, there was a clear hierarchy of medical interventions (Album 1991). Performing brain surgery, organ transplants or treating heart disorders is ranked on the top of the hierarchy and is far more prestigious than dealing with everyday disorders like varicose veins and haemorrhoids.[5] Disorders of the intestinal and digestive system (gastroenterology) score about half as many points in this ranking list. Until a few decades ago gastro-surgery dealt mostly with the upper and middle parts of the intestinal system.[6] Problems further down received very little attention; indeed, they went practically unnoticed. This however is a domain in transition during the last 10-15 years.

In our culture bowel incontinence is an extremely stigmatizing disorder that causes shame among those affected. A dysfunction of the bowel, bowel or anal incontinence, may have several causes. Women constitute the majority of the affected and the most frequent cause is damage incurred during childbirth. Though in some cases neurological mechanisms are involved and sometimes there is no identifiable cause, which may be the case when the patient is an older woman. The assumption is that current problems are the delayed effect of complications

---

[4] Intensive care is an interesting case, in that technology and intimate care has to be combined and there seems to be a high male turnover.

[5] The study has been replicated recently and the findings are surprisingly stable according to author. The article is yet in print.

[6] Private communication from a surgeon.

occurring during childbirth (Gleditsch, Nesbakken and Nygaard 2001). A bowel dysfunction alters the natural reflex sequences. The patient may pass stool without being aware of it or, on the other hand, may be given fallacious signals of an ongoing bowel movement that is actually not happening. All degrees of incontinence are found, and only a small proportion require advanced surgical intervention.

To explore the nature of the work three of the few very specialists in this surgical area were interviewed. One of them explained that his personal interest in bowel surgery, was that 'the pelvic floor and rectal system are interesting, but neglected anatomical structures in surgery'. The pelvic floor is constituted by a series of muscles with openings in them, one for faeces, one for urine and muscle contractions when in labour. The exceptional thing about the pelvic floor, he explained, is that the muscles are not attached to a bone structure, as elsewhere in the body. The absence of supportive hooks means that the so-called 'soft structure' is particularly vulnerable to blows, pressure and traumas. The delicate muscular and neuromuscular structures act in a finely balanced way. A female surgeon said that her interest in the area was wakened by the many female patients she had met who had suffered for many years, due to lack of medical treatment and disinterest of medical doctors. She saw it as a challenge to develop new knowledge and improved treatment methods to help these women back to a more normal existence.[7]

The diagnostic examination procedures related to bowel dysfunction are extremely intimate. In contrast to, for instance, gynaecological examinations, which also concern the body's intimate areas, there are often malodorous liquid and formed stools to deal with. In the most severe cases, the patient has to be examined sitting on a toilet chair with a mirror reflecting the anal area. A contrast medium is injected into the bowel and the patient is watched often by several people while he or she defecates. Diagnostic procedures often require the insertion of the (gloved) hand into the rectum to inspect and control bowel functions and follow the passage of the contrast medium through the colon. One could hardly imagine a more intimate examination of the body and its functions than in this case.

Recent technological developments have resulted in a number of new diagnostic tools and methods, which in turn may spur a further developments. Many patients today can be helped with relatively uncomplicated surgery, for others a more advanced regime is called for. For example, only a relatively simple operation is needed to repair a dysfunctioning anal sphincter, and with new surgical techniques a dysfunctioning reflexive system can be completely restructured. In the most severe cases, it is now possible to attach a pace-maker to the inside of the thigh to control the sphincter (this is important, even though a

---

[7] The motives and interests of these two surgeons differed in a gendered way, but the scarce interview material does not allow drawing any conclusions. However, they shared a professional interest in constituting a new field as an area of proper surgical knowledge and intervention.

pace-maker installed in the heart is likely to be ranked higher). With new techniques available, medical help can be offered to larger numbers of patients.

The increased activity in the field has had both academic and practical offshoots. Firstly, during the course of the past decade, a growing number of scientific articles have been published at home and abroad. Secondly, the discipline has now become a separate area of expertise with its own networks, collaborative ventures, international conferences, etc. In one respect bowel incontinence is a surgical success story, where medical technology plays a key role. And the effect has been to enhance the status of the disorder itself as well as that of the doctors working in the area. For instance, Rikshospitalet (the Norwegian national hospital) has given priority to developing the surgical field of anal incontinence.

A gendered context of dirty work

We all have mental pictures of the job professional doctors and nurses do. It is acknowledged that in a modern health system nurses need comprehensive theoretical training to achieve the required level of competence. Still, below the surface the level of theoretical training nurses really need, remains an open question. The implicit assumption is that their tasks are, and will always be basically practical and concrete, learned by doing, more than derived from theoretical books. Still women are regarded the 'natural' carers who are born to take on such tasks. The capacity to care is embedded in their genes and culturally a part of what it is to be a woman. Concerning the doctors, the medical examination involves physical work on actual bodies. Most people are aware of this, often from personal experience. But in spite of this widespread knowledge, the dominating mental image remains that of a theoretically and physically remote profession. The contrasting mental images are in turn a power relationship that serves to keep intact the demarcation line between high and low esteem.

Examination and treatment of patients with bowel incontinence is an excellent case with which to illuminate the particularities of intimate bodily intervention in a medical context: it is dirty work both literally and figuratively. But what makes this work different from the other dirty aspects of caring work in the health sector, is exactly the context and the purpose of the work performed on the body. The medical definition of the situation implies that tasks are performed within a scientific frame of reference. The doctor's main job is not to *remove* organic waste products from the patient's body, but to correct a medical disorder through intervention. The context is a crucial distinction that defines the symbolic boundary and constitutes a dividing line between the doctors' 'honourable' dirty work and the low status dirty work performed by the care workers.

The fundamentally gendered nature of work in the health sector requires us to question the relationship between theory and practice in many different ways and to explore the mental work that perpetuates symbolic gender divisions (Acker 1992). It is also important to note that the two working contexts are related to different knowledge regimes. Within the medical context, the justifications for all treatment methods are basically scientific, despite the many exceptions to this principle in practice. Moreover, historically, abstract and scientific knowledge has always tended to carry masculine connotations. Taken together, medicine is regarded a theory-driven practice, it is positivistic and evidence-based in nature, and the knowledge travels *from* theory *to* practice. Nursing and care theory on the other hand is derived from practical knowledge, i.e. from caring practices. Practice constitute the basis for theoretical reflection, and the route knowledge takes leads from practice through reflection and theory back again to practice. It is a form of grounded theory. That knowledge is fed back into two different – i.e. theoretically and practically – embedded systems of knowledge, reshapes and perpetuates in this particular case a symbolic divide in terms of gendered power and ranking. In his analyses of professional systems, Abbott (1988) regarded this division as a crucial aspect, inasmuch as theory-derived practical skills represent abstract knowledge, while theory derived from practice remained closer to the concrete.

The abstract/concrete distinction concerns basically the distribution of positions in a professional hierarchy. Feminist scholars have shown that women's knowledge more often is perceived as practical, almost irrespective of its actual content, form or character (Acker 1992; Witz 1992).

When an intimate examination procedure is linked to medical science and contextualized, the body waste ceases to be concrete. The 'shameful' bodily product is transformed from matter *out of place* to matter *in place*, from a concrete to abstract diagnostic matter, by virtue of its inclusion in medical expertise. Still, when the task of the nurse is to remove that same matter from the patient's body, making the patient clean in that process, that task involving waste products is encoded as concrete and feminine and equated with low status. Thus nursing and care work are caught in an ambivalent space and relegated to a lower rung on the status ladder: on the one hand the work is essential; on the other it is dirty, invisible and shameful.

Conclusion

The body plays a key role in health practices. The symbolic meanings and cultural encoding of physically intimate tasks are important. The body cannot be escaped, but understanding the nature, ranking and implications of health work is far from easy. We still need theories to explore the nature of the gendered split between treatment and caring work from new and fresh angles. Taking rectal surgery as an example, I have tried to show that it is not proximity to bodies and bodily waste alone, nor technology or the practical nature of such work that determines the status of the tasks. Doctors do a lot of intimate work with the patient body which causes neither embarrassment nor an exodus from the profession. One important place to start may be to contextualize the intimate tasks and the structures within which the work is done. It could stimulate the generation of more encompassing theories and help us understand the battleground and why the gendered division of labour persists as a ranked system. The work with bodies in the health sector is part of a gendered structure and a hegemonic system of meaning.

Medicine has precedence and definitional power. The divisions travel in criss-cross fashion, however, and while many boundaries have given way others remain firmly in place. There is good reason to believe that gender boundaries and the valuation of tasks will be challenged by future developments and the new gender balance in medicine. Here I would like to mention two likely dimensions of change. While men will probably continue to avoid 'women's work', i.e. intimate caring work, women will increasingly join them and march out of the low status healthcare jobs in growing numbers. Secondly, more women are now entering the medical profession. It remains to be seen whether this female 'invasion' into traditionally male medical territory will challenge the separation of practical and abstract work, as women are culturally associated with practical work. A redefinition of medical work as merely academic and abstract may be an element in an ongoing process of transformation. What should also be taken into account is that as technology becomes more widely incorporated in modern nursing functions it may lead to mounting tension between practical caring work and technological aids. Whether this will undermine the exclusive–trivial balance altogether, is a question still in need of a good answer.

The extent to which newcomers today decide to leave the profession before they really get a foothold is unknown. What the statistics do tell us, however, is that working with the elderly has become less attractive both for general and auxiliary nurses. To solve the crisis of shortage of providers, we are heading in a direction where increasing numbers of tasks are being performed by unskilled workers, both women and men, from different ethnic backgrounds.

References

Abbott, A. (1988): *The System of Professions. An Essay on the Division of Expert Labour.* The University of Chicago Press.

Acker, J. (1992): 'Gendering Organization Theory', in: Mills, Albert, J. and Tancred, P. (eds): *Gendering Organizational Analysis.* London: Sage.

Album, D. (1991): 'Sykdommers medisinske prestisje', in: *Tidsskrift for den norske Lægeforening* no. 17.

Annfeldt, T. (1998): *Kjønn i utdanning. Hegemoniske posisjoner og forhandlinger om yrkesidentitet i medisin og faglærerutdanning.* Dr. polit. thesis, NTNU, Pedagogisk institutt.

Annandale, E. (1998): *The Sociology of Health and Medicine. A Critical Introduction.* Cambridge: Polity Press.

Bakken, R. (2001): *Modermordet. Om sykepleie, kjønn og kultur.* Oslo: Universitetsforlaget.

Dahle, R. (1991): *Arbeidsdeling, makt, identitet.* Dr. philos. thesis, University of Trondheim. Den Almenvitenskapelige høgskolen.

Dahle, R. (1992): 'Kan betydningen av kjønn trylles bort?', in: Andenæs, A. (ed.): *Epler fra vår egen hage.* University of Trondheim AVH, Senter for kvinneforskning, Report no. 4.

Dahle, R. (1993): 'Inntrengere eller nyskapere. Flere kvinnelige leger?', in: *Tidsskrift for den norske Lægeforening.* 113; 2597–600.

Dahle, R. (1994): 'Å være Dame over liv og død', in: *Nytt Norsk Tidsskrift* 11/1.

Dahle, R. and Iversen, M. (2001): 'Relasjonene mellom sykepleiere og hjelpepleiere, en grensetvist', in: *Tidsskrift for velferdsforskning*, no. 4.

Dahle, R. og Isaksen, Widding, L.: 'Sjukvård som maskulinitetsprosjekt', in: *Kvinnovetenskaplig tidskrift* 2-3.

Davies, K. (1997): *Embodied Practices*. London: Sage.

Davies, K. (2001): 'Disturbing Gender' Lund, *Studies in Sociology*, vol. 4.

Douglas, M. (1966): *Purity and Danger. An analysis of the Concepts of Pollution and Taboo*. London: Routledge and Kegan Paul. Norsk utgave (1997): *Rent og urent*. Pax forlag.

Ekeland, T.-J. (2001): 'Den biomedisinske arkitekturen som maktdiskurs', in: *Fokus på familien*. Oslo: Universitetsforlaget. Vol. 29, 308-323.

Gjerberg E. (2002): 'Maktrelasjoner i helsetjenestens yrkeshierarki', in: Ellingsæter, A.L. and Solheim, J. (eds.): *Den usynlige hånd? Kjønnsmakt og moderne arbeidsliv*. Oslo: Gyldendal Akademisk.

Gleditsch, D., Nesbakken, A. and Nygaard, K. (2001): 'Sfinkterplastikk ved traumatisk betinget inkontinens', in: *Tidsskrift for den norske Lægeforening* no. 16; 121; 1908-10.

Hughes Everett, C. (1984): *The Sociological Eye*. Transaction Books, New Brunswick and London.

Kubie L. (1937): 'The Fantasy of Dirt', in: *Psychoanalytic Quart* 1937; 6: 388-424.

Kvande, E. (1998): 'Konstruksjon av mannlighet i organisasjoner under endring', in: *Sosiologi i dag* no. 3.

Isaksen, L. Widding (2002): 'Masculine dignity and the dirty body', in: *NORA*, no. 3, vol. 10.

Johansson, T. (1999): 'Vad gör vi på gymen? Drømmen om en hård kropp', in: *Tvärsnitt. Humanistisk och samhällsvetenskaplig forskning*.

Lawler, J. (1991): *Behind the Screens – Nursing Somology and the Problem of the Body*. Pearson Professional.

Malterud, K. (1990): *Allmennpraktikerens møte med kvinnelige pasienter* Oslo: Tano. NOU no. 13 – 1999: *Kvinners helse i Norge*.

Parsons, T. (1951): *The Social System* London: The Free Press of Glencoe.

Rasmussen, B. (2002): 'Hjemmesykepleien som en grådig organisasjon', in: *Tidsskrift for samfunnsforskning* 41(1): 38-58.

Ross, D.W., Hirt, M. and Kurtz, R. (1968): 'The Fantasy of Dirt and Attitudes towards Body Products', in: *The Journal of Nervous and Mental Disease* 146, 4.

Shilling, C. (1993): *The Body and Social Theory* London, Sage.

Skårderud, F. (1994): 'Idéhistorier om kroppen', in: *Tidsskrift for den norske Lægeforening* 114, 2: 177-84.

Solheim, J. (1999): 'Makt som grense'. Lecture in NFR-conference *Kjønn i endring*.

Sudman, T. (1998): 'Kjønn er (også) en jobb', in: *Fysioterapeuten* no. 5, vol. 65: 12-19.

Sørhaug, H.C. (1994): 'Dær går grænsen!', in: Arnstberg, K.-O. (ed.): *Førbjudet, farligt, frestande. Om tabu i vår tid*. Carlsson bokförlag.

Turner, B.S. (1992): *Regulating Bodies: Essays in Medical Sociology*. London: Routledge.

Twigg, J. (1999): *Carework as bodywork*. Paper read at the IV European Congress of Gerontology, Berlin.

Wærness, K. (1984): 'The Rationality of Caring', in: *Economic and Democracy*, vol. 5.

Witz, A. (1992): *Professions and Patriarchi*. London: The International Library of Sociology.

Widerberg, K. (1995): *Kunnskapens kjønn: minner, refleksjoner og teori*. Oslo: Pax.

Chapter 7

Professional Knowledge and Symbolic Care Relations in the Danish Cancer Field

Tine Rask Eriksen

Using two constructed histories based on interviews and questionnaires I outline how cancer patients act, think, and orient themselves based on their lifestyle when encountering a serious illness.

With my reconstruction of the social order in the field of cancer, I illustrate how different types of care relations between patients and health care professionals are socially and culturally determined. Furthermore, I demonstrate how the social order that patients encounter in the cancer field is incorporated in professionals as a habitus that operates 'without their knowledge' and which seems to communicate the interests of the dominant experts (i.e., symbolic violence). My point is therefore that patients and professionals often act against their own respective objectives to receive and provide care.

Introduction

A substantial dilemma of the Nordic field of professional care is the fact that most of the theoretical research in care (Eriksson 1987, Martinsen 1987), as communicated within the educational system today, has a normative character. It thus does not have sufficient explicative power when it comes to the problematic conditions in the practical care work in public institutions.

The relation between nursing care and the conditions in which that care is given has been the driving force in my research. My research in the 1980s was focused on qualifying care in health care education (Eriksen 1992, 1993). More recently, I have been studying the health care sector from the patients' perspective. This chapter is based on my investigation of 500 cancer patients' psychological and social problems in connection with cancer. At the time of the study, all 500 patients had been receiving treatment for cancer during the preceding year (Eriksen 1996 p83).

The aim of this chapter is:

- to demonstrate that cancer patients' life experiences form an essential basis for the way they react when they develop a serious disease,
- to demonstrate the extent to which care relations between patients and professionals are structured by the professionals' knowledge, language, and work routines,
- to demonstrate whether the professionals' knowledge and work routines function as a form of symbolic power over the patients and their (psychological) approach to their new situation, and
- in this way, to create theoretical insight into the complex aspects at work in the field of paid care work in the modernized welfare state in the Nordic country of Denmark.

Theoretical framework of the study

The framework for this study is Bourdieu's (1990, 1996, 1997, 1999) cultural theoretical approach to human behaviour. Bourdieu's cultural theory explains how socially determined circumstances structure the ways in which human beings live and behave. Human beings are woven into a social context that represents the symbolic reality constituting their understanding of the world. As such, human beings neither create nor select their worldview, they are embedded in it. Bourdieu's work and his key concepts are useful for uncovering these complex structures in specific fields.

Field, habitus, and capital are the central organizational concepts in Bourdieu's work which includes studies of the fields of artists and intellectuals, class lifestyles, power of law, and so on. In analytic terms, a field can be defined as (Bourdieu and Wacquant 1992 p97):

> a network, or a configuration, of objective relations between positions. These positions are objectively defined, in their existence and in the determinations they impose upon their occupants, agents or institutions, by their present and potential situation in the structure of the distribution of species of power (or capital), whose possession commands access to the specific profits that are at stake in the field, as well as by their objective relation to other positions.

The function of the concept of habitus is to sidestep the alternative between the individual and the society. To speak of habitus is:

> to assert that the individuals, and even the personal, the subjective, is social, collective. Habitus is a socialized subjectivity. (Bourdieu and Wacquant 1992 p126)

In each field, the agents have a specific class socialized habitus and a specific cultural and symbolic capital. Symbolic violence plays a pivotal theoretical role in understanding the domination in individual fields. It can be defined as: 'the violence which is exercised upon a social agent with his or her complicity' (Bourdieu and Wacquant 1992 p167). To express it more rigorously, social agents are knowing agents who, even when they are subjected to determinisms, contribute to producing the efficacy of that which determines them insofar as they structure what determine them. That is, the agents recognise a violence that is wielded precisely inasmuch as one does not perceive it as such.

Although Bourdieu has never analysed the logic of practice in nursing, I have been using his theory and his key concepts in my research, aiming to understand the logic of the care relations between cancer patients and professionals in the health care system (Eriksen 1996). Nevertheless, it has been necessary for me to prolong' his theory with other similar theories that are more capable of explaining, for instance, gender (Widerberg 1995), gendered body (Knizek 1993), and the field of memory (Gammelgård 1996).

When human beings develop cancer, they are examined and treated within the health care system. They enter into what for them is a new or specific context: a field. This field has its own history, institutions, agents, idioms, norms, rules, and routines (Bourdieu 1996 p85). The field that cancer patients enter today is characterised by continuing conflicts about funding, methods of treatment, types of knowledge, care cultures and relations (Eriksen 1996 p25). There are certain 'rules' of the game; and participation in the field of conflict demands, above all, a certain habitus, a certain competence, resources (or capital), and a good position in the hierarchy. The agents' positions often depend upon the participants' gender, social class, and educational background. In these conflicts, language is one of the structuring factors for the above-mentioned knowledge, types of relations, and communication. Language functions as a form of symbolic violence or power, that is, as the power to construct reality (Bourdieu 1996 p40) and thereby to construct the social order in the field of cancer. This same social order is made to seem 'natural' for the participants (here professionals and patients), as it is gradually incorporated or socialised as a habitus. The habitus is a physically and mentally incorporated practice form that determines how agents react, think, and orient themselves in a specific context (the cancer field). Thus, the specific social order is perceived as legitimate by its participants, e.g., in the cancer field. We are here speaking of a process by which the dominant group, 'the experts', forces its specific interests upon others (the patients). As mentioned above, Bourdieu characterizes such a process as symbolic violence (Bourdieu 1996, 1997 p104).

Material and methods

In the current study, quantitative methods were used to collect the data, as well as a subsequent series of qualitative interviews. Using two questionnaires (distributed with an interval of 6 months), the 500 cancer patients' life stories, case histories, extent of social and psychological support, and patterns of everyday life were mapped out (Eriksen 1996 p89). Subsequently, 20 patients were subject to life-history interviews, in which the patients related their experiences of everyday life and of the support relationships in which they participated. The data were analysed using statistical, phenomenological, and structural methods. The results of the analyses were entered into a construction of the social reality of the life of cancer patients and their care relations with the professionals.

In my work with quantitative and qualitative data, I have followed Bourdieu's principles by going beyond the 'Antinomy of Social Physics and Social Phenomenology' (Eriksen 1996 p49). Bourdieu suggests that the task of sociology is:

> To uncover the most profoundly buried structures of the various social worlds, which constitute the social universe, as well as the 'mechanisms' which tend to ensure their reproduction or their transformation. This universe is peculiar in that its structures lead, as it were a 'double life'. They exist twice: in the objectivity of the first order constituted by the distribution of material resources and means of appropriation of socially scarce goods and values; and in the objectivity of the second order, in the form of system of classification, the mental and bodily schemata that function as symbolic templates for the practical activities – conduct, thoughts, feelings, and judgments – of social agents. Social facts are objects, which are also the object of knowledge within reality itself because human beings make meaningful the world, which makes them. (Bourdieu and Wacquant 1992 p7)

A science of society is thus understood as a bi-dimensional 'system of relations of power and relations of meaning between groups and classes' and of necessity must affect a double reading Or, to be more precise, it must craft a set of double-focus analytic lenses that capitalise on the epistemic virtues of each reading while skirting the vices of both. The first reading treats society in the manner of a social physics: as an objective structure, grasped from the outside, whose articulations can be materially observed, measured, and mapped out independently of the representation of those who live in it. Breaking with common sense perceptions enables the uncovering of the determinate relations within which men and women necessarily enter to 'produce their social existence'. Thanks to tools of statistics, ethnographic descriptions, and musical scores, the actions of agents (each one believes that she is improvizing her own melody) are organised and ascertain the objective regularities they obey.

The aim of the 'double-focus analysis of my material' has been to reveal the objective structures of the relations between patients and professionals and to uncover the regularities of their patterns (habitus) of actions and experiences in the field of cancer.

One of the goals of this study is thus to illustrate the extent to which experiences (habitus) in the cancer patients' life histories gradually change their confrontation of their illness and their interactions with professionals in the field of cancer, including methods of patient support and care. Using six constructed stories, I attempt to establish the patients' behavioural patterns: before diagnosis, at the time of diagnosis, and in the following period. The life histories are based on selected patient typologies taken from the entire data set (Eriksen 1996 p120). Each life history is introduced with a short quantitative presentation of the objective characteristics of this particular group of patients. This is followed by a constructed story, which is based on similar types of life history interviews (Gergen 1988).

Using these constructed cases, I have tried to show (Eriksen 1996 p120) how different types of relations between patients and professionals are gender-related and socially differentiated, and how particular forms of symbolic power function in care work in the cancer field.

In these 'patient' histories, I have found significant differences in the ways that men and women react when relating to self and to others and when coping with the concrete and symbolic break from the way they behaved before the disease was diagnosed. In this chapter, I include 'a summing up' of two constructed patient-histories (Peter Jones and Ann Brown) to show some of the objective structures of the different care relations for men and women.

Constructed life stories

A man's history

Peter Jones has cancer of the colon. He is fifty-two years old, married, middle class and lives in a large provincial town (Eriksen 1996 p159). He grew up in a family with two siblings. His father was a bricklayer who had his own business when Peter was a child. When Peter was ten years old, the family moved to a larger provincial town, where the parents had a sweet shop for more than thirty years. His mother was a housewife and helped out in the shop. The family's values were marked by the necessities of managing their own business – the values of being independent and making the best of things were considered important. Peter describes the relations of his childhood as having been 'good'. Several pauses and contradictions during the interview suggest, however, that Peter at early age had to learn to take care of himself, as he was mostly left to his own devices.

After nine years in school, Peter was apprenticed in trade, in the same town. He is today a senior clerk in the same, now large, business. He has been able to employ the strategies he learned as a child to make the best of whatever possibilities presented themselves. He is married to a woman working in the same business and they have children, now adults.

The division of labour within the family is traditional. The married couple share common values of a 'good family life'. Peter talks about the importance of taking part in the children's upbringing, although he worked up to twelve hours a day for many years. Peter's way of describing illness in his childhood is contradictory. He says that he did not have any previous experience of illness, but at the same time, he has several fleeting memories of characteristic hospital odours and of how he once fainted when hospitalized as a child. As an adult, he still finds it difficult to talk about his sister's cancer more than twelve years ago, and fights back tears when speaking about it during the interview.

At the time of diagnosis For some years, Peter has not reacted to physical symptoms, just as he speaks of his body as an 'instrument' of strength and action. When it malfunctions, he tries to deal with the problems by means of rational action. When he discovers blood in his stool, he asks his wife what he should do, as she is the one who knows about illness. It is also his wife who makes sure that he sees a doctor. After a few days in hospital, he is told that he has cancer of the bowel. His old modes of coping become apparent when he talks about his illness: a disregard of his body and his emotions as a way of tackling the illness. There are also, however, some 'new' reactions, such as feelings of powerlessness, physical restlessness and uncertainty about the new situation.

In meeting professionals in the field of cancer, Peter's old patterns of behaviour are activated. He wants to act practically to get the best out of the situation. These patterns are reinforced by the professionals' pragmatic and technical way of dealing with the problems related to his colostomy. However, Peter's rational way of confronting male doctors gradually changes, and he lets his wife take over in the relations with which he has difficulty. Because of their shared values of 'good family life', his wife participates in the circumstances of his illness, and in the practical concerns related to his colostomy,[1] but not in his emotional reactions. Peter knows that it helps his wife if they talk about things, so they talk and talk. However, it is an instrumental or empty talk that does not help Peter to accept his new condition or to confront his anxiety.

Daily life with cancer A year and a half after a colostomy, Peter Jones' social and economic life has been more or less sustained, and he has learned to live with and manage his colostomy. However, he has not yet been able to share his feelings of horror and powerlessness with either family or professionals. Instead, he uses one of his old competencies to avoid painful situations. He suppresses his thoughts and emotions by doing practical things.

But before going to sleep, difficult thoughts emerge. This feeling of powerlessness is increased because of damage to some nerves during the operation that has rendered him impotent. Because he has not gotten any support from professionals on how to solve this particular problem nor advice on how to live with it, he distances himself from professionals in the field of cancer by not showing up for his out-patient appointments.

Summary Peter Jones tells his life story and describes his illness as he wants to see and communicate it. The analysis of the case history also includes the story of a man's powerlessness in this situation. This man has a certain social status, and the ability to act and deal with practical problems concerning his illness. He also ex-

---

[1] In connection to some diseases of the colon, the colon is brought out on the abdomen. Here the intestinal membrane is attached to the skin, and an artificial opening of the alimentary canal is formed. The fecal discharge is deposited in a bag attached to the abdomen. This bag can be changed as needed.

periences closeness with and solidarity from his family and place of employment. In spite of these resources, however, he is left without any real possibility of gaining insight into his own situation or of learning how to live with his illness. At the same time, a certain change in his mode of behaviour is noticeable. An example of this is a change from a non-feeling mode to a state of feeling something in relation to his present situation (it is an example of how his habitus has been changed).

A woman's history

Ann Brown has ovarian cancer. She is fifty-one years old, married, middle class and lives in the suburbs (Eriksen 1996 p132). She grew up in a small block of flats in a city with her parents and two younger brothers. Her father grew up in the country, in a family of agricultural labourers. He was a worker in a large factory. Ann's mother lost her mother at an early age. Ann's mother was not educated, but worked as a 'housemother' at a nearby school. In her family life, Ann developed a number of gender-determined abilities centred on the importance of being a part of the family group, and always being available to its members. The division of work was characterized by her mother having a dominating and controlling personality. The social relations of her childhood were therefore inconsistent as Ann had a close but difficult relationship with her mother and a close relationship with her somewhat weaker father. From early childhood, Ann experienced a feeling of not doing things well enough, just as she today describes herself as a compliant woman.

After graduating from tenth grade at the local, lower secondary school, Ann was trained as an office worker in an insurance company. She married an engineer, and they now have two grown-up children. Even though she has a job, the division of labour within the family is traditional. Ann is available to help other people and she tries to maintain order in a complex daily existence by controlling other people and by not forwarding her own demands. These contradictions gradually lead Ann to try to cope by means of pills and alcohol (Eriksen 1996 p34). Her mode of talking about her experiences with illness in childhood is marked by a taboo attached to her mother's cancer – that which could not be controlled was not talked about. Ann learned a mode for handling serious illness – by not talking or thinking about it.

At the time of diagnosis The way in which Ann talks about the treatment of her ovarian cancer shows that forms of ambivalence remain noticeable throughout the long period of treatment. She gets the year of the outbreak of the disease wrong; when talking about its treatment, she says that it has been long and that dead cancer cells are still being found in recent biopsies. When she was told that she had cancer, she broke down completely (Eriksen 1996 p136). At the same time, she says that she cannot remember what happened for a long time. This 'don't remember' mode is often repeated during the interview. Presumably, this indicates an activation of childhood modes that taught her to treat the uncontrollable as taboo.

In Ann's contact with professionals, some life biographical relation modes are also detected, particularly the importance for her to be accepted as a person. This results in her seeking personal instead of professional relationships with the professionals. However, it also means that she is passive both in relation to her treatment and in gaining insight into the body's pathophysiology.

In relations with her family, she maintains her life-historical way of making a taboo of the 'terrible'. Ann does not remember how her family reacted to her illness. At the same time, she resists any attempt on their part to talk about the 'terrible' – the cancer. This distances her from her husband and children. It also results in a repression of her own emotions and the sense of her physical being.

Daily life with cancer About a year after her diagnosis, Ann's social and economic life is partially sustained. She is back at work, although working part time. The division of labour within the family is unchanged, but supplemented with paid help in the house and garden. Ann tells of a life characterized by contradictions between old and new ways of behaving. New strategies include positive thinking and living, inspired by self-help books for cancer patients. Old strategies include the idea that the 'terrible' must be kept at bay by engaging in an endless series of activities. For Ann, these contrasts gradually lead to a lack of concentration and increasing uneasiness. However, she still cannot accept the difficulties. Instead, she worries about others, in this case her husband. At check-ups at hospital, Ann still maintains her old mode of behaviour. This means that she still does not want to know anything about the status of her illness, but seeks acceptance as a woman who is behaving correctly in relation to her situation.

Summary Ann Brown relates her life history as she sees it. Nonetheless, the analysis of the history reveals an ambivalent woman, who is marked by a life in which she has always tried to relate to other people on their terms. As she has little previous experience with serious illness, other people's ways of handling illness are adopted as her own strategy. This strategy counteracts, so to speak, Ann's possibilities of finding her own way of dealing with her present situation.

Empirical structures for care relations

Relations within the family

These constructed stories provide a sketch of how two middle-aged, middle-class individuals act, think, and orient themselfves based on their lifestyles when encountering a serious and prolonged illness such as cancer. Certain common features are seen, but there are also differences in the gender-related way of interacting with professionals, family and self, and in how they specifically and symbolically handle the series of disruptions in their lives.

In their own families, both Peter and Ann manage to maintain 'old' ways of mutual support. Their experiences of sharing difficult feelings related to serious illness are either lacking or are of an subconscious nature. However, neither Peter and Ann nor their families can accept these new feelings about cancer, emotions such as anxiety and feelings of chaos. On the contrary, both Ann and Peter employ socially and culturally determined 'defense practices' to minimize existential pain. These practices enable them to 'replace' painful feelings with something else, so that fear and uncertainty 'disappear'. However, this pattern of repression prevents them from learning anything about their new existential conditions (Gammelgaard 1996 p78). The conclusion is therefore that changes in the incorporated lifestyles of both patients are minimal.

Cancer exists in the body and, as it is primarily the biological body that has been treated in both Ann's and Peter's cases, their bodies have been partly transformed into objectified and deformed bodies negating gender and sexual function. Since throughout their lives these same bodies have been socialised by incorporating a series of practices, changes in the physical body, gradually, will become a basis for new and different experiences (Knizek 1993). The concrete disruption of their physical condition is simultaneously reinforced by the social order of care work for cancer patients, where patients are gradually exposed to a long series of relationships with many types of professionals in treatment, in the wards, and in outpatient clinics.

Relations to professionals

At the empirical level, these two life stories also suggest that there are gender-related differences in the way Peter and Ann confront the social order and in the way professionals function. For Peter, his relations with professionals constitute a means of gaining insight into the treatment of his illness and of learning how to cope with practical problems with his colostomy. Through language, he obtains information about the illness. In this way, Peter finds himself able to relate to female nurses by means of rational competence – they give him some books so that he can read about the changes that have taken place in his body. These relations 'open up' for a possibility to learn how to deal practically with his new physical condition – the colostomy. In his relation with the nurses, his physical discomfort, his preconscious horror and powerlessness ensure the beginning cognition of his present situation (Eriksen 1996 p163).

For Ann, interaction with professionals is a means of gaining acceptance as a suffering woman, with the possibility of exchanging feelings about her difficulties. She uses language to establish 'ego-supporting' relations with the professionals. Thus, Ann is unable to relate to a male surgeon who directly addresses her and tells her that he has removed a tumour from her ovary. In this situation, her biographical habit of turning the 'terrible' into a taboo is activated. Thus, the surgeon's 'assaulting' form of relating to her comes to function as symbolic violence (Eriksen 1996 p137).

The social order in the field of cancer

In this section, I will use a reconstruction of the empirical patterns found in the patients' histories and the types of patient groups based on the entire sample in order to show – via the cultural theory – how the social order in the cancer field is producing some routinized care relations between patients and professionals.

Care relations and symbolic violence

According to the quantitative survey of 500 cancer patients, approximately 50 percent have been hospitalised three times or more, and more than half of the 500 patients have received two or three types of treatment for cancer (Eriksen 1996 p91). The main form of treatment that patients seek in the field of cancer is biomedical, focusing on the diseased part of the body. The diseased part is removed by being cut out or destroyed with chemotherapy or radiotherapy. The cancer field's division of labour among various specialists (and forms of conflict) structures the ways in which the patients' treatment is divided among specialists. The consequence of this objectification and division of labour for the patients is an alienation from their physical bodies (Knizek 1993). At the same time, professionals talk about the physical forms of treatment in codes and non-physical forms of communication. In this process, the patients' suffering remain virtually unrecognized or secondary. Thus, routines of treatment can function as symbolic violence in relation to the patients' existential situation and to the care relations in the field.

Using my reconstruction of the social order in the field of cancer, I will now illustrate how different types of care relations between patients and professionals are socially and culturally determined. Furthermore, I will demonstrate how the social order that patients encounter in the cancer field is incorporated in professionals as a habitus that operates 'without their knowledge', and how the professionals seem to communicate the interests of the dominant experts (i.e., symbolic violence).

Care relations are different for men and women, as well as for different social classes. The following different types of relations have been found to be the objective structures for the types of relations that occur between patients and professionals.

First, male patients with high social status relate to professionals in a verbal and objective manner, using rational abilities. This way of relating acts as a challenge to professionals, as the patient meets biomedical logic on the own premises of field. Thus, this type of male patient participates actively in his treatment. However, these treatment-oriented relations, verbal and rational, prevent this group of high-status patients from dealing with psychological problems related to conditions of life with cancer (Eriksen 1996 p180). This pattern is different for women with similar high social status.

Female patients from the middle class relate to professionals by becoming an object in the professionals' institutionalized support relations. Here, the symbolic violence functions as the passive subordination of the women to the dominant forms of support. This means that the professionals' support and care fail to relate to the female patient's life-historical precondition for functioning as a patient.

Male and female patients from the middle class with a high biological intensity of illness and great bodily changes are extremely dependent upon support. This group, particularly, receives technical and routine based support from the professionals. In these cases, this kind of support 'produces' a form of symbolic violence that limits the patients' ability to internalize their greatly changed body and conditions of life (Eriksen 1996 p181).

Finally, male and female patients from a lower social level, who have the competence to handle psychological problems by doing practical things, have a tendency to evade support from the professionals. Here the patients' socially determined compulsion to act makes them turn to their material existence instead of to their feelings as patients. This denial of oneself as a patient prevents the professionals from becoming a support relation for this group.

Symbolic power and care work

The quantitative survey of the patients' need for support indicated that the need for sharing worries with others is the greatest need cancer patients have (Eriksen 1996 p96). Using Bourdieu's theory of human behaviour, I have analysed the different relations that mitigate against the establishment of the kind of care relations within which patients and professionals can share the difficult feelings of fear and chaos in the course of the illness. I have also shown how the patients' previous experiences cannot always be used in relation to the situation of their illness. In order to examine further these complex conditions that make it difficult to establish care relations, I will place my reconstruction of the field of cancer and its actors in the perspective of forms of power that are in the field (Bourdieu 1996). By doing so, I wish to illustrate why patients and professionals act against their own respective objectives to receive and provide care.

According to Bourdieu (1997 p123), the most brutal power relations are symbolic relations and acts in which one obeys and submits to some given power.

It is precisely these symbolic relations that disguise the complexity of power relations, and the process that transforms them through continuous conflict and confrontations (Flybjerg 1992 p112). The participant does not discover how the relations of power find each other through the creation of networks and systems, and implement the relations of power in different institutions. In these systems, ideological structures also play a role in the struggle for the right to define the social order of the field. Here, symbolic power is the power to constitute the given order by means of, for example, cognitive and ideological concepts, thus endueing others to believe in this order. Thus, symbolic power is almost magical, making it possible to achieve that which can be achieved by means of economic power (Bourdieu 1996 p45). Symbolic power works as long as it is accepted. This means that symbolic power defines itself both by those who exercise it, and those against whom it is exercised. It functions in the very structure of the field where power is produced and reproduced.

Earlier in the chapter, I outlined the cognitive structures that produce the social order in the field of cancer. Further, I described how the ideological and cognitive structures define themselves through the professionals' knowledge and gradually also through the patients, as a necessity for holding one's aim as a patient. In the field of cancer, cognitive structures are furthermore defined in a masculine universe, where the relation between power and gender (Widerberg 1995 p13) is important when analysing the relations that structure care work. The masculine domination (Bourdieu 1999) in the field is partly symbolic power and included in the cognitive structures that suggest that actors must be able to function by means of the so called 'masculine logic', that is, through the means of a verbalization of care expertise. Therefore, the relationship between practical logic – to give care – and cognitive logic – to verbalise care – needs further modification.

In my earlier research (Eriksen 1989 p12), I showed how care competence primarily is constituted by historically determined female 'characteristics'. These characteristics have been attributed to women based on biological gender and reproduced from generation to generation as part of the 'natural' division of labour between the sexes in the family. Here the content of care is to nourish and give life to others. It is important to illustrate what happens when these care abilities are used by middle-class women employed in highly specialized institutions. In the relations between patients and professionals in the field of cancer, the professionals' care-related discourse about human relations is a part of the symbolic relation in the way care-work is organized. Similarly, professionals have also developed 'theories of relations work'. In these theories, patients are defined in relation to the profession's own knowledge and it is ascribed to them the lack of what the profession can offer them in the field of cancer (Eriksen 1996 p188). Thus, certain symbolic power relations are established that can make the patients more ill, or ill in ways that correspond to the dominant forms of treatment and support in the field of cancer. The same symbolic power relationship is thus partly responsible for reducing patients to objects, where their need for support is limited to what can be dealt with as a matter of routine in existing modes of relations and support.

Conclusion

To conclude, the results of this study of care relations between patients and professionals in the field of cancer indicate that the care relations establish a string of technical and routine based support relations, which are defined by cognitive, ideological, and productive structures in the field. This is partly made possible by the patients' lack of biographical qualifications for coping with a serious illness within an institutional framework and because the biological body is undermined and psychological orientation strategies do not function for the patients. Furthermore, female care workers are socialized to function within the field's productive and masculine structures, which have transformed their female care abilities into a knowledge that verbalizes care. At the same time, they are not aware of the forms of symbolic power they themselves communicate in a symbolic power that prevents them from attaining their objective – the establishment of authentic care relations. Authentic relations are those in which the professionals with expertise can meet patients on the patients' terms and share their feelings of fear and chaos. Perhaps the professionals can break through the cognitive and ideological concept of care work in the field of cancer and recognize that nursing and treatment of cancer patients do not at present contain an aspect of care, but more often a verbalized care.

References

Bourdieu, P. (1990): *The Logic of Practice.* Cambridge: Polity Press.
Bourdieu, P., Chamboredon, J.-C., Passeron, J.-C. (1991): *The Craft of Sociology.* Berlin and New York: Walter de Gruyter.
Bourdieu, P. and Wacquant, L.J.D. (1992): *An Invitation to Reflexive Sociology.* Cambridge: Polity Press.
Bourdieu, P. and Wacquant, L.J.D. (1996): *Refleksiv sociologi – mål og midler.* Copenhagen: Hans Reitzel.
Bourdieu, P. (1996): *Symbolsk Makt.* Oslo: Pax Forlag.
Bourdieu, P. (1997): *Af praktiske grunde. Omkring teorien om menneskelig handlen.* Copenhagen: Hans Reitzel.
Bourdieu, P. (1999): *Den maskuline dominans.* Copenhagen: Tiderne Skifter.
Eriksen, T.R. (1986): *Sygeplejekultur i erhverv og uddannelse.* Næstved, Denmark: Kontekst.
Eriksen, T.R. (1989): 'Kvindeverden og offentlig sektor', in: *Social Kritik* nr. 3, Copenhagen.
Eriksen, T.R. (1992): *Omsorg i forandring.* Copenhagen: Munksgaard.
Eriksen, T.R. (1993): 'Er plejekulturens kundskabsformer funderet i en omsorgsrettet eller i en behandlingsrettet rationalitet?' Oslo: Norges Forskningsråd NAVF.
Eriksen, T.R. (1996): *Livet med kræft.* Copenhagen: Munksgaard.
Eriksson, K. (1987): *Pausen. En beskrivning av vårdvetenskapens kundskapsobjekt.* Stockholm: Almquist & Wiksell.
Eriksson, K. (1995): *Vårdandets idé.* Stockholm: Liber Utbildning AB.
Flyvbjerg, B. (1992): *Rationalitet og magt,* vol. I. Copenhagen: Akademisk Forlag.
Gammelgaard, J. (1996): 'Brændt barn skyer ilden', in: *Spor i tiden. Erfaringer i et humanistisk og sundhedsvidenskabeligt perspektiv.* Copenhagen: Munksgaard.
Gergen, M. (1988): 'Narrative Structures in social explanations', in: *Analysing Everyday Explanation.* London: SAGE Publications.
Knizek, B.L. (1993): *Den psykiske krop.* Copenhagen: Gyldendal.
Martinsen, K. (1987): *Omsorg, sykepleie og medicin.* Oslo: Tano.
Martinsen, K. (1993): *Fra Marx til Løgstrup. Om etikk og sanselighed i sykepleien.* Oslo: Tano.
Muschinsky, L.J. (1993): 'Vent ikke på bedre tider. Om de kulturelle betingelser og de professionelles ansvar for en ny politik', in: *Dansk Pædagogisk Tidsskrift* nr. 3, Copenhagen.
Widerberg, K. (1995): 'Sociologins makt – maktens sociologi', in: *Sociologisk Forskning* 4, Oslo.

Chapter 8

On Health Professionals'
Construction of Dying Bodies:
The Case of Palliation Services for
Cancer Patients in Denmark

Helle Timm

Introduction

The welfare of terminally ill persons has come into focus in Denmark over the past
20 years. Terms such as 'hospice', 'hospice philosophy' and 'palliation' have become a part of health professional, organizational and political efforts in the care
for the dying, foremost for incurably ill cancer patients.

While working as a sector researcher, I followed the health policy debate, the
development of guidelines and laws as well as concrete institutions and practice.
Simultaneously, with others, I have undertaken studies in which cancer patients,
their relatives and care-nurses' experiences with terminal illness and death have
been highlighted. The issue, which continues to interest me (as a sociologist in the
health field), is *the reasons why the health field is the way it appears today; are its
ongoing development efforts optimal for the ill and dying and their families?* This
chapter frames these issues into a specific question, i.e. *what images of the ill, dying body are constructed in and with the development of palliation as a health specialty? How do these images match with the experiences of the ill and dying and of
their relatives with respect to illness and death?*

The body (including the sick or dying body) can be seen as a physical entity, a
biological organism that constitutes a delimited proportion of an individual. This
understanding dominates the collective medical field and health sciences generally.
In practice and in more recent health science traditions such as social medicine and
nursing care, emphasis is placed on the relationship between the physical body and
psychological and social factors. The palliation field attempts to understand and
consider the seriously ill and dying as a 'whole person' (not simply as a sick body).
Pain and relief are understood in physical, psychological, social and spiritual dimensions (Twycross, 1995). Danish national reports/statements, guidelines, etc.
have adopted the WHO definition of palliative care:

Palliative care is holistic active care of patients whose illness does not respond to curative treatment, and where control of pain and other symptoms and of psychological, social and spiritual issues are prioritised. The aim of palliative care is to achieve the highest level of life quality for the patient and his family. Many aspects of palliative care are also useable in the illness process in connection with cancer treatment.

Palliative care:
1. confirms life and sees death as a natural process;
2. does not delay or expedite death;
3. relieves pain and other symptoms;
4. integrates psychological and spiritual dimensions in care;
5. offers support for the patient to live as actively as possible before death;
6. offers support to the loved one's family during his illness and during the grieving period.

(Danish National Board of Health, 1996, pp.17-18)

In this chapter perceptions of the body are understood as social constructions, as specific images of the body. The images of the body determine the space of acting and being in relation to serious illness, death and dying.

The chapter begins with an introduction to the concepts 'social constructionism', 'action' and 'body' and to sociological theory on late modernity and death. Subsequently the chapter consists of three parts; the first part is an analysis of a discourse on 'the good death' as it appears in the Danish Health Care System. The second part is reflexions on lay perspectives on death and the dying. And the third part consists of reflexions on the level in between the societal discourse and the subjective lay perspective – which is where the everyday cultural practice of palliation is found.

Theoretical concepts

Social constructionism and action

Social constructionism can be defined as a major indicator of more recent theories about society and culture. The common scientific theoretical approach can be framed as follows: knowledge is socially constructed via human acting and being in the world (Berger and Luckman 1966, Järvinen and Bertilsson, 1998; Hacking 1998, Winther Joergensen and Philips, 1999). This, in part, is due to our knowledge about and ideas on what 'good care' for incurable, dying people is about.

In the chapter 'the care for dying people' is interpreted as a symbolic and social order (characterized by certain norms, habits, routines), which professionals and lay people act within and upon – and thereby reproduce and change.

The Italian sociologist, Crespi (1992) suggests an acting term in a social constructionist frame of understanding:

The whole dimension of action can be recognized only by stressing the ambivalence of the attitude of the actor towards those structures, which, although guaranteeing social predictability and intersubjective order, are at the same time limiting his possibilities. (Crespi, 1992, p. 33)

Crespi speaks of the power to (i.e. people's ability to and possibility for) act/acting at different levels – about individual power (i.e. associated with personality and life history) and cultural power (i.e. associated with being a part of a specific social, ethnic, gender or age group) and of structural power (i.e. connected to social position to maintain existing order). However, at all levels power is associated with people, subjects and actors. In the article the power to take part at different levels in the social construction of 'the care for dying people' is discussed.

The body as a social construction

In order to understand the body, illness and death as socially constructed phenomena, we must understand them to be natural and biological 'givens' and simultaneously as socially created and interpreted. The Australian sociologist, Turner (1984) says that the body can only be understood as a combination of opposites, i.e. the body is both impersonal and personal, an objective and subjective phenomenon, a natural and a cultural phenomenon. Human beings have bodies and are bodies, which are socially constructed i.e. socially interpreted. The dying body and the dead body is understood (and treated) differently in different cultures and at different times.

The English sociologists, Williams and Bendelow (1998), propose that the historical and social dualism between the physical body and the spiritual and acknowledged soul/psyche must be deconstructed via the sufferer's narratives.

Narrative, we suggest, is central to this enterprise. It is here, on this uncertain biographical terrain, that the dialectical relationship between nature and culture, meaning and significance is played out and the disrupted relationship between nature and culture, meaning and significance is played out and the disrupted relationship between the body, self and society symbolically repaired. (Williams and Bendelow, 1998, p.163)

Late-modernity and death

Sociologists have also focused on death. First and foremost, this has occurred in England over the past 15-20 years where death has been researched and theorized upon in the late-modern society. This is not relevant to the same extent in the Nordic countries. In Denmark, for example, there are very few examples of sociologists who have explicitly focused theoretically and empirically on death (Hviid Jacobsen, 2001, 2002; Timm, 1999).

According to recent socio-psychological and sociological theorists (Ziehe and Stubenrauch, 1983; Beck, 1992; Giddens, 1990) late-modern social order is influenced, amongst other factors, by globalization, the speed of change and cultural freedom from institutional norms and action patterns. The individual's relationship to the existing order is influenced by reflection and the absence of things which one can take for granted. This is also true about death and dying. The late-modern society is characterized, to a large extent, by general individualization. Cultural freedom and increased reflection give the individual, on the one hand, more choice in lifestyle (and perhaps in death) within a given space of acting and, on the other hand, an increased burden and demand in relation to having to do something. Another essential characteristic of the late-modern society, according to Giddens (1990, 1991), who portrays the layman's viewpoint on experts, is that the experts that represent the 'system' are also framed in reflexivity as questions and doubts about their competence and authority are raised. At the same time, dependence on these same experts is increased both because society becomes more and more complex and allegedly because less and less is known in advance.

The English sociologist, Walter (1994) describes three ideological types of 'space of acting' in relation to death and dying: the traditional, the modern and the late-modern. These can be seen as historical spaces of acting that dominate at different historic periods, i.e. spaces of acting dominating in different late-modern cultures of everyday life.

Table 8.1
Ideal types of the cultural responses to death

	Traditional	Modern	Neo-modern
Bodily context	Death quick and Frequent	Death hidden	Death prolonged
Social context	Community	Public vs private	Private becomes public
Authority	Religion	Medicine	Self

Source: Walter 1994, p.47

According to Walter, the ideal type of late-modern death is characterized by (1) being prolonged (the longer-term illness give the ill person the possibility to reflect and take stock of his life and death); (2) privacy becomes public (relationships, social conventions and physical arrangements from the private sphere partially become an ideology in the public sphere, such as in hospices and palliative units in hospitals. The private sphere (i.e. the home) becomes partially the workplace for health experts whose task it is not solely to focus on the ill person but also on his entire family); and (3) the self (the autonomous individual) is idealistically the highest authority in the experience of an incurable illness and in arranging his own relief and care.

Current sociological and health foci on care for the dying can be said to spring from reflections of the modern death. The English physician, Cicely Saunders, amongst others, has written and acted on this subject since the 1950s and has given birth to what is today defined as the English hospice movement. Elisabeth Kübler-Ross, a Swiss physician, dedicated a publication on the subject of *On Death and Dying* in 1969 and the German sociologist, Norbert Elias wrote about it in his 1985 book *The loneliness of the dying*. Each in their own way can be said to be pioneers in promoting awareness of the poor conditions which 'modern death' offers the dying. For Elias and, to some extent, for Kübler-Ross the turning point was the taboo of death and the increased feelings of loneliness that followed from this taboo. Saunders focused on care as well as on the loneliness of the dying person, with relief in its broadest understanding as the turning point.

Refusal and taboos surrounding death in modern society vs. openness and staging of death in the late-modern society are a main focus of sociologists who, amongst others, tackle the subject. According to Walter (1991) and Mellor (1993), death in the late-modern society is no longer seen as a taboo. Death (in the concrete and fictitious sense) is covered in the media, in art, literature, research, etc. as well as in health policy and practice where much attention is paid to the incurably ill and the conditions involving the dying. Simultaneously however, death (as in the modern order of things) is hidden from the public where we also live our lives (e.g. in work places, residential areas, etc.) and is referred to special institutions (e.g. hospitals, nursing homes) or a private space (e.g. home). Those accompanying the dying remain the closest relatives and the health professionals.

One can conclude that even if a breakthrough has not occurred, then a softening at least of the modern order or the modern 'space of acting' in death and dying is present. This can be seen at a collective level in the speaking of and staging of death in various ways, and at the individual level where allegedly death for the terminally ill can be constructed today in more ways than ever before.

Palliation of the dying body – the discourse on 'a good death'

Discourse can be defined as '*...a horizon of intelligibility and possibility delimiting what is possible and what can be said and done*' (Dahl, 2000, p.324).

There is a connection between characteristics in the late-modern society – i.e. between the late-modern ideology of the 'space of acting' in relation to death and dying; the hospice philosophy; and the actors who dominated the development of 'care for the dying'; and the palliative specialty (at least in Denmark).

This chapter started by stating that care for the terminally ill came into focus in Denmark approximately 20 years ago. One can pinpoint the year because, at that time – the start of the 1980s – there was strong public critique regarding existing health care practice that, to a large extent, was centred in the medical discourse. The critique manifested itself in the unsatisfactory conditions for the dying within curative institutions, foremost within hospitals. More specifically, the critique turned its focus to the issue that the dying did not receive the care that they required. The hospitals were, to a large extent, specialized treatment institutions at that time and so-called terminal patients were not considered curable cases and were therefore not a priority target group for hospitals. The consequence of this was allegedly that the incurably ill too often were just left to 'lie around' without receiving care, relief or perhaps even treatment that they may have needed.

Those who came forward with this critique and who became actors at the social level were first and foremost experts with power at the structural level. They were people in leader positions within the health care system in alliance with (especially health) professionals in the central administration, politicians with personal or professional interest in the subject and patient organizations with health professional dominance such as *Kraeftens Bekaempelse* (The National Cancer Society).

It is mainly the actors with their roots in the medical discourse (and anchored in medical practice) that probably were both pressed and inspired to make change by a political discourse of a more market-oriented health system. On the other hand, international experiences, and especially the British hospice movement inspired these actors. In 1990, some of the actors and the movement of which they were a part, became more visible with the establishment of the *Danish Society for Care of the Dying* – (following a Nordic Forum, equally dominated by doctors and nurses). Since then, the active members of this society, among others, have made special efforts to define a profile of what can be said to be a strategy and a discourse on 'a good death' in Denmark.

Today, at the beginning of a new millennium, a health policy strategy has been developed for care of the dying in Denmark, which can be seen as a compromise between involved discourses and actors in the field. The strategy on 'a good death' is a compromise constructed in a struggle foremost between 'what existed before' (the treatment-oriented and modern health care system with its predominantly medical orientation) and attempts to change and develop. There has also been struggles within this movement, e.g. between professions (e.g. doctors and nurses), between specialties (e.g. oncology and the struggle for and against medical specialties within palliation); between hospices and palliative hospital wards (e.g. the civil society vs. the public health care system), etc. (Busch et al., 1997).

The development can partly be described in movements – power struggles which produced changes in the field itself and which have been reflected in various ways, including through use of language. One example is the term 'care of the dying' which, over a couple of years (from 1996-1997) in public documents, conference programmes, etc. was replaced by the term 'palliation'. Palliation means providing relief vs. curative measures (i.e. treatment). During the same period, the concept of 'terminal care' was replaced by 'palliative care' (Busch et al., 1997, Danish National Board of Health, 1996, 1999). The term 'palliation' is used as a medical term used to express relief for the dying when treatment is no longer possible. The change in language reflects a struggle between actors, which emphasized respectively the hospice philosophy and the medical orientation approach. Consequently, care of the dying as a medical specialty within the public health care system (palliation) was developed. There was not necessarily any discussion regarding the actors having different goals but rather different understandings of how to reach the same goals.

Another example is that the discourse on 'a good death' came to involve specifically people dying of cancer. The Danish people also die from other causes including cardiovascular disease or even simply from old age. However, dying of cancer seems to be in a special category and more of a problem for the health professionals. People with cardiovascular diseases and other serious illnesses live with chronic and life-limiting suffering as well. Yet, their forms of life and death may be different from those of the cancer patient and the constructed ideologies for a good death, i.e. the planned, prepared for and meaningful death.

A final example is the hospice philosophy's approach to the autonomous person, i.e. the ill person and his family's autonomy and life situation. In the discourse on 'a good death', respect for the ill person and his family's perspective is considered only in the relief provided and in user investigations (e.g. satisfaction studies). The needs of the ill person and his family, their desires and experiences are interpreted and integrated in the daily palliative practice by health professionals.

One can conclude that the discourse on 'a good death' in Denmark, has its roots in the hospice philosophy's ideologies regarding relief and a meaningful death at the physical, psychological, social and spiritual levels and in the ill person's and his family's autonomy. Simultaneously, the health professional's role is given considerable priority due to its link to the health policy discourse dominated by concepts of quality development, standardization, education, multidisciplinary collaboration, leadership and organization (Busch, et al. 1997; Danish National Board of Health, 1996, 1999). The discourse on 'a good death' originally sprang from a critique of the modern 'space of acting' for death and dying, and included criticism of the medical discourse and its practice. However, the discourse on 'a good death' does not fundamentally affect the medical domain. Perhaps the contrary is true, because the discourse, to a large extent, uses health professional expertise not only in care and treatment but also in psychosocial and spiritual care. 'A good death' requires many different types of well-educated experts (at different levels).

Using Walter's approach and characteristics of the ideal type of space of acting for death and dying, one can say that in Denmark the discourse on 'a good death' takes the form of a rather sketchy space of acting and is permeated by a concrete health professional construction which builds on both a hospice philosophy and a health professional approach. Table 8.2 illustrates this by placing the discourse on 'a good death' in Denmark between both the modern and the late-modern ideologies of a good death.

Table 8.2
The discourse on 'a good death' in Denmark – between ideal types of cultural responses to death

	Traditional society	Modern society	The discourse on 'A good death' in Denmark	Late-modern society
The ideal of 'A good death'	Forgiveness and peace	The sudden, easy and private death	The individualized, psychologized, and pain relieved death	The lived, open and meaningful death
The dying person	The sick	The patient	The user	A unique person
Care for the dying	Care	Terminal care	Palliative care	Palliation
Bodily Context	Death quick and frequent	Death hidden	Cancer death	Death prolonged
Social context	Community	Private versus public	Private and public professionals as well as family	Social network Multidisciplinary team
Authority	Religion	Medicine	Professionals, user and family	Self
Ethical Foundation	Love of next kin	Justice	User-involvement and patientsatisfaction	Autonomy

Inspired by: Walter, 1994, pp.47-48

The terminally ill person is understood in this discourse not only as a sick and dying body but as a person who, separate from his (physical) illness, also suffers mentally, socially and spiritually, and as such requires relief in all of these dimensions. Through a cross-professional approach, the understanding of what it is to have a body, a suffering body, that should be relieved from pain, is supplemented with an understanding of how the ill person also suffers mentally, socially and spiritually. However, the physical component is still understood as the baseline, separable from the other dimensions. The medical understanding of the body is not really changed or extended in and with the hospice movement or the development of a palliation specialty.

To have and to be a dying body – the dying person's and his family's perspective

The layperson's perspective of illness and death is subjective, oriented towards illness and everyday life (Timm, 1997a). That is to say that the layperson's knowledge, experiences, viewpoints and actions are influenced by who she is as a person and by what daily life she lives.

Everyone has an everyday life – a life that we live every day (Bech-Joergensen, 1994). Everyday life connects the individual with society. The individual is affected by and affects society via actions and ways of being. In other (social constructionist) words, through everyday life people create and recreate the societal structure. Simultaneously, everyday life makes an order, or rather patterns of action and ways of being (e.g. habits, norms, routines) that provide meaning for the individual's existence (e.g. at home or in the hospital ward).

When one has a life-threatening disease it contests the validity of the daily course of life – of everything that we take for granted when every day functions and life takes its natural course. More generally, a life threatening disease breaks an individual's life story, leaving the life course more or less affected (Bury, 1991; Timm, 1997a; Williams and Bendelow, 1998). Moreover, the illness and the fact that one may die from it becomes a part of the rest of the individual's life – will I get better? Will I die of this disease? How can I continue to live with the fear of a relapse and anxiety of death? Will I be different after the treatment and when/if the illness progresses? What will my life be like and for how long? As human beings, we do not just have bodies – we are our bodies and with the body, via physical acting and being we create and recreate not only the order of daily life (and with that societal order) but we also create who we are (identity). This is yet another everyday truism that becomes affected when we become seriously ill. We are shaken and shocked over existence as a whole but also over who we are; we are not quite what we used to be to ourselves or to others.

The fact that the layperson's perspective is subjective, oriented toward illness and everyday life can imply many things. It could mean that suffering is individually and socially determined; the same diagnosis and prognosis has different meanings for different people who receive them and what life situations they are in (Gannik, 1999). It could also mean that distinguishing between physical, mental, social and spiritual dimensions of suffering may not be so clear-cut (if you are not part of a palliative team). Suffering is not experienced as either one dimension or the other.

In another context, I tried to illustrate that we are our bodies by the manner of speaking about how we feel: I feel tense and uneasy, I am bleeding, I am sweating, I am in pain, I sit poorly, I am pushed around, I feel tearful, I drag my self around. I feel joy overcome me (Timm, 1997b, p.32). All of these expressions show that emotion and physical experiences are not separate from each other or the context in which we experience them.

In relation to an evaluation of the Danish law on care for close relatives who look after a terminally ill and dying family member, I interviewed people who were dying and their relatives who were granted compassionate leave compensation under this law (Timm, 1999). For this chapter I selected two cases that illustrate that laypeople have and are their bodies and that their suffering should be understood as both subjective and cultural. The two cases involved cancer, death and the compassionate leave compensation law. While the cases are different from each other, they both illustrate that suffering and relief from a lay perspective is not experienced in separate dimensions. Through narratives, it becomes clear that, for example, phenomena such as pain and anxiety are not experienced or treated as separate factors of physical, mental, or social dimensions but rather as phenomena that are related to how people are in the world and to their relationships with each other.

Peter and Marian

The first case involves a 57-year-old man who is dying of cancer. He is a psychologist and has lived with his wife for the past 17 years. She is a doctor. The first interview took place approximately two months prior to the man's death. The interviewed couple was very determined to explain to me how much it meant for them to be attached to the home hospice service where, allegedly for the first time, they were met by health care professionals who held a holistic approach to their work and had respect for the patient's autonomy and where the patient and his spouse could seek advice and support 24 hours a day.

> **Marian:** It was fantastic. It allowed Peter and me to have a regular relationship – pain and anxiety were the two things that were the worst. If those two things were controlled, one could cope with the rest.

> **Peter:** Yes, the pain totally consumes me. I don't know if I am more sensitive than others. They are horrifically serious pains – and just that feeling of helplessness and doubt. Nothing has a meaning anymore. 'Try to look out at that lovely garden' but I can't see any lovely garden. The only thing that exists is pain and the fear that it is all going downhill. It is only negative, negative, and negative. The contrary of what people believe, morphine treatment will give you a positive experience – it gives me a lift so that, as a person, I can enjoy life more. So that I am pleased with life. (Peter and Marian, 1998, 1.int.p.34)

Peter described his pain as horrific. He felt helpless and full of doubt. He was blind to anything beautiful and his life spirit had disappeared. Pain and fear were the only things that seemed to exist for him. Peter was his cancerous body. The correct dosage of morphine allowed him to experience life joy.

Some weeks after Peter died, Marian told me about the last 24 hours when she, Peter's two sons and a nephew were with him:

> He experienced some hallucinations which caused the whole situation to turn humorous. It did not seem to bother him that we laughed. He suddenly sat up and imagined that he was in a train with a large crowd of people. We were to distribute cigarettes out to each of them – and then he wanted beer, coffee, vanilla cream, cigarettes, ashtrays and lip balm. He was used to giving orders – one knew exactly what he wanted – but as we were four, we could laugh at this and share the role of the fool who was being ordered about. We arranged things so that they could be there when he wanted them and this quieted him down. It was clear that it was an inner tranquility. (Marian, 1998, 3.int., p.4)

Peter was his cancerous, hallucinating body but at the same time was Peter – a special cancer-ridden, hallucinating body that existed, took actions and was met and understood from the perspective of his own subjective and life historic reference.

Peter and Marian were/are intellectual, highly educated, middle-class people with ideals, living in a way that, to a large extent, resembled those which characterized the ideal type of the late-modern space of acting. They were in a social-economic situation and had the bargaining power to accomplish their roles in collaborating with professionals from the home care and home hospice services. They had a good social network and supportive work places and accomplished, to the fullest extent, their roles as autonomous, reflective, open and effective users of these services.

Karl and Edith

The other case involved a 52-year-old man who also died of cancer. He was an invalid pensioner due to diabetes and his illness and death experience was shared by his wife of 17 years. She is a civil servant in a public institute. Edith's story is one of loneliness and an experience of disappointment with her social network and with the professional treatment and care system they used. It is the story of a man, Karl, who did not want to speak about his feelings or his illness and who put all of his trust in the hospital.

> **Edith:** – and he had to go up there and get the results and came back home, set the table with beer and aquavit and everything else. And then he said, 'You must not be upset – it is cancer'. We then sat down quietly and calmly spoke about it and then he said, 'One thing that I do not want is that you start to cry'. 'No', I said. 'You will be cured.' (Edith 1998, p.2).

We were never informed how sick Karl was. I believe that it was because they knew how sick he really was and did not want to tell us. A half-year later he died, but it started to go downhill very quickly. Karl did not want any medication. He never got fresh air but slept all the time. I believe that if he came out on the street and got fresh air and the like – but it was like he did not want to let others know how sick he was. (Edith 1998, pp.3-4)

Interviewer (HT): And what about pain killers?

Edith: Only suppositories and I administered these to him.

Interviewer (HT): But you got them from your own doctor?

Edith: Yes, we did. We got so many and I had no idea how many he was supposed to have each day. He just had to have them when he felt pain. That is probably why he slept through everything, don't you think? When I asked him if he felt pain, he could not explain where the pain was located. He just had pain. Or else he just wanted that morphine in order to sleep through the whole ordeal. Whether he wished for a fast death or not, I just don't know because when we found out that the end was near, we no longer spoke about death – We spoke about his desire to go to the 'unknown' (HT:part of the graveyard) and that there should not be any funeral or anything of the sort. (Edith, 1998, p.23)

Over the last three weeks prior to his death, Karl was admitted to hospital. He requested that this be done. Karl was at home on a visit one week before dying and during the last 24 hours he received an increased dosage of morphine intravenously and Edith was with him.

Like Peter, Karl was his sick and dying body, which was and acted and was met and understood from his own specific subjective and life historic reference. I am only aware of Edith's story and as such, her own interpretation of Karl's way of being sick. It is clear that Karl and Edith were/are not intellectuals. They were/are unskilled, with limited education and part of the working class whose ideals and way of being on death and dying fit best into the ideal of a modern space of acting. Both Karl's and Edith's loneliness left a large impression. They had a very sketchy social network and remained rather private about their situation. Yet they achieved, to the fullest, the image of the modern patient – one who believes in authority, trusts, has expectations and remains passive.

The point here is that Karl's and Edith's experiences with care for the dying are very different from the ideals put forward in the discourse on 'a good death'. Firstly, Karl's ways of acting and being does not fit into the ideals of the discourse; Karl does not want to talk about death and dying, he wants treatment (to be cured), and when he is not granted that, he withdraws from social life. Secondly, Karl is met by professionals who, to a great extent, leave him alone (and to Edith). Whether the professionals act from respect, from lack of knowledge or powerlessness I do not know – but it does not fit with the ideals of the discourse.

In other words: In the case of Karl and Edith, the discourse on 'a good death' seems to be a far off ideal, which has no connection with their lived experiences. They are 'outside' the discourse. And they are left to one another.

Both Peter and Karl had cancer. They both had pain and they both feared dying. However, their illnesses and death processes were very different as were their suffering and relief. Suffering, pain and anxiety are subjective and constructed in everyday culture and cannot be separated from the ill person and those who accompany (or do not accompany) him.

Palliation in practice – between the discourse and the dying person's experiences

Care for the dying on a daily cultural level (i.e. between the social discourse, the general strategies and the subjective experiences of the dying person) must be investigated concretely and empirically, from the angle of local practice. It is at this level that the ideal of 'a good death' must be practised and negotiated from what already exists and what is already being done – and what makes sense. As mentioned before, many actors in the construction of the social discourse on 'a good death' belong to the health profession. Their critique and desire for change springs from experiences with and insight into unsatisfactory practice in general. These experiences are now switching back, so to say, to the daily culture practice level as the discourse on 'a good death'. The discourse raises some general ideals, norms and values for concrete death processes as well as for the people who are involved. The discourse, however, exists in relation to different everyday cultures, lifestyles and individual conditions (ref. the above-mentioned case studies), e.g. with the understanding and practice of what a good life is, what death means and how one dies best (including relationships between people). Everyday life culture and individual experiences and competences in the individual family setting and among the professionals have a bearing on what the discourse will mean. In some cases (and sometimes), the ideals match those one already possesses. In other cases (and at other times) there may be a large difference between the general ideals and concrete practice. In Peter's case the discourse on 'the good death' fits into the ideals, norms and values which already structure his life; Peter is open about his disease and his suffering, he is demanding and organizing in his personal relationships and in his relation to the health professionals. The opposite is seen in Karl's case; Karl is not used to talking about him self or about suffering, he is a very private person with only one close relation (to Edith). Karl does not know how to react to being dependent on other people. Karl is caught up in his sick body. And the discourse on 'the good death' brings no help or relief to him.

One example is of physical pain relief. Physical pain relief is central to the palliative effort because it is understood as the basis of relief in relation to the other dimensions of pain (Danish National Board of Health, 1996, 1999). However, the health professional's differ greatly concerning their knowledge and understanding of what pain is and how it is relieved. From Peter's case where pain relief was offered 24 hours a day and regulated by professionals whenever needed – to Karl's case where pain relief was left to his wife, who did not know anything about the disease, the pain or pain relief. Medical knowledge may vary regarding which forms of pain relief work and under which circumstances. Knowledge and understanding of how physical pain is associated with mental, social and spiritual pain (including what a suffering person is) also differs. The extent to which one can and should relieve pain associated with cancer can be said to be a general question, the answer to which is that one can and should. The real question, however, is whether one has the necessary knowledge and experience to do so.

Another example is the ideal regarding openness about death and the fact that a person is dying. Interviews with nurses from hospital wards and in municipal home care services, suggest that there is variation in the degree to which nurses who care for the dying speak about death with the ill person, his relatives and each other (Timm, 1999). There are hospital departments where people die from cancer and in which the words 'death' and 'cancer' are not used. That shows a lot about the discrepancy between the discourse on 'a good death' and daily practice (although there is no implications made here about the quality of care for the dying). The discourse should function in a daily practice, strongly influenced by an organizational (sectorial and professional) division of labour. The ideal is recognized and accepted, however, in practice concrete openness is set aside for as long as possible (especially until the hospital regime is completed). The Danish anthropologist Plough Hansen (1995), in a study on care of cancer patients in a hospital ward, documented the extent to which nurses corroborate to maintain the existing institutional order and simultaneously how these same nurses practice a communication order (regarding the ideology) which is different from the practical order. Nurses are constantly pressured between a demand for closeness and the demand to keep a distance from the patient.

Another example is provided here as an extension of the forenamed ideal of clarity and acceptance by the dying person. 'A good death' is a conscious and proclaimed death; a death ruled by action and existence that fits the character of the person who is used to reflecting on and speaking out about his life, self and feelings. However, these ideologies may not necessarily suit everyone – be this the ill person, a relative or a health professional. There is a hypothesis that 'psychologizing' death in Denmark has met with suitable conditions, for various reasons. The general social tendency to individualize and psychologize when understanding people's problems and actions has been supported from many angles. Psychology is one of the courses that nurses in Denmark have leaned toward in an attempt to develop a more theoretic baseline in their practice. Existential psychotherapy has had a special Danish version of its own in popular books about 'grief and crisis' (Davidsen-Nielsen and Leick, 1987; Davidsen-Nielsen, 1997) and finally the powerful patient organization *Kraeftens Bekaempelse* (The National Cancer Society) assumes a psychological orientation in its approach to patient support and guidance. Another hypothesis is that the ideals of openness, clarity and acceptance are especially meaningful for people from a specific (middle) class and a specific (female) gender. In any event, many studies on the ill and dying point to the fact that these ideals hold very different meaning for different people (Jacobsen et al., 1998; Rask Eriksen, 1996; Timm, 1997b, 1999).

A final and more general example involves the terminally ill who die while under the care of medical practice but who are neither dying of cancer nor dying 'a good death'. These are people, for example, with long-term illnesses such as sclerosis, chronic lung disease, cardio-vascular ailments whose illnesses and dying processes must also be constructed within practice, in a caring relationship between the professionals and the patient. They do not currently lean toward the discourse on 'a good death'.

One can conclude that at the daily cultural level, it is clear that the discourse on 'a good death' seems more like a cluster of ideals. In reality, people live their death as they do their concrete everyday life and life stories. On a daily cultural level it is also clear that professional knowledge and experiences (and engagement therein) are often decisive as to how a concrete death process will be expressed. Simultaneously, it is at the daily cultural practice level that this will take place, and also here a large theoretic understanding of the ill person, the dying body, must find its inspiration. This is where people are sick and dying and where they give and receive care and relief in the construction of a concrete death process.

Summing up

Can one, through health policy and the health profession, do something more than what the hospice philosophy approach currently offers as ideologies and attempts in practice to optimally relieve suffering? This would include defining what suffering is in its broadest sense, i.e. as physical, psychological, social and spiritual. Can one avoid that death remains a lonely experience? Perhaps not! Perhaps we have a 'red thread' for developing practice in the discourse on 'a good death'. I do not answer these questions; this chapter only attempts to put into perspective the establishment and development of palliation in Denmark by exposing it from the angle of a social constructionist understanding. I thereby insist that the existing construction is only one of several possible.

The palliation specialty (like all other specialties) is constructed within specific social conditions and by health professionals with power at the structural level. These health professionals have grasped and shaped a social construction which has limited form and content. The palliation field is dominated by the medical approach to the dying body (cancer patients) and by an individualized and psychologized understanding of death (grief and crisis). Each part, to a large extent, is detached from daily cultural experiences with life and death. Both parts should be seen as meaningful for specific groups (middle class, women) within the cancer field.

The palliative death is a medicalised expert death. It has partial consequences for understanding the sick and dying person who is perceived and treated from a medical approach, supplemented by the psychological, social and spiritual dimensions. There are partial consequences for the development of a professional vs. daily cultural space of acting on death, dying and care of the dying. While the professional space of acting is strengthened, that of the layperson's daily cultural space of acting and being is not.

Table 8.3
The meeting between lay realities and professional ideals in late-modern society

Lay- (realities)	Professional- (ideals)
The loneliness of the dying	Autonomy (individualization)
Lack of everyday cultural settings and rituals	Palliative care (the experts' good death)
Having a body and being a body	Understanding of physical, psychical, social, spiritual suffering and relief

The development of care for the dying should, in the future, consider to a larger extent, the layperson's experiences with and conditions for death and dying. The health profession's dominating understanding of palliation must, to a much greater degree, come into dialogue with a more culture theoretic and daily life based understanding of death and dying in late-modern Denmark.

References

Beck, U. (1992): *Risk society: towards a new modernity*. London: Sage.

Beck-Jørgensen, B. (1994): *Når hver dag bliver til hverdag* (When every day turns into everyday), Copenhagen: Academic Press.

Berger, P.L. and Luckmann, T. (1966): *The social construction of reality: a treatise in the sociology of knowledge*. Garden City, N.Y.: Doubleday.

Bury, M.R. (1991): 'The sociology of chronic illness: A review of research and prospects', in *Sociology of Health and Illness*, vol. 13, no. 4: 451-468.

Busch Juul, C., Cramon, P. and Timm, H., Wagner, L. (eds.) (1997): *Palliativ indsats i Danmark* (Palliation in Denmark), DSI – Danish Institute for Health Services Research, Copenhagen

Crespi, F. (1992): *Social action and power*. Oxford: Blackwell.

Dahl, H.M. (2000): *Fra kitler til eget tøj – Diskurser om professionalisme, omsorg og køn* (From white coats to own clothes – discourses on professionalism, care and gender), Aarhus University: Polticas Ph.D serie, Institut for Statskundskab.

Danish National Board of Health (1996): *Omsorg for alvorligt syge og døende: redegørelse: om hospiceprogrammer og andre initiativer inden for den palliative indsats* (Care of the seriously ill and the dying: report: hospice programs and other initiatives within the palliative work), Copenhagen: Danish National Board of Health.

Danish National Board of Health (1999): *Faglige retningslinier for den palliative indsats: omsorgen for alvorligt syge og døende* (Specialist guidelines for the palliative work: The care of the seriously ill and the dying). Copenhagen: Danish National Board of Health.

Davidsen-Nielsen, M. and Leick, N. (1987): *Den nødvendige smerte – om sorg, sorgterapi og kriseintervention* (The necessary pain – about grief, grief therapy and crisis intervention). Copenhagen: Munksdgaard.

Davidsen-Nielsen, M. (1997): *Blandt løver: at leve med en livstruende sygdom* (Amongst the lions: living with a threatening disease), 1st edn. Copenhagen: Munksgaard/Rosinante.

Elias, N. (1985): *The loneliness of the dying*. London: Basil Blackwell.

Eriksen, T. Rask (1996): *Livet med kræft: i et støtte- og omsorgsperspektiv (Life with cancer – in a support and care perspective)*, 1st edn. Copenhagen: Munksgaard.

Gannik, D.E. (1999): *Situationel sygdom: fragmenter til en social sygdomsteori baseret på en undersøgelse af ryglidelser* (Situational disease: Fragments for a social theory of diseases based on a study of 'symptoms of the back'), 1st edn. Copenhagen: Samfundslitteratur.

Giddens, A. (1991): *Modernity and self-identity: self and society i the late modern age*. California: Stanford University Press.

Giddens, A. (1990): *The consequences of modernity*. Cambridge: Polity Press.

Hacking, I. (1998): 'On Being More Literal about Construction', in: Velody, I. and Williams, R. (eds.): *The Politics of Constructionism*. London: SAGE Publications.

Hviid Jacobsen, M. (2001): *Dødens mosaik: en sociologi om det unævnelige* (The Mosaik of Death; a sociology on the unmentionable), 1st edn. Copenhagen: Gyldendal.

Hviid Jacobsen, M. (2002): 'Dødens Sociologi – seneste skud på den sociologiske grundstamme?' (The Sociology of Death – recent sociological theory?) *Dansk Sociologi* 4/98: 67.

Jacobsen, B., Dalsgaard Jørgensen, S. and Eilenberger Jørgensen, S. (1998): *Kræft og eksistens: om at leve med kræft* (Cancer and existence: about living with cancer), 1st edn. Copenhagen: Danish psychological Publishers.

Järvinen, M. and Bertilsson, M. (1998): *Socialkonstruktivisme: bidrag til en kritisk diskussion* (Social Constructionism; a contribution to a critical discussion). Copenhagen: Hans Reitzel.

Kübler-Ross, E. (1969): *On death and dying*. New York: Macmillan.

Mellor, P.A. (1993): 'Death in high modernity: the contemporary presence and absence of death' in: Clark, D. (ed) *The sociology of death: theory, culture, practice*: 11-30. Oxford: Blackwell Publishers.

Ploug Hansen, H. (1995): *I grænsefladen mellem liv og død: en kulturanalyse af sygeplejen på en onkologisk afdeling* (At the interface between life and death: a cultural analysis of nursing care in a cancer ward), 1st edn. Copenhagen: Gyldendal.

Timm, H. (1997b): 'At have en krop og at være en krop: om sundhedsfremme og sygdomsforebyggelse' (To have a body and to be a body; on health promotion and prevention of disease), in: *GRUS*, vol. 18, no. 52: 24-36.

Timm, H. (1997a): *Patienten i centrum?: Brugerundersøgelser, lægperspektiver og kvalitetsudvikling* (Patientfocused?: Userinvestigations, lay perspectives and development of quality), DSI – Copenhagen: Danish Institute for Health Services Research.

Timm, H. (1999): *Plejeorlov: en evaluering af plejeorlovsordningen for uhelbredeligt syge og deres nærmeste* (Compassionate leave: an evaluation of relief care services for the terminally ill and their families). Copenhagen: The University Hospitals Centre for Nursing and Care Research.

Turner, B.S. (1984): *The body and society: explorations in social theory*. Oxford: Blackwell.

Twycross, R. (1995): *Introducing palliative care*, 1st edn. Oxford: Radcliffe Medical Press.

Walter, T. (1991): 'Modern death: taboo or not taboo', *Sociology*, vol. 25, no. 2: 293-310.

Walter, T. (1994): *The revival of death*. London: Routledge.

Williams, S.J. and Bendelow, G. (1998): *The lived body: sociological themes, embodied issues*, London: Routledge.
Winther Jørgensen, M. and Phillips, L. (1999): *Diskursanalyse som teori og metode (Discourse analysis as theory and method)*, 1st edn. Copenhagen: Samfundslitteratur.
Ziehe, T. and Stubenrauch, H. (1983): *Ny ungdom og usædvanlige læreprocesser: kulturel frisættelse og* subjektivitet (New youth and unusual learing processes: Cultural liberation and subjectivity). Copenhagen: Politisk Revy.

PART IV
DIFFERENT FORMS OF KNOWLEDGE AND DILEMMAS OF CARE EDUCATION

Chapter 9

Caring Experience and Knowledge – Inside and Outside of Danish Classrooms

Betina Dybbroe

What characterizes the socialization, formation and learning processes taking place in educations related to care work inside the present Danish welfare system? And how does this prepare students for and construct caring practice? Students, teachers and educational institutions face conflicting and competing rationalities in the care sectors under the influence of modernization – in what ways do they bring this confrontation into the classroom as subjects of learning? These are the main questions posed in this article.

A theoretical precondition for discussing the dilemmas and conflicts in care is, that care implies both 'taking care of' and 'caring for' (Eliasson-Lappalainen 2000). It is therefore never possible to reduce care to routines governed by specific regimes, i.e. institutionalized values of health, hygiene, social competences etc. Care implies acknowledgement of others, as well as being acknowledged, establishing interdependency of civilization (Honneth 1992) as a constant symmetric and asymmetric interaction, on both the intimate, professional and societal level. It may create conflict, especially in a society with asymmetric power relations. It implies taking responsibility for other human beings and their needs, also when their positions are weak. Kari Wærness defines this as a mixed/joint political and ethical rationality, which is constantly present as a civilizing demand on society, but also needs political and cultural interpretation (Wærness 1987). This also has to be interpreted and translated professionally and contextualized practically through knowledge of needs and problems of specific groups of citizens. As a rationality in public care work it expresses human dependency (as opposed to the political concept of self-care) and a political responsibility for helping The Other with what is needed based on The Others perception of present needs (Wærness 1989).

This rationality of care is currently under the pressure from principles and rationalities of political modernization, economic commodification and the cultural rationality of individualization and bureaucracy, and at all times under different professional interpretations. (Hjort 2003). The rationality of care is thus not merely the professional ethos. Education for the caring sectors also plays its part in channeling these pressures.

Through an analysis of a specific case from the Danish Education of Pre-School teachers and Social Workers (DEPS in the following), I explore how students are professionally motivated by their life historical knowledge and understanding of care and how this appears inside educational spaces in different ways related to the way modernization is reforming their education. This motivation only minimally becomes subject of qualifying for care inside schools, in the various classrooms. This argument is analysed by way of a variety of educational factors: curriculum, organization, positions of teachers, qualification requirements of students etc. The case is presented as specific and exemplary at the same time, because the traces we see here are part of a general trend of changes that has been going on in the caring education during the last ten years in Denmark.

The educational agenda in modernization of the public sector

Education was important, but not directly addressed in the reform to modernize the public sector in Denmark. Education was a tool among others in the effort to professionalize in order to be able to control output, where top-down control systems and hierarchies had formerly been the solution. Here it became expedient to delegate abilities to solve problems, evaluate results and take professional responsibility (Hjort 2001). This new paradigm also implied that professionals should be able to translate directives of economic effectiveness into professional standards, and to create balances between managerial and economic principles and those of the profession (Christensen 2003).

During the 1990s the focus in educational planning in care education has subsequently been on professionalizing and creating a theoretical knowledge-base for the profession, drawing on both the natural sciences as well as humanities in order to meet the new qualification demands. Simultaneously and to some extent nonconsciously they are trying to hold back the dominance of the new foreign and somewhat threatening principles and rationalities. New educational reforms evolved, changing educational thinking, curriculum, and working conditions inside learning spaces. They were all created under the pretext of *qualifying existing thinking about and construction of* practice, but have also contained elements designed to *change the understanding and practice of work as well as education,* which is the focus of this chapter.

The Danish 'pedagogue' is a new construction, created by the 1992 reform (DEPS). Before 1992 there were three different educations in this area in Denmark, care being directed at three different groups of citizens in three different kinds of institutional care and attention. It expressed the idea of shaping education focused on the specific needs and social conditions of the citizens to be cared for and taken care of. There was a professional understanding of the need to contextualize care. Specialization was not only practical and professional but also became political.

Since introducing DEPS the aim of the leading strata of the profession as well as educational planners had been to qualify practice as well as giving the professionals their 'own' knowledge base, i.e. trying to give the young the capacity to participate in the creation of this knowledge base through education. However, the excluding dynamics of the modernized welfare state are adversaries in this attempt. In order to gain credibility, the pedagogue must be able to argue and fight for her professional thinking and negotiate it with and against other agents: citizens (consumers/'users'), managers, and other professional groups, politicians etc. She has no legitimacy 'just' taking care of and caring for children. In this way, the excluding dynamics become embedded inside the educational schemes, as the more sensuous, practical, bodily qualities and craftsmanship in caring loose status.

The modern pedagogue is visualised as less focused on 'the shop-floor work' with children and colleagues, and is seen instead as someone sharing her working time between this and: 'office work', educating, coordinating and communicating with parents and agents outside the workplace. The relationally orientated pedagogue of the eighties and nineties is superseded by a new vision of the professional. She is to possess professional methods and tools of a more abstract character. The category of reflection begins to replace even the category of 'pedagogical work'. This creates a conflict with at least two other factors of the modernization process. It creates *a conflict with the ability to negotiate care and service with consumers/citizens*, because this can only take place in specificity and on a basis of action with citizens. So there is a conflict with the need to act practically, bodily and emotionally. Secondly the new vision of the pedagogue is partly *in conflict with a very production oriented culture of work,* which has been enhanced throughout the nineties. In this production oriented working culture of the modernized institutions, the criteria of success are often the numbers of children in the kindergarten, the turnover on the wards, the amount of elderly returned to their own homes etc. and does not always include time and space for expressions of the reflective practitioner (Vabø 2003).

The first evaluation of the implementation of DEPS on a national level was completed as soon as 1998 (Johansen, Kampmann and Weber 1998). It revealed that modernization was clearly influencing the educational reform in ways that did not exactly follow its articulated pedagogical aims. Yet the educational thinking of the DEPS reform exceeds the limits of budget control, the ideas of new social contracting etc.and is at some points in conflict with the managerial and economic principles. In the following case we see an example of the professional translation of modernization, blending modernization reform of economic, managerial, and democratic domains, with parts of the educational strategy of DEPS intended to professionally challenge modernization.

A local educational development project

This case description is based on an investigation of the educational changes implemented during a study term of a specific educational institution of the DEPS in

2000-2001 (Dybbroe 2001 a).[1] The object of investigation was the local transformation of the DEPS in combination with various smaller modernization reforms in leadership and financing into a two year process of planning and implementation of educational changes in curriculum, methods of study, teachers profile, and educational organization. The institution in focus was in the vanguard in attempting to introduce the category of reflection as a focal point of education, and connecting this with a progressive thinking about democracy, participation and students sharing responsibility for curriculum and the plan of study.

The research design attempted to capture the processes of transformation in their subjective expressions and it had a theoretical framework of life history. Theoretically, it combines analysing life historical material as an expression of socialization, and psychodynamics created in past as well as present interactions with others. *And* analysing them in the present context, as reality oriented handling of real-world phenomena present in their stories as well as in the stories of others. The expressions of life histories in the total meaning of the word allow us to explore the subjective tensions between all that is sensed by a person and that which is conscious. This is the basis for the wish oriented practice of life (Lorenzer and Orban 1978) and studying this can give us clues as to how social factors are translated and shaped into lives, knowledge, professionalism, rationalities of practice etc. Using linguistic analytical methods on the theoretical area of socialization both enlarges and surpasses the scope of biographical analysis. In this type of analysis everything is analysed for meaning, even through linking the language patterns and language games to conditions of socialization.

The research focused on various themes such as democracy, educational planning, communities of practice etc. However, the present focus is on the unseen relations that might exist between external demands of the modernization process and the internal educational reformation initiatives and thinking; and the nature of the relationship between specific educational changes sparked off by the DEPS reform inside the schools, here a specific institution, and students' ability to build life historical knowledge of care.

The educational institution in which the investigation took place, is a well functioning and well renowned educational institution of medium size which recruits students from a large geographical area. The institution is seen as educationally progressive in the professional field and has been in front in several educational initiatives, lately in the national educational reform of 2000 (CVU-reform). The initiative to create educational changes was taken by the principal, as a translator of the political rationalities, but also as a leading representative of a professional ethos trying to renew itself. The project was explicitly intended to combine cost-effectiveness (a cheaper way to educate a constant amount of students) with

---

[1] The research included observations of all forms of education present: lecturing, student's presentations, group-work of students, consultancy and monitoring, staff meetings, plenary seminars between all students and staff. It included analysing written material from curriculums and studyplans, educational papers from the staff, students reports, state regulatives etc. This was supplemented by 24 in depth lifehistorical interviews, with eight students and four teachers twice, in the beginning and at the end of term.

decentralization of responsibility (students responsibility for learning, and teachers responsibility for professionalization) and with new ways of educational academization. But the project was also intended to challenge modernization.

The institution articulated an aim of developing quality in their institution in accordance with leading professionals in the field, stressing the need for higher qualifications of a more generalist, theoretical, social *and* personal character in order for the pedagogue to make independent professional choices, maintain professional standards and manage in a changing society. The whole staff accredited flexibility, autonomy and reflexivity very high value as qualification requirements for candidates, and articulated this as the aims of educational change. The students who had already completed half a year of trainee time, and one year of teaching in the disciplines were to start on a self-directed period of study. The specific pedagogical translation of reflection as the core in this new professionalization of the pedagogue, was this:

> To have a didactic effect, we need for the students to focus on the methods we use to explore that part of reality which becomes the subject of our education. From this stems the idea of focusing on the procedures of investigation methods.... (Interview with principal, Dybbroe 2001 a, p.33).

This institution translated the qualification of generalists, not just in relation to the requirements of the labour market, of documentation etc., but also in order to create innovative and self-assured professionals. The radical step was to establish a democratic project, where students were stimulated to create their own knowledge, independently of the teachers and the disciplines, focusing on the methodical rather than subject matter. Teachers and students were given almost separate learning spaces, so that teachers could lecture, but the students were free to choose supervision from teachers or not.

The principal articulated the new pedagogical discourse in this way:

> Pedagogical authority is transferred to the subject-matter, working with the subject-matter and the way we process the subject-matter. We become dependent on our subject and material and in this way relationally orientated on a more material foundation. Mostly with regard to the relations between the material and humans and to a lesser degree the relations between people (Dybbroe 2001a, p.35).

This implied severing the usual interaction between teachers and students, and students were 'set free' from the life historical horizons of their much older teachers, the personified interpretations of subjects and disciplines by teachers and teacher's translations of professionalization in care. They were seemingly set free to include their own life historical interpretations and experiences in choices of subjects and methods – or were they?

Autonomy and separation

Returning to one of the questions of this chapter: how the implementation of these new discourses affects the socialization of students – and specifically in relation to care. This started with planning of the study term, and the role that socialization of students played here.

During a year of preparation for the educational development project, the teachers and principal never reflected on or discussed the background, experiences and expectations of students in relation to the curriculum they were preparing. (This is parallel to the tendency of the earlier national evaluation.) They did not try to reflect in what ways the new curriculum might be inclusive or exclusive to specific groups of students, or what sort of learning processes might be impeded and which might be enhanced. Instead of understanding this as professional incapacities it could be suggested that the institution was trying to set new standards on the market of education in accordance with the academic ambitions of the reform of 2000 (CVU-reform). Selling an educational product that could attract some groups of students and discourage others.

The expectations and background of students in relation to learning were framed by both their former experiences as non-educated staff in child- and care-institutions, and as pupils of the compulsory school system. Many of them may have been very competent care-workers for several years, but once the students are inside, being educated, they position themselves as pupils, to some extent in a re-production of the traditional school relation between pupil and teacher. This may be said of other vocational and professional education for the young, but is of specific interest in the present analysis in combination with a reformed concept of the relation between students, teachers and subject.

Curriculum and didactics were designed to create freedom for students to construct their own knowledge, stay independent of teachers' and traditional professional ideals, and students were invited to negotiate frames with staff. As education will produce codes of power that signify included and excluded values and meaning in learning (Bernstein 2001), this was questioned in the investigation. How did educational codes impose themselves? How were educational codes apprehended by students in specific classrooms and inside educational frameworks? And how did this affect learning and the creation of knowledge in care?

The students reacted specifically according to their background in the school system and according to a number of social and life historical factors that I will not expound here. Existing social hierarchies inside education were deepened during the process, whereby the scholarly most successful became even more successful, and the lesser successful even less. But during the first part of the process, the students generally tried to comply with the new demands, although many had difficulties in understanding the ideas and aims behind this. They took the liberty of constructing their own knowledge at face value, they freely created themes related to their working experiences and deeply felt motivation, and they felt free to do this.

The students had expectations of meeting knowledgeable professionals and being supervised by teachers. They expected to have problems of practice and the professional field translated and interpreted, allowing them subsequently to become full members of a new practice. Likewise, their life-historical background as participants of the school system was transparent, showing students themselves neglecting their own practical experience of working with care. They did not insist on presenting their practical knowledge in the classroom, or hold on to experiences that they found relevant to the theoretical themes discussed in lectures.

But students did establish their separate learning spaces, the group work, projects, plenary presentations of students work etc., as the intention of the educational change had been. Here everything except the methodical focus seemed open for negotiation, and they started to add and reflect on their experiences. Life historical experiences and expectations deriving also from the conflicts in caring practice and sensing of the practical realm of both life and care work, would appear.

The teachers on the other hand established their separate learning spaces. They lectured and did not just teach as before. Teachers performed with their self-chosen subjects and disciplines and thrived, indulging in self-directed learning process with their disciplines and subjects, not with students, not with colleagues. This was the intention of curriculum.

The socialization process of students and *of teachers thus became much more separate than before and in this process of separation, a process of social exclusion seemed to be gaining in speed. This was an unintended, but very clear tendency. The learning spaces inside the classroom and outside classroom, seemed to be competing at the same tim. The two learning spaces were not only becoming more autonomous, but also more heterogeneous and parallel.*

Identification, connection and fascination in care

The competition and heterogeneous process of professionalization was focused on care and caring qualifications. In the following, I will present a single example from my findings that is an illustration of the patterns in which socialization of students for caring practice became divided between the two learning spaces. It shows how students tried to undertake their own socialization towards care.

A large part of the 70 students chose to concern themselves with the theme of children experiencing deprivation of care in various ways and focused on different aspects of this: aspects of methods in care work, understanding specific situations and needs of citizens, reflecting on perceptions of care etc. A group of students argued their choice in this way in their report:

> During our education until now and generally in our work with children, we have had the experience that many pedagogues don't really have sufficient knowledge of care deprivation, and wherever that knowledge exists, it is only with difficulty translated into practical work with children. So we think that the child deprived of care, feeling a lot of frustration and pain, doesn't really get adequate help. Does this mean that the institutions practice 'public deprivation of care'? We think that at present, one can complete the entire education and only touch superficially on care deprivation, and that's a

problem because in all educational work with children you can meet with care deprived children. That's why we've chosen to work more intensely with this subject this term... (quoted in Dybbroe 2001 b).

Based on their experience, the students felt that here was an urgent professional problem from practice, which they did not have the background to approach. They wished to avoid finding themselves in the situation of many of their educated colleagues, whom they experienced as inadequate in dealing with the problems of these children. The teachers looked at it quite differently, and thought the students were repeating themselves, and that their interests were of low academic value:

> Many students, already at the first term exam, when they start to choose subjects to work with, they start talking about single mothers, child victims of incest, child abuse, deprivation of care, the most extreme things are the ones they choose to work with from the start. I mean, the most miserable corner of reality... Well the whole social pornographic field nearly, and I think that's a problem, that they are concerned with this in such a superficial way, that it's a good story, that it's awful and pitiful... (Interview with teacher, Dybbroe 2001 a).

Teachers had a professional preconception which also contained attitudes and ethics, just like the students. When reading through all the student reports of this term, certain 'social pornographic' perspectives do appear, but they are far from dominant. In nearly all the projects about deprivation of care, there was indignation concerning pedagogues who did not fulfil what parents had failed to do. In this sense, the students had high ideals and not always a clear vision of what the capacity differences and relations are in public care in relation to family care. This was partly what they wanted to find out.

There was much and evident uncertainty about understanding their own methods of learning in the work of the study groups, because they sensed that they were linking it with personal experiences, emotions etc. Was this wrong knowledge?? In the end, much time in groups was spent on how to argue and even legitimize their interest in deprivation of care, as here in the group discussion about being discussants for another group in class. The report they were discussing was an analysis of the case of a family of fugitives, where both deprivation of care and mental illness were part of the problem. They had been told by teachers to focus on what is professionally relevant for the pedagogue:

> Hanne: What is pedagogical-professional relevance, really? Isn't it something directed at each of us as persons?
> Lone: But why does it at all have to be pedagogically-professional? You certainly also need cultural understanding, and it says that the mother is mentally ill. Well, then it isn't a pedagogue she needs. There are far too many things in this case that are not reflected upon.
> Kirsten: Isn't there a teacher, who has read these reports who can help us evaluate this?
> Lone: But when a child has a social capital of being able to contribute to the welfare in the family, and when this child is told in the day-care institution that they shouldn't do anything, then that is symbolic violence.

Karen: That's just like the child I had, whom nobody in kindergarten understood, and the mother said he helped her with a lot of things.
Lone: It's funny what happens when you recognise something. When we were reading John Halse (BD: on children deprived of care) then it is like working with children, recognition is an important emotional dimension.
Hanne: But I don't understand it, how can we discuss that with them.
Kirsten: We can't extract anything general from this.
Lone: You have to approach it more professionally and separate the personal and use the theoretical concepts.
Hanne: No, we must express it in everyday language so that we understand it.
(quoted from Dybbroe 2001 b).

The group is searching for an understanding of the subject matter, and at the same time searching to understand how the professional is related to the personal and emotional – and they feel lost! Kirsten wants teachers as authority in this dilemma. Lone wants to construct her own knowledge and continues the discussion, when the others try to draw themselves out of it. Hanne desperately needs to stay in the everyday understanding in order for her to grasp anything, and she believes the pedagogical-professional to be an individual ability of feeling and deciding the right thing to do. Lone is not afraid of trying to use the new theoretical language and the concepts she has been taught, as she wants to raise the subject to a more abstract level. But Lone is ambiguous, because she wants to separate the personal from the professional, and at the same time talks of the personal and emotional aspects of learning care. This ambiguity is too difficult for the group to handle, and in the later presentation in class not a word is mentioned about it, or anything related to experiences or attitudes of the members in this group.

Lone afterwards recalls:

I had the experience, and maybe that was because our group was special, because the three of us worked really well together, but one of us was actually working with emergency brakes all the time, and that really surprised me, we used an awful lot of energy on that ... and in the first term paper she had had enormous problems, she had been very unhappy, and then you sit there and think, could I maybe give her a good experience. We've talked a lot about how you are as a person, and what sort of experiences we have and how our childhood has affected us, and I mean, Hanne, she told us some things where I thought, no that can't be true, but then it's obvious, she is having a hard time when we're working with something that affects you emotionally, then she may be obliged to use her self-defence. (Interview with student, Dybbroe 2001 b).

Both Hanne and Lone are examples of the connection between the personal life history, the shared life historical conditions of professionals and citizens, and the competences and professional qualifications in care. (The life historical dimensions of caring knowledge in pedagogical work are illustrated more deeply in Dybbroe 2003). The mutual recognition, and to some extent identification, between Hanne and the citizens they are working with, between Lone and Hanne, and between Lone and the citizens, containing engagement and direction, in joyful as well as often painful ways, is part of learning in care. The students in this group were not very special, but like all the other groups trying to get hold of how to be committed and empathic and yet professional in reflecting the problems and needs of citizens. This little extract of empirical data from the learning process in care outside the classroom, contains elements of the classical dilemmas in the formation of professionals of care. Formation can be here seen strung out between the theoretically based authority and personal authority (Martinsen 1994). Furthermore, it can be seen as symptoms of what has been discussed morally and ethically under the theme of relations between heart, hand and head, or under the theme of balancing between recognition of and identification with the other (see Dahl, 1998, and her discussion of Noddings, Benhabib and Leira).

Another perspective is to see the participants' experiences and discourses of distance and closeness related to their caring practice, in which they are obliged to trespass on the borders between the intimate and the public as spheres with different rationalities that are blended in care work (Christensen 2003, Dahl 1998, Dybbroe 1999). Theoretically, one perspective is to understand this psycho-dynamically as a pre-condition for maintaining and defending subjectivity, so that the primary socializational dilemma between autonomy and intimacy (Chodorow 1978) is doubled. Care workers cannot care for and take care of without being intimate and giving up on some of their autonomy, and yet cannot be professional and gain caring authority if they do not – to some extent – act autonomously in public care. A very complex process ensues, where care workers must seek recognition for themselves, as well as the citizens they care for (Honneth 1992) while balancing closeness and distance. This is a fundamental condition in working in the public care sectors. These are the dynamics that structure the experiences in care work as repelling and attracting at the same time, creating connectedness and relations, but also threatening professionals with loss of subjectivity.

Various investigations into care work with elderly in their own homes can be seen in this theoretical perspective (Jensen 1992, Christensen 1997, Thorsen 1998, Vabø 1998). The care workers show symptoms of the psycho-dynamical difficulty of this balance through infantilizing their relations with citizens, becoming aggressive, or rutinized and distant etc.

From the case above we can understand, that Hanne was to some extent threatened in her subjectivity by the working process, not through identification with specific citizens she was taking care of as the educated pedagogue she was to become. But in the educational frame Hanne was being challenged through meeting citizens in a complex of social phenomena, through investigating, analysing and trying to reflect on this, and lastly trying to take theoretical responsibility for plans of action for these citizens. This was what the group had been working with, and this was what many of the other students had been working with as well. All groups had similar experiences of students being confronted with emotional and identifiable material, and probing in darkness as to what this had to do with professionalism in the sense of curriculum and the educational thinking in their institution. Their socialization for professionalism in caring was clearly taking place inside this passionately strong, personally engaging, disturbing and partly incomprehensible horizon of experiences. But they were beginning to become divided, creating imbalances between the personal and professional. They were beginning to internalize a set of codes for practice, where the affective, bodily and personally engaging aspects of care were being reserved for the learning space outside the classroom.

Excluding care

The teachers were not supposed to interfere with the subjects the students had chosen. The subjects chosen by students surprised the teachers who were not in a position to question or negotiate them. In the curriculum, supervision was methodically focussed and in consultation with teachers, subjects and ethical/political questions of care could not be discussed, because the teachers were disengaging themselves from this. The students were to construct their own knowledge.

But as the term was ending, discussions, negotiations and even quarrels with teachers about results and standards of work started to alarm many students. At the end of term, the students presented their work and were strongly criticized by teachers, who found that the methodical focus was not presented strongly enough in the reports, and that the quality of work was too poor. The contents of reports were most specifically criticized for not taking on macro-social perspectives and for lacking professional distance to problems of specific citizens – and to stay at the 'socio-pornographic' level. There was too much personal engagement in the subjects, too many unsolved ethical problems. A teacher here explains her position:

> I prefer not to go too much into the normative domain, where you suggest ways to handle and act, the correct pedagogical practice, but the students are always looking for this, and I think that every time they speak up, or try to say: must I understand it this way then? Then they make the theoretical theory into a practical theory. So at the same time as I am trying to remember what to teach them, I keep on thinking: why do they want it so concrete? But I suppose that's because they are looking for methods and some answers (Dybbroe 2001 b).

But the normative domain is also the emotional and inter relational domain where students are subjects to strong feelings. It is in these domains that the psychodynamics of closeness and distance, as analysed above, will express themselves. These domains and mechanisms and the possible theorizations about care that could arise from this, were thus excluded from class and left to trainee periods. But here they also seemed 'out of place':

> Somebody comes out to visit you in the institution, from this school, but it's more like, how are things going, are you fulfilling my standards and all that, but directly sort of get monitoring, you don't get anywhere ... so I haven't had the experiences rearranged and reflected, or had it talked through with anybody except for my fiancée (interview with student, Dybbroe 2001 a).

The students were slowly learning how to hide and devalue these parts of the qualification process for care.

Creating the individually responsible, depersonalised care-worker – and how it doesn't work

How can we interpret the relation between the new discourses of the education of pedagogues and their unintended practical consequences? Wasn't it just an unhappy coincidence, related to bad management or bad teaching? The answer must be no, the actors actually performed quite well – it was the script, that was causing the changes and trouble.

The minimization of an 'educational meeting' between reflection and experiences with specific citizens in their emotional, professional and ethical aspects had become a larger problem with the new curriculum. First of all it now became a larger problem, because the separation between students and teachers in the process created separate responsibilities. Commitment was deposited in two different 'boxes': the teachers were engaged in elaborating reflexivity in relation to their disciplines, as they also were being asked to enact autonomy. They could evaluate the effect of this only through the projects of the students – and here the signs of their lectures were hard to find. The students on the other hand were engaged in trying to get their work recognized as their own contribution and construction. A gap in understanding was inevitable.

Secondly, the idea of studying reflexivity as generalization and educationally focused could not work, because students were intent on becoming more knowledgeable practicioners. The students were more interested in reflecting on pedagogical work, not as method, structure or organization, but as craft involving entire persons. Furthermore, the students had been preoccupied with learning about the problems and needs of specific citizens. The following case of a student illustrates what the life-historical dimension in qualifying for care is about. It is about the personal, sensuous and engaging meaning of care:

> I thought I could actually cope with a lot of influence from outside, see a lot of shit and stuff without it sort of touched anything in me, but then in connection with my practical trainee period, where I really found out, where I *really* found out how bad those children can be. Where I saw some children that are so destroyed... that was tough, that was damned, what they could... could do to you, how bad a mood they could set you in, when you came home... but also getting to know yourself (interview with student, Dybbroe 2001 a).

The experience is situated in the present, past and future at the same time. This student expresses what can be seen as the life historical subjective meaning of professionalizing in the deprivation of care. *Sensing* deprivation of care, he also *senses* aspects of his personal as well as professional self, that have to do with his own upbringing, and *senses* his way of relating, in this case specifically to the children deprived of care. Life historically he is confronting himself with the question of how to *reflect on* this, how to create knowledge/experience about deprivation of care, how to work with these specific children professionally, and letting it touch and develop him personally at the same time.

Teachers perceived the interest of students in the subject matter as sensation seeking and shallow. An alternative way of interpreting this is to see the students´ knowledge, and not their interest, as shallow. Fascination can be interpreted as part of an ambivalence in relation to social problems, as repelling and desirous at the same time. This is typical of all kinds of students working in care, although not so often seen with the experienced workers. It is another way of highlighting the mechanisms that are often recognised as practice-shock of new candidates. Students are non-routinized participants in the maintenance of the unquestionable order of everyday life (Beck-Jørgensen 1994) in caring institutions and related educational institutions, and they meet those governing rationalities partly as outsiders.

The confrontation with needs and problems of citizens, in this case the deprived children, becomes more than what it seemingly is to the theoretically based teacher or the trained professional. From a life historical horizon of being young and 'outside' professionality, identification with children and reaction towards the grown-up professionals and the institutions is inevitable. In this specific case, the identification allows the ambivalent feelings of students to be exposed through the case of the deprived children. This does not imply that the students necessarily feel as deprived children or believe that all children are deprived of care.

For the students, both the subject matter and professionalism were personal and emotional as well, and they had no professional ethos or instruments to control and guard the seesawing between closeness and distance. They wanted a space to reflect and ponder on this, maybe just a breathing space in the sense of Thomas Ziehe, where time for sensing and being is seized and does not seize you. (Ziehe 1978) They (mis)used this opportunity to construct their own knowledge, a personified knowledge about care. They were punished for this (mis)use, not by formal examination, but through a week of presentations and discussions in classes and in big plenary sessions that were very painful. The symptoms of failure and collective shame were present in all the interviews with students after the end of term.

Only a few students who had worked mostly macro-sociologically or written about the study-methodical practice were praised and felt self-assured at the end of term. In this way, a process of exclusion had been the result of a study period, which started by opening the learning space for everybody and his or her conception of the importance of different aspects of pedagogical practice. The seemingly noncoded learning space turned out to be very much coded. Teachers and the institution had expected specific learning that focused on the category of reflection, as the leading professionals in the field have defined it. Teachers also wanted it presented in specific ways, where they still could recognise their own disciplines in the work of students, whereas students had felt absolutely free to choose other knowledge bases.

Curriculum and the organization of the term had created an ambiguous situation, where disciplines for the students had become de-personalization, and the classroom was becoming more de-personalized with weakened relations between students as well as between students and teachers. Teachers were regressing to disciplines and the theoretical realm, partly hiding their personalities here. And students were regressing to the social substance of pedagogical work, in the more individually personified form of cases, personal experiences and specific relations in their present lives as students and care workers. The meeting between the theoretical horizons of knowledge bases unknown to students, and the experiences and knowledge of students, through specific teachers and students meeting to interpret and create themes of experience together in the classroom, did not take place.

And so knowledge in care was only created in patches, in spite of curriculum, and mostly excluding the personal as a source of energy for engagement in caring practice.

Final comments

A curriculum that encourages focus on the category of reflection and 'academic' cognitive and verbal methods, *without including* the relational, specific, bodily and emotional aspects of the category of experience in care, can have at least two consequences for learning in care. First of all, knowledge areas that are experienced by students as interwoven and joint in their own lives as well as in training and job experience, are here coded as separate in the class room. Division and fragmentation of knowledge of phenomena is created instead of connecting and integrated understanding, especially suppressing emotionality. Secondly, educational processes will invite students to understand the knowledge base of the education as dichotomized between the more theoretically organized mono-disciplinary approaches, as being more 'right' and fundamental and the practical knowledge related to citizens and the ways their needs are expressed, to be of lesser educational value.

The experiences of caring *for* as well as *about*, of relating to and acting with children, disabled psychiatric patients etc. in caring institutions – as both disturbingly sensuous, bodily based knowledge and unreflected sensing – as practical, unquestionable everyday routine actions, and not least, as reflected personal moral knowledge – are analysed in this chapter to be more the focus of a qualification process 'outside school'. A rupture is created between pedagogical knowing and theoretical substance inside education. The rupture, however, is not openly between the practical sense in care and theory of care. So students will compensate to some extent in their more self-directed learning processes, but these processes will create exclusion of many students and lowering of self esteem amongst students, as seen in the case.

Taking a brief look at the possible connection between the qualification requirements in the work places under modernization and the qualification process of students in education, we can see some parallels. This is just one example. At the political level, the social contract with citizens today is both governed by the demand for standardization and de-personalized service, as something all consumers are paying for/buying regardless of specific needs – and at the same time culture is individualized, forcing negotiation of service/care between individuals. This requires personal authority and personal relating, at the same time requiring a professionally and politically standardized de-personalization of problem solving in the same services/care. This becomes one of many conflicting points of confrontation between the principles of economy and of bureaucracy and of the rationality of care.

In this same way, we may understand the presence of conflicts between the personal and methodical/theoretical way of defining the substance of education.

De-personalization of the subject matter and educational process, which was the explicit goal of the studied institution, is also the goal in reforming other curricula in several caring educations in Denmark presently (i.e. the education of social workers, and the education of nurses). Focus on methods of the theoretical/educational practice was in the case part of the chosen curriculum, as an interpretation of the shift in the DEPS reform towards reflection, and from specialization to generalization in the educational profile. Traces of modernization could be seen in the case as having specific importance for the socialization, formation and learning process in care. They were represented by a number of factors, both intended and unintended, and most important: *distance* to caring practice in the class room, *exclusion of knowledge* about citizens' needs and the emotional sides of care in the class room, *de-personalization* of classroom learning – and on the other hand strong *personalization* of learning outside classrooms. The studied case can thus be understood as exemplary of part of what is happening to the caring educations at present.

References

Andersen, A.S. and Sommer, F. (2003): 'Reform på reform – voksen-, erhvervsrettet- og professionsrettet uddannelse', in: Andersen and Sommer (eds.): *Uddannelsesreformer og levende mennesker,* Erhvervs- og Voksenuddannelsesgruppen. Roskilde: Roskilde University Press.

Arvidsson H., Berntson L. and Dencik, L. (1994): *Modernisering och välfärd – om stat, individ och civilt samhälle I Sverige.* Göteborg: City University Press.

Bech-Jørgensen, B. (1994): *Når hver dag bliver hverdag.* Copenhagen: Akademisk Forlag.

Bernstein, B. (2001): 'Pædagogik, diskurs og magt', in: Chrourouaraki and Bayer (eds.): *Pædagogik, diskurs og magt.* Copenhagen: Akademisk Forlag.

Chodorow, N. (1978): *The Reproduction of Mothering, Psychoanalysis and the Sociology of Gender* California: University of California Press.

Christensen, K. and Syltevik, L. (2000) (eds.): *Omsorgens forvitring, Antologi om utfordringer I velferdsstaten.* Bergen: Fagbokforlaget.

Christensen, K. (2003): 'De stille stemmer', in: Widding Isaksen, L (ed.): *Omsorgens pris-Kjønn, makt og marked i velferdsstaten.* Trondheim: Gyldendal Norsk Forlag.

Christensen, K. (1997): *Omsorg og arbejde. En studie af ændringer i den hjemmebaserede omsorg.* Afhandling i sociologi. Bergen: Institut for Samhellsvetenskap.

Dahl, H.M. (1998): 'Den følsomme stat?', in: *Grus* nr. 54, Aalborg: Aalborg University.

Dybbroe, B. (2003): 'Professionality and Gendered Learning', in: 'Care: What's so Feminine about it?', in: Dybbroe, B. and Ollagnier, E. (eds.): *Challenging Gender in Lifelong Learning.* European Perspectives. Roskilde: Esrea and Roskilde University Press.

Dybbroe, B. (2003): 'You´ve got to give all the love you have, and yet consider it to be a job' – Care Work in a Gendered and Life Historical Perspective, in: Jørgensen and Warring (eds.): *Adult Education and the Labour Market* vii, Volume B. Roskilde: Esrea and Roskilde University Press.

Dybbroe, B. (2001 a): *Genvej til selvstændige læreprocesser?* (Shortcut to autonomous Processes of Learning?). Skriftserie fra Erhvervs og voksenuddannelsesgruppen nr. 122, Roskilde: Roskilde University Centre.

Dybbroe, B. (2001 b): 'Uddannelsens behagelige lethed og arbejdets smertelige tyngde – om at lære omsorg i det pædagogiske felt' (The Delightful Lightness of Education and the Painful Weight of Work – about Learning Care in the Pedagogical Field), in: Andersen, A.S et al. (eds.): *Bøjelighed og tilbøjelighed – livshistoriske perspektiver på læring og uddannelse.* Roskilde: Roskilde University Press.

Dybbroe, B. (1999): *Som var det mine egne – omsorg som kundskab og arbejde i to kulturer* (As if they were my own – Care as Knowledge and Work in two Cultures) Ph.D. thesis, Roskilde University Centre.

Eliasson-Lappalainen, R. (2000): 'Etik och moral i äldreomsorgens vardag', in: Christensen and Syltevik (eds.): *Omsorgens forvitring?* Bergen: Fagbokförlaget.

Eriksen, T. Rask (1992): *Omsorg i forandring.* Copenhagen: Munksgaard.

Hjort, K. (2003): 'Viden som vare?' in Hjort (ed.): *De professionelle.* Roskilde: Roskilde University Press.

Hjort, K. (2001): *Moderniseringen af den offentlige sektor.* Institut for Uddannelses-forskning, Skriftserie fra EVU-gruppen, Roskilde University Centre.

Honneth, A. (1992) : *Kampf um Anerkennung.* Frankfurt am Main: Suhrkamp Verlag.

Jensen, K. (1992): *Hjemlig omsorg I offentligt regi.* En studie av kunnskapsutvicklingen i omsorgsarbeitet. Oslo: Universitetsforlaget.

Johansen, E., Kampmann, J. and Weber, K. (eds.) (1998): *Omgå eller omgås – modernise-ring og uddannelsestænkning i pædagoguddannelsen.* RUC i samarbejde med BUPL og SL, Skriftserie fra Erhvervs- og voksenuddannelsesgruppen no. 67, Roskilde University Centre.

Just, E. (2002): 'Viden og læreprocesser i sygehuse', in: Laursen, E. (ed.): *Viden om læring.* Aalborg Universitet.

Larsen, K. (2000): *Praktikuddannelse, kendte og miskendte sider* – Et observationsstudie af praktikuddannelse inden for sygeplejerskeuddann. Ph.D. thesis, UHCF, Copenhagen.

Lorenzer, A. and Oban, P. (1978): 'Transitional Objects and Phenomena: Socialization and Symbolization', in: Grolnick and Barkin (eds.): *Between Reality and Phantasy.* London: Jason Aronson.

Martinsen, K. (1994): *Fra Marx til Løgstrup: Om etik og sanselighed I sygeplejen.* Dansk udgave. Copenhagen: Munksgaard.

Nielsen, S.B. (2002): ' 'Modernisering' og 'feminisering' i velfærdsstaten – omsorg, profes-sionalisering og kønsmagt under forandring', in: Borhchorst, A. (ed): *Kønsmagt i forandring.* Roskilde: Roskilde University Press.

Noddings, N. (1984): *Caring: a Feminine Approach to Ethics and Moral Education.* Berke-ley: University of California Press.

Thorsen, K. (1998): 'Den pressede omsorgen. Kvaliteter i hjemmehjelpstjenesten for eldre i lokal kontekst' in *Nova Rapport* 18, Oslo.

Vabø, M. (2003): 'Forbrukermakt i omsorgstjenesten – til hjelp for de svakeste?', in: Wid-ding Isaksen, L. (ed.): *Omsorgens pris – Kjønn, makt og marked i velfærdsstaten*: 102-127. Trondheim: Gyldendal Norsk Forlag.

Vabø, M. (1998): 'Hvad er nok? Om behovsfortolkninger i hjemmetjenesten', in: *Nova rap-port* 8, Oslo.

Wärness, K. (1989): *Et program for omsorgsforskning,* Skriftserien *Occasional Papers.* Bergen: Sociologisk Institut.

Wärness, K. (1987): 'The Rationality of Caring', in: Sassoon (ed.): *Women and the State.* London: Hutchinson.

Ziehe, T. (1978): 'Om læreprocesser', in: *Kontekst* 35, Copenhagen.

Chapter 10

Youth Culture –
A Source of Energy and Renewal for
the Field of Nursing in Norway

Karen Jensen and Bodil Tveit

The future of our health care system is dependent on many factors. Among these are factors related to recruitment or, more pragmatically framed, to the ability of core professions to attract students to the field and to evolve a foundation for work which is motivational and binding over time. Without a sufficient number of persons willing to perform the practical work which health care involves, investment in all other aspects would indeed be in vain. Recently published data indicate, however, that this key factor is increasingly under strain. They show that younger generations in particular prefer to work in new and more 'trendy' fields and are more prone to career shifts and occupational flight than were previous generations. Among the fields hit hardest by this development is nursing. Over the last ten years the number of younger applicants to this profession has dropped dramatically (National application statistics 1996–2003). In addition to the concern this has caused, research indicates an increase in burn-out rates as well as other signs of dissatisfaction. According to a recent study a large number of all nurses regret their choice of occupation and would prefer to work within other fields (Statistics for Norwegian Nurses Association 1999). The urgency of the situation has been underlined by projected figures which indicate a dramatic increase in demand for health care personnel in the near future (Econ-Rapport nr. 49/1999, Hagen 2000). This article presents data from a larger research project that has questions related to recruitment and moral motivation as its core theme.[1] In the project special attention is paid to discussing sources of motivational energy and renewal.

[1] This research is supported by The Norwegian Research Council, The Centre for the Study of Professions, Oslo University College, and The Institute for Educational Research, University of Oslo. We wish to thank the other members of our research team, Associate Professor Berit Karseth and Senior Lecturer Bjørg Fossestøl for valuable discussions contributing to this paper. We would also like to thank Professor Arne Johan Vetlesen and Professor Harald Grimen, for commenting on the manuscript.

Images of nursing

Research into professional cultures indicates vast differences in the images professions project and in the ability they have to create a sense of identity and belonging
(Biglan 1973, Becher 1994, Knorr Cetina 1997). Professions not only have their
own traditions and categories of thought which provide members with shared concepts of theories, methods and techniques, but also with a moral order – that is, a
value system which helps to define what is considered right, good and desirable as
opposed to bad, improper and immoral (Harré 1983, Ylijoki 2000). These distinctions contribute to the identity of professions as well as to the broader image they
project. A brief glance at the images projected by the nursing profession indicates a
growing tension between the values portrayed as important by the profession on
the one hand, and by youth culture on the other.

   Nursing is among the oldest of the health care professions, and one that today
also plays a major role within most branches in the sector. Having evolved through
different phases of history, nursing has come to embody a host of images and ideals. These range from the notion of nursing as a religious calling, to more modern
conceptions of nursing as a profession. Although these traditions are different and
contribute to a plurality in modes of thought on many issues, they find common
ground in the primacy they give to 'the other', and in a tendency to downplay the
ethical value of self-related motives and concerns. Within the early religious tradition, this manifests itself in an appraisal of values related to self-sacrifice and to
abiding by the law of Christian love and duty. An excerpt written in 1868 describes
nursing as an occupation, which requires:

> ...a relinquishing of self which enhances the will to abide by the given law and gives
> strength, without remorse or longing, to deprive oneself of worldly goods and pleasure
> as well as one's own comfort and life habits; a solemn and tireless patience to be com-
> mitted to the sick, day after day (quoted in Martinsen 1984, p. 53).

Though many things have changed in the course of history, nursing is still characterised by a strong other-orientated rhetoric and ideology. Inspired by the work of
relational philosophers – for example Emmanuel Levinas's (1991) face-to-face-
ethics, or Løgstrup's (1969) theory of ethical demand – researchers have evolved
theories of care which grounds ethical responsibility in 'being'. Defined as a prop-
erty of being, responsibility for the other is not something we can discard, question,
or step in and out of. It is a non-optional fact of life and a responsibility we simply
have as persons. Though this view has much merit, it contributes to an understanding of moral responsibility as uncoupled from the logic of reciprocity as well as
that of roles and social institutions. As expressed by Vetlesen (1997, p. 10), in responsibility understood as being, there is no decision, no asking, 'What's in it for
me?' No pondering, 'Shouldn't I rather stay outside of commitment?' According to
this view, all that matters is 'the other'. Echoing this view, nursing theorists have
evolved an image of nursing as a selfless and quite demanding activity (Martinsen
1993, 2000; Nåden and Eriksson 2000, 2002; Nordtvedt 2001).

In recent years these ideals have also come to inspire nursing education. In the year 2000 a new National Curriculum for Nursing was introduced in Norway based on an ethos of care (Karseth 2002). Some quotes from this document (General Plan and Regulations for 3-year Training Programme in Nursing, 2000) may serve to illustrate the level of ambition which currently prevails. The goal of nursing education as stated in the document, is to ensure the capacity of nurses 'to provide total care for a patient based on an understanding of what it feels like to be ill and threatened by disease' (GP, p. 27), develop an 'ability and will to establish, carry out and persist in inter-human relationships' (GP, p. 29), and to evolve 'a competence to meet patients and next of kin, with sensitivity, empathy and ethical responsibility and concern' (GP, p. 33). To be a caring person, it says, is to be emphatic and understanding, and to act in solidarity with the patient or client.

Though the understanding of nursing as 'first and foremost about caring for the patient' or what we more generally have termed as 'the other' has considerable moral merit, contemporary research suggests that it is far too narrow to capture the multitude of interests and concerns that seem to guide future generations.

Changes in patterns of commitment

Though social research is a field often fuelled by diversity in opinion, most researchers agree that modernity has contributed to a shift in orientation, in particular among the younger generations. Rather than being guided by the values of duty and self-sacrifice there is, they maintain, a growing trend among youth to orientate themselves subjectively and to give primacy to their own feelings and state of mind (Shusterman 1988, Bell 1992, Abrahamson and Ingelhart 1995, Hellevik 1996). At the level of everyday life, this is demonstrated by what researchers describe as a shift of focus from the ethical to the aesthetic: While 'being of use' was characteristic of earlier generations, the desire 'to find oneself' is more central today (Gullestad 1996).

Though researchers tend to agree on the general nature of this development, their views on the effects that it has on morality vary considerably. According to some social theorists, this trend has had a devastating effect on morality (Sennett 1977, Lasch 1979, Shusterman 1988, Bell 1992). The aesthetic turn, they maintain, has lead to the emergence of a narcissistic and self-indulging culture void of moral quality. Others, however, are more optimistic and underline the ambivalent nature of today's situation. Among these is the German youth researcher, Thomas Ziehe (1989; 1993; 2000). According to Ziehe the aesthetic trend among youth carries a seed not only to self-indulgence and preoccupied behaviour, but also to an increase in self-knowledge and in life energy. He identifies three modes of orientation, which are typical of today's youth. The first is a tendency to seek meaning and self-knowledge through intimacy. This mode of orientation represents an attempt among young people to escape from what they perceive to be a cold, harsh and superficial world through cultivating warm and close relationships. What is valued here is developing as a true and authentic person. A second form is what he calls an ontologizing tendency. This represents an attempt to regain some of the certainty and predictability previously provided by religion. Though this can be achieved in several ways, the most typical, according to Ziehe, is to engage either in new religious movements, or in the truth-seeking processes of modern psychology. The third form is what he terms fictionalization. This mode of orientation points to the trend whereby meaning is regarded as something to be created rather than sought. What is valued within this mode of orientation is the ability to adapt, transform and experiment with different modes of being. The aim of the game is neither to find certainty nor to uncover the depths within oneself, but to have fun, to enjoy, to thrive. According to Ziehe, all these forms represent unorthodox and creative modes of being which ultimately lead to an increase in motivational energy and the ability to find meaning in everyday life (Ziehe 1989; 1993; 2000). Though he emphasises the life-affirming potential that lies in this development he also draws attention to the pitfalls involved. If pushed too far, preoccupation with the self may, he cautions, leads to the erosion of moral language and culture. Why bother to ponder or elaborate on a situation when merely referring to what one likes, feels and subjectively desires are considered sufficient grounds for action?

In this article we present data from a project, which explores the gap between the current culture and the ideals and images projected by the nursing profession. What is it that attracts younger persons to this field in the first place? Are they guided by the traditional values of duty and self-sacrifice? Or have other more self-related concerns come to dominate? Is there a tension between the desires, attractions and motives of today's students and the norms and values professed as important in nursing school? In the project special attention is paid to identifying sources of motivational energy and renewal. Are there lessons to be learned from youth culture? Does youth culture offer a release from the image of nursing as a limitless and selfless profession?

A narrative approach

In order to gain insight into the motives, desires and attractions of today's students, a narrative approach was chosen for the study. This approach takes advantage of people's natural capacity for making sense of their lives by way of stories (Bruner 1987, Polkinghorne 1996). In every day life human beings use conventional narrative means to give shape to their lives. Questions related to desires and motives are an integral part of these narratives. By following a select number of students from the time they start their education throughout their studies we are able to gain insight into the motives and concerns that guide student choice as well as some of the transformations that take place in the course of their educational programme.

The nurse students we followed, fifteen in number, were all from Oslo University College.[2] Each student was interviewed three times. The first interview was conducted in the fall semester of the year 2000, only a few weeks after semester start. The second interview took place in fall of the year 2001 and the third in the spring of 2003. The interviews lasted on average an hour and a half and were all audio-recorded. The analysis was conducted by way of a three-step procedure. First we analysed each interview separately. The aim of this initial analysis was to identify patterns related to three themes: What characterizes the motives, desires and values the students hold? Is there a tension between students on the one hand and the school on the other? In the second step we focused on the group as a whole, and identified patterns typical for different phases of their educational study. What motive types and tensions were typical for students in their first, second and third year of college? As a third and final step, we describe patterns of transformation and change, both at the level of the individual and of the group.

In this article we focus on group patterns rather than individual learning trajectories. We start by presenting data from the first interview and the student's initial motives and desires. We thereafter combine data from the second and third interview and focus on the issue of change.

Initial motives and concerns

The narratives point to a variety of motives and motive types. Rather than form a pure and consistent motivational pattern, the narratives suggest a move towards unorthodox combinations where different motive types appear in new and interesting combinations. Among the factors virtually all of the students underline as important are issues related to job security and to securing a balanced life with time for family and friends. Nursing has an advantage over other occupations in the sense that it can easily be adapted to other activities and play a major or minor role in life depending on circumstances. As Elisabeth expresses it: 'If you want for example to stay home with your kids or something, you can either work shifts, part-time, or not at all for a while. It doesn't matter – you are guaranteed a job anyway.' In addition to the value students place on flexibility and security, it is interesting to note the importance they attach to travel and to the transferability of credentials. Tina wants to go to Africa while Christian wants to join the Red Cross or the army, anything that enables him to move around for a period. Like most of the students they value the opportunity nursing provides to obtain jobs in other countries, to be flexible and feel free. As Linn expresses it: 'Nothing can stop me from going to Australia for a year, if I want to.'

---

[2] The project includes 63 students from four different occupational groups, all working within the field of health care: nurses, physiotherapists, social workers and child welfare personnel. This article reports data strictly from the interviews with 15 nurse students, ten female and five male students.

In addition to being guided by practical and material concerns the narratives suggest a strive for a deeper meaning. The qualities students seek are related to personal development and the quest for work, which they find meaningful and engaging. Though some are more dominant than others one can see traces of all the three orientation forms described by Ziehe in our material.

Intimacy and closeness

The opportunity to work in close contact with other people attracts the students. Almost all the narratives contain statements related to the value of personal contact and relationships. What kind of relations the students seek varies. Some students want to work with people more or less because they want to avoid being alone. Lars is one of them: 'I prefer being with people all the time. I don't like it when I am alone too much,' he says. Others, like Toril, are in search of somebody to talk to: 'I'm really a chatterbox, so nursing is just perfect for me,' she says. Other students are more demanding in their quests. What they seek are more authentic forms of intimacy. What attracts them is the possibility the profession provides to 'get really close to people...to enter into the souls and hearts of others.' Anna illustrates this when she compares the advantages nursing has to other jobs she has had: 'You also meet people if you sit in the checkout counter in a shop, but as a nurse you get a much deeper and closer contact.' Elisabeth goes even further in her expectations. She wants to become friends with her patients and to gain their full confidence and trust: 'I want us to be good friends and that they may perhaps open their hearts for me, that they trust me and talk to me about everything.' In addition to providing a unique possibility to get to know others, intimate and close relationships are viewed as a source of self-knowledge: 'What's exciting about working with people, Tina says, is that as an individual I can learn from their experiences... By meeting other people and watching them develop, you learn something about yourself.' Getting close to other people's inner life is considered a way in which to gain insight into the otherwise concealed and hidden labyrinths of both one's self and life in general.

Ontological modes of orientation

The material indicates that very few students show allegiance to metaphysical meaning systems in any sense or form. On the contrary the narratives suggest a resistance among students towards being associated with motives of this type. This holds particularly true for motives suggesting nursing as a calling. David is among these: 'The very concept of calling makes me freeze,' he says. 'It's old fashioned.' Christian is another example: 'I may have an inner drive, sort of... to help people, but I don't feel a calling. Not like that you read and hear about in history. I don't feel that at all.' The resistance they show goes however beyond the notion of nursing as a calling. Viewed as a whole the narratives indicate a reluctance towards anything that indicates the choice as one-sided and selfless: 'It's not just idealism,'

Tina says. 'You never do anything without getting something in return.' Anna also reacts to what she calls 'the myth of the idealistic nurse striving to save the world… It's no more honourable to be a nurse than to be anything else.'

Rather than depict their choice of study as a result of their religious beliefs or any other form of patterned expectation for that matter, several of the narratives convey a tone of destiny. In order to understand the mechanism at work here, one must understand the role more psychological modes of understanding play in the students' descriptions. In an attempt to describe their choice the students often refer to traits in their personality or what they portray as psychological determinants. Remarks typical for the students are: 'It is kind of me … I don't know, but I think it fits with me in a sense; I have an inner drive, sort of … to help people; it just seems natural for me.'

Though this mode of thought deviates in many ways from the notion of a calling, it conveys a tone of necessity and destiny that resembles that expressed by Luther in his famous statement 'Here I stand: I can no other'. Rather than being called by God, however, the students are called by themselves, metaphorically speaking, and their search for a life true to what they experience as their true being. Though the case of Tina is a somewhat extreme, it illustrates what is meant here. Tina describes her choice as a matter of course, and as something she simply had to do: 'Though I have frequently wanted to want something else… it's the only thing I ever could and really wanted to do. It's just me, I guess.' In her description she depicts her path as mapped out from early childhood: 'I've realised it since I was a little girl. It's simply a part of the care I have inside me.'

Lars also turns to his past for an explanation. In his narrative he points to the fact that he is raised in a Christian home. Though he himself feels free from the bonds of religion – the values of care, he maintains, have been subtly transmitted to him by his parents and grand parents. As he expresses it: 'Because I always have felt close to and respected my family, their values have in many ways also become mine [...] making nursing a rather natural choice for me.' In contrast, however, to many other truth and certainty-seeking movements this mode of thought does not portray the future as given. On the contrary, it portrays everything, even the past as capable of reconstruction and susceptible to change, dependent on a person's will and the capacity for self-reflection and a constant self-probing in the dynamics of both the past and the present.

Aestetization and fictionalization

According to the students one of the greater challenges in life is to avoid boredom. Anything is better than 'having to sit day after day behind a desk'. Although the students recognise, that nursing also may have its dreary moments, it is not, as Linn expresses it, 'all routine at least'. Beyond this, several of the students describe an action-oriented motive. What they look forward to are the more particular, exciting and thrilling moments they expect to experience in nursing. What attracts them is drama and action, and seeing what they, as individuals, can endure. The trend to seek meaning through intensity and excitement corresponds to what Ziehes terms as 'aestetization' and 'fictionalization'. Two examples may serve to illustrate what is meant by this. What attracts Linn is the thought of emergency situations, the ability to act, or rather perform with decisiveness and skill, to stay cool and keep calm: in short, to be master of the situation. She is trapped by the excitement when everything has to happen very fast. The urgency and pressure in critical moments like those she has seen on TV where it's a matter of life and death, fascinates her. Surgery, wounds and blood attract her too: 'Everything that has to do with cutting, stitching and things like that, I find it very exciting'.

Christian is also drawn by the intensity he expects to experience in nursing. In his leisure time he is interested in outdoor activities and loves extreme challenges like rock climbing and rafting. Although he wants to work with people and be active and useful, he also visualizes possibilities to pursue his hobby even into his working life: 'Imagine dangling on a rope under a Sea King helicopter, rescuing someone injured from a rock face!'

Linn and Christian picture future job-scenes, allowing themselves more or less central positions in the event. Christian projects dramatic situations featuring himself as the hero; Linn's position is more inclined to place the doctor in the position of the hero. Although she is not the hero she portrays herself as important. In order to secure this role she plans to study hard: 'I intend to have enough knowledge to know what the doctors are talking about. I won't let them push me aside.'

As indicated, many of the students describe rather illusory fiction images of nursing. The narratives indicate that these, at least for the time being, serve an important function as a source of motivation and energy. An example of the motivational impact these rather unreal pictures have may be found among the many visions of life as a midwife: The mere thought of babies is enough to excite June: 'Oh, I just love babies, they are so cute', she says. 'Imagine going day in and day out surrounded by all those beautiful tiny wonders. It's my dream!' Giving injections, stitching, blood and so forth, are also parts of being a midwife, but are aspects to which she has given little thought. All this she finds awful and are aspects she has pushed to the back of her mind. For the time being, however, she's enjoying living in the illusion of an occupation full of sweet smells, cute babies and joy. Why worry, when 'you don't even know where you will end'.

In summary, the data from the initial interviews confirm the descriptions provided by social researchers of today's youth. Rather than relate their choice of study to the desire to help others, the students underline ways in which nursing can contribute to their own plans, desires and needs. This development is as pointed out ambivalent. It has an energizing effect on the students, inducing them to take their studies seriously. Irrespective of whether one wants to save lives, care for babies. or to explore the inner depths of the self, hard work is required. It also contributes to a positive vision for the future and an ability to resist the denigrating effect the massive negative rhetoric surrounding work of this type might otherwise project. The students know what they want and need, and accept that others may have different preferences and views. In occupations plagued by high burn-out rates and emotional drain, these qualities may prove to be an important resource. They may help the students to maintain the 'spunk' necessary not only to survive, but to set goals, to achieve, and even enjoy their work. As pointed out by moral theorists however, the moral worth of expressive and self-related motives is contingent upon the capacity we, as individuals, have to extend our sensitivity towards our own needs and desires, towards the needs and desires of others (Bauman 1997, Taylor 1994). This requires a language rich in qualitative distinction – a language, which enables us to distinguish between what is important rather than trivial, admirable rather than base, worthwhile rather than superficial, good rather than bad. The narratives provided by the students in the early phases of their education indicate that such a language is wanting. Superficial expressions such as 'I like', 'I want', 'I think it's fun', or 'I can't stand', and so forth often serve as the only reasons they give. A brief look at the way in which the students discuss the prospect of working within the field of elderly care exemplifies the problems that flow from the lack of a more self-reflective vocabulary. Many of the students express reluctance towards working with elderly persons. Their reluctance applies in particular to work within homes for elderly. Though many mention the need for innovation and revitalization within this field, it is on the bottom of most priority lists. Although there may be good arguments for this the students do not offer any. With a mere shrug of the shoulder they dismiss this line of work with phrases like: 'It just doesn't appeal to me'; 'I don't have enough patience for that'; 'To me it sounds far too boring'; 'If you end up there you stop developing, you loose momentum and become side-stepped'. A brief glance at the students' narratives towards the end of their education indicates what is being done within an educational framework to develop a language that is reflected in a wider set of concerns.

Transformation and change

The results of the study indicate that towards the end of their education the students are still highly motivated for work within the field of nursing. Though many admit to having found parts of the curriculum boring and poorly organized, none of the students report regretting their choice of study. Rather than reveal signs of resignation and discouragement, the stories they tell and the descriptions they give of their educational experience are, for the most part, positive. This holds particularly true for experiences related to the moral dimension of nursing.

According to the students, the ethos of care is reflected at all levels of their educational programme: in the lectures held, in the practical assignments they are given, as well as in frequent discussions they have with their teachers. Rather than alienate the students however, the rhetoric and ideology characteristic of this mode of thought has contributed to a stronger sense of occupational pride and social purpose. They have become more orientated towards the needs and concerns of others and reflexively aware of the moral responsibility being a nurse involves. Many of the narratives contain descriptions of normative and personal change. In an attempt to describe the shift in orientation they experience, the students often employ concepts they have learned in school: Tina describes herself as 'more focused on showing respect for the individual', and 'more concerned to gain the patients trust'; Toril as 'more caring and emphatic'; Christine describes herself as more 'humble and tolerant' as well as 'more concerned with the moral values she expresses through her behaviour'; Linn has learned 'to approach people with sensitivity and respect', and David has become 'a better listener'. Though it is difficult to access how deep-rooted the changes actually are, the narratives indicate the development of a richer language used to express themselves. Examples of concepts that are employed with ease by the students are care, empathy, trust, respect, compassion and moral responsibility.

The narratives also indicate an increase in reflective awareness among the students and a sharper focus on issues related to care. Some cases illustrate this. While working in a nursing home for dementia patients, Elisabeth experienced several episodes where, in her view, patients were ridiculed and treated with lack of respect. After summing up her experiences, she explains: 'These are things we notice'. Christian confirms the importance that the development of a language of care has been not only for him, but for all the students. 'I think', he says, 'we all have developed a more critical eye...We have become, he says, quick to pick up on people who do not show empathy and respect.'

The narratives also contain examples of an increased capacity for 'strong evaluation'. Though the case of Kaja is particular it serves to illustrate this point. In her first interview she admits to being prejudiced towards persons with a different racial background to her own. She notices that being around them annoys her and that she has little patience with their problems. Through discussions with others as well as through literature offered in school she had become conscious of the need to curb her spontaneous emotions and inclinations. It is absolutely wrong for her as a nurse, she says, to treat patients with prejudice. Her opinion as a private person is one thing, she says, but her professional role demands that all patients are treated with openness and trust. Though she admits that it is not easy for her to change on this point she sees it as her responsibility to do so.

For many of the students the shift in orientation has come partly as a surprise. They have changed more than they expected. To begin with, Linn explains, she didn't notice any difference. Though she read a lot and was active in other ways, she experienced a gap between what was taught and what she herself felt. Gradually and almost unnoticeably she started to change. Things looked and felt different than before. 'It's not that I have become an idealist, nor that I go around thinking of how important it is to give a lot and be compassionate. ... It has just sneaked itself in on me and become part of who I am and what I do.'

Old concepts – new meanings

In a manner similar to Linn many of the students describe the shift in foci they have experienced as effected by way of small, barely perceptible steps. According to their account the initial gap between the norms and values they themselves held, and those professed as important by the profession, was quickly filled, paving the way for a learning process virtually void of conflict and tension. In general the descriptions the students give of their learning process suggests a rather passive submission to the moral order of the profession. The frequent use of handed-down concepts, word forms and phrases supports the assumption of a quick and quiet adaptation to the ideals of care. As pointed out by cultural theorists however, even when people act in traditional ways they might think in new ways (Cohen and Taylor 1992, Fornäs 1995). 'A culturally modernised self-image can hide behind conventional social actions or the other way around' (Fornäs 1995). In today's society resistance may take on many forms, from the manifest opposition of well organised movements to more subtle forms of cultural reinterpretation and resistance (Fornäs 1995, Ziehe 1991). In situations characterized by conflicting interests and concerns more partial forms of cultural release may be sought. By cancelling out the meaning of old concepts and infusing them with new meaning, a culture may be radically revitalized without even a ripple on the surface. A more in-depth analysis of the narratives suggests that this may be the case here. Two elements single themselves out as zones of difference in opinion. The first refers to the role of the self in nursing while the second relates to the theme of moral responsibility.

The role of the self in nursing

As indicated above current theories of care depict nursing as largely other regarding nature, and down-play the moral worth of self-interest and concern. The narratives indicate that this is not an image the students share. The more experience the students gain, the firmer their resistance towards models which portray nursing as a one-sided affair. The concept of care they opt for is more inclusive and underlines the moral worth of self-related motives and concerns. Among the students most eager to argue the need for a more inclusive concept of care is Elisabeth. In her experience, caring for the self has nothing to do with egoism, neither does it stand in contrast to caring for others. It is, she argues, an integral part of caring for 'the other'. In an attempt to explain her position she compares nursing with another activity in which she is involved – blood donation. In contrast to blood donation, which can be done without paying attention to the self, nursing requires a presence and an ability to preserve the openness necessary to treat each and every patient as a unique person. In order to ensure such a quality, particularly over time, it is, she maintains, important to know who you are and where your limits go. 'If you don't learn these things', she says, 'you will burn out and no longer be of use to anyone'. Christine supports her claim.

> If you experience helping others as something you do solely for others ... everyday life as a nurse will become unbearable. There has to be something you feel you can develop within, something that interests you. But if self-interest is all there is to it that would be unbearable as well. In order to survive and thrive, she says, you have to combine the two concerns – get them to pull in the same direction.

In her experience, however, achieving this requires a mellowing of interests and concerns.

> To begin with, she says, my motivation was more of a practical nature. It just fitted my life in a way...but in the course of time things changed... I experienced what a rich and exciting experience being to use for others can be.

Anna's account reflects a similar development. She describes helping others as 'personally satisfying' and as something that gives not only her work, but life in general 'a new dimension'.

Though the manner in which the students envisage the balance between self and other varies, the narratives clearly indicate an interpretation of care which deviates from current models of care. Rather than view concern for the self as immoral – something selfish, narcissistic and an escape from rules, they depict care for the self and care for the other as two sides of the same coin. By infusing the concept of care with a new and more inclusive meaning the ideal of care is no longer perceived as foreign but rather as something the students feel that they can 'develop within' as Christine expresses it.

Moral responsibility

The other point of tension we identify centres around the theme of moral responsibility. Though the students do not discuss questions related to moral responsibility explicitly, the narratives indicate that this is a theme, which concerns them. During their training the students have developed a stronger feeling for the responsibility nursing implies. 'I wasn't aware, Elisabeth says, of how much responsibility being a nurse involves. It's not that it matters or anything. It's just that it requires more commitment than I expected.'

The students' response to this is ambivalent. They feel challenged but also hesitant and alarmed. What alarms them the most is standing alone with responsibilities, which are too heavy to carry. Models, which portray their responsibility as unconditional and limitless, are at risk of adding to the burden.

This point is clearly illustrated in the students' reflections regarding their future occupational choice. As pointed out in the first interview the students are generally reluctant to work in homes for the elderly. Though the reasons they give have become more self-reflective and elaborate in the course of their study, the narratives indicate that this a position in which they stand even firmer than before. Among the factors that contribute to the reluctance to work within this field is the fear of being landed in a situation where they are made personally responsible for factors, which they experience as being beyond their control. The case of Elisabeth illustrates what is meant here. '(...) It might, she says, be wrong of me not to take it as a challenge...but the standard in nursing homes is far beyond dignity: everything is old and worn out; there is no money, no resources, nothing (...) This makes me reluctant to work there despite the constant reminder we get in school of our duty as nurses to give priority to underprivileged groups in society. Elisabeth supports her claim of nursing homes as desperate sites: The halls in nursing homes, she says, are dark, dreary and smell of urine (...) beyond anything I would consider working within.'

Like all professionals nurses are exposed to special demands. In virtue of their role they are made responsible not only for one unique Other, but a multitude of unique Others. Although they may have both the expertise and will to solve the problems at hand, they are often exposed to situations where there simply is not enough to go around. Situations like this give rise to a series of questions. What direction should their responsibility take? Who, in the midst of need is the most needy? It also becomes pressing to allocate their time and effort efficiently. Should they give priority to patient contact, or should they work to improve the conditions that surround them? What role should they play in the larger world of economy and politics? Where do the limits for their responsibility as individuals and as nurses go? When it comes to addressing problems like these however, current models fall short. They depict a moral landscape which stretches between the I and the Other. Within this narrow and tightly circumscribed space there is, as Bauman (1997) criticises, room for only two actors. There is no room for social institutions, roles or even other persons. As the narratives point out, however, this is too narrow a space as far as professional work goes. The infinity of moral responsibility, the unbounded moral demands simply cannot be sustained within economically and socially deprived systems. In order to enlighten the problems that confront the field of health care today it is not sufficient to focus on relational issues alone. What is needed are models that go beyond the nurse/patient dyad and draw attention to those factors which facilitate, and those which hamper, the chances of taking up the responsibility health care implies.

A strategy for transformation and renewal

The concept of care, and the ideals and images it projects, constitutes a core within the nursing profession. It contributes to binding members of the profession together and to enhance a sense of social purpose and occupational pride. But there is a reverse side to the coin. The ideals of care also contribute to a certain rigidity within the profession and to an image of nursing as isolated from new impulses, trends and culturally modernized visions of what constitutes a good life. The students' response to this dilemma suggests a way out of this situation. The strategy they employ represents a compromise solution between two contradictory needs: the need to belong and preserve, and the need to renew and expand. Nursing offers a language rich in normative distinction. By using this language the students mark their loyalty and commitment to the profession while simultaneously gaining access to a tool, which helps them to navigate more efficiently within the field. Although it is, of course, difficult to measure the power of this new language, the results from our study suggest that the language of care has been 'internally persuasive' as well as externally effective. It has affected the way the students think and feel about their work. The results, however, point to areas in which the models are insufficient. Rather than form a subculture, and attempt to rejuvenate outside the frame of current culture, the students employ what Ziehe (1993) terms as a 'more fluid strategy'. By widening and transforming the meaning of core concepts within the profession in a direction more congenial to the spirit of the times, they revitalize the culture of nursing in important ways. Though not all their attempts of renewal can be immediately applauded or subscribed to without reducing the field of nursing to a playground for experimentation, the dilemmas the students point to and the solutions they suggest should motivate thought.

As pointed out by Ziehe it is possible to react to modernity in two ways. One is to continue as before and pretend nothing has happened. Another is to affirm at least some aspects of modernity and test its creative possibilities. The students have employed the latter strategy. The profession as a whole would be well advised to do the same.

References

Abrahamson, P.R. and Ingelhart, R. (1995): *Value change in global perspective*. Anne Arbour: The University of Michigan Press.

Bauman, Z. (1997): 'Morality begins at home – or: Can there be a Levinasian Macro-Ethics?', in: Jodalen H. and Vetlesen, A.J. (eds.): *Closness. An ethics*. Oslo: Scandinavian University Press.

Becher, T. (1994): 'The significance of disciplinary differences', in: *Studies in Higher Education*, 19 (2): 333-346.

Bell, D. (1992): 'Modernism, postmodernism, and the decline of moral order', in: Alexander, J. and Seidman, S. (eds.): *Culture and society*. Cambridge: Cambridge University Press.

Biglan, A. (1973): 'The characteristics of subject matter in different academic areas', in: *Journal of Applied Psykology*, 57 (2): 195-203.

Bruner, J. (1987): 'Life as narrative', in: *Social research*, 54 (1): 11-32.

Cohen, S. and Taylor, L. (1992): *Escape attempts: the theory and practice of resistance in everyday life*. London: Routledge.

Econ-rapport 49/99: 'Kostnader ved sykepleiemangelen'. ECON – Senter for økonomisk analyse.

Fornäs, J. (1995): *Cultural theory and late modernity*. London: Sage.

General plan and regulations for 3-year training programme in nursing. (2000) Ministry of Education, Research and Church Affairs.

Gullestad, M. (1996): *Everyday life philosophers: modernity, morality, and autobiography in Norway*. Oslo: Scandinavian University Press.

Hagen, K. (2000): 'Sosialdemokrati 2000. Tema: Velferdspolitikk', in: *Arbeiderpartiets Programdebatt*. Oslo: Det norske arbeiderparti.

Harré, R. (1983): *Personal Being*. Oxford: Basil Blackwell.

Hellevik, O. (1996): *Nordmenn og det gode liv. Norsk Monitor 1985-95*. Oslo: Universitetsforlaget.

Karseth, B. (2002): 'Desire to do good – an educational ethos?' Paper presented at the 30th Congress of Nordic Educational Research Association (NERA) in Tallinn, Estonia.

Knorr Cetina, K. (1997): 'Sociality with Objects', in: *Theory, Culture & Society*, 14 (4): 1-30.

Lasch, C. (1979): *The culture of narcissism: American life in an age of diminishing expectations*. New York: Warner Books.

Levinas, E. (1991): *Totality and Infinity*. Dordrecht: Klüwer.

Løgstrup, K.E. (1969): *Den etiske fordring*. Copenhagen: Gyldendal.

Martinsen, K. (1984): *Freidige og uforsagte diakonisser. Et omsorgsyrke vokser fram 1860 – 1905*. Oslo: Aschehoug/Tanum – Nordli.

Martinsen, K. (1993): *Fra Marx til Løgstrup: om etikk og sanselighet i sykepleien*. Oslo: Tano.

Martinsen, K. (2000): *Øyet og kallet*. Oslo: Fagbokforlaget.

National Application Statistics (Samordna opptak) 1996-2003. Ministry of education and research – statistics: University of Oslo.

Nordtvedt, P. (2001): 'Profesjonell omsorg – dyd eller ferdighet?', in: Ruyter, K.W. and Vetlesen A.J. (eds): *Omsorgens tvetydighet*. Oslo: Gyldendal akademisk.

Nåden, D. and Eriksson, K. (2000): 'The phenomenon of confirmation: An aspect of nursing as an art', in: *International Journal for human caring*, 4 (3) pp23-28.

Nåden, D. and Eriksson, K. (2002): 'Encounter: A fundamental category of nursing as an art', in: *International Journal for human caring* 6 (1) pp34-40.

Polkinghorne, D. (1996): 'Narrative knowing and the study of lives', in: Birren J.E., Kenyon G.M., Ruth J.E., Schroots J.J.F. and Svensson T. (eds.): *Aging and biography. Explorations in Adult Development*. New York: Springer.

Sennett, R. (1977): *The fall of public man*. New York: Knopf.

Shusterman, R. (1988): 'Postmodernist Aestheticism: A New Moral Philosophy?', in: *Theory, Culture & Society*, 5, pp337-355.

Statistics for Norwegian Nurses Association (1999): Norsk Sykepleierforbunds medlems-undersøkelse. Norwegian Gallup Institute A/S.

Taylor, C. (1994): *Sources of the self. The making of modern identity*. Cambridge: Cambridge University Press.

Vetlesen, A.J. (1997): 'Is Man a moral being', in: Jodalen H. and Vetlesen, A.J. (eds.): *Closness. An ethics*. Oslo: Scandinavian University Press.

Ylijoki, O.H. (2000): 'Disiplinary cultures and the moral order of studying – A case-study of four Finnish university departments', in: *Higher education*, 39, pp339-362.

Ziehe, T. (1989): *Ambivalenser og mangfoldighed. Tekster om ungdom, skole, æstetik og kultur*. Copenhagen: Politisk Revy.

Ziehe, T. (1993): *Kulturanalyser: ungdom, utbildning, modernitet*. Stockholm/Stehag: Brutus Östlings Bokförlag Symposion.

Ziehe, T. (2000): 'School and youth – a different relation', in: *YOUNG – Nordic Journal of Youth Research*, 8 (1) pp54-63.

Chapter 11

Learning through the Body in Danish Nursing Education

Kristian Larsen

Introduction

Every day professional work is carried out in workplaces (e.g. in hospitals) around the world, and simultaneously, knowledge is transferred from experienced persons in the work contexts to those who have yet to gain knowledge. While student nurses in practical training have unique and specific experiences, they share similar characteristics with other professional groups associated with the hospital system as well as outside of it. From a research perspective practical or workplace training is not well developed nationally or internationally, a fact that can be explained historically, socially and technically. Admittedly, it is a complex task to define who and what is entailed in the learning process and just what happens in the span between the poles of consciousness and body, theory and practical knowledge, thought and action. These two poles will be discussed by radicalizing Dreyfus (conventional model) and Bourdieu (alternative model).

The first model is the dominant and often implicit theory of education (later called the doxa about education) in the Western world. It involves institutions such as universities and schools, fields of practice/workplaces and agents relevant in an educational context, such as teachers and students. The knowledge transmitted between the agents is experienced as verbally transmitted. In this chapter I will, however, try to present another and to some degree provoking, alternative model. It provides opposite perspectives on who or what the teacher (also) is. I will also introduce alternative perspectives on the kind of knowledge and how it may be transmitted. My focus will be on presenting a number of findings of empirical research based on educational theory. There will only to a limited degree be discussion related to other research on the area or to theory or methodology.

However, I will start by briefly presenting some studies on Nursing and learning within Nursing. This area is dominated by research that shares many characteristics with the model, here called the conventional model. Then Aims, methods and data from the empirical study are presented, including a brief introduction to Nursing education in Denmark. The last part of the chapter presents findings in the research including some reflections about consequences and future perspectives.

Table 11.1
Two models for learning within nursing

Central in the study of practical training/ learning in practice	Conventional model Model inspired by Dreyfus (1986)	Alternative model Model developed as part of the study and inspired by Bourdieu (1977)
Theoretic status and relationships between theory and practice	Theory developed by researchers *for* practitioners (normative theory) Theory and practice as a continuum	Theory developed by researchers *about* practice (descriptive theory) Theory established by breaking with the spontaneous experience
Central to research	The baseline is the profession's, the educational programme's and the agent's construction Primary data sources are experiences of key persons, i.e. masters, doctors, nurses and students, collected through interviews The subject, consciousness, reflection and the experienced reality are central Training is seen as a deficit in relation to the educational objective	The researcher's theorectical construction of the object Primary data sources are the dynamics between persons and things seen (observation) in relation to each other The context (relations to things and persons), the materialised practice and relationships are central Training is seen as adequate in the field

Studies on nursing and learning within nursing

Inspired by Schön's (1983, 1987) studies of reflection and especially Carr and Kemmis' (1986) studies of critical theory, Cox et al. (1991), Ghaye and Lillyman (2000), Thompson (1987), Street (1990) and Newton (2000) have shown how nursing is part of a (male) medical system including a certain technical rationality. They focus on the possibilities for and the limitations to reflection as dimensions of developing nursing and nurses, including nursing education, within this system. Street (1990) says oppression is embodied and as it is non-conscious, it cannot necessarily be reached through a process of reflection. Colliere (1986) and Hickson (1990) point out that the dominant idealistic theories in nursing fail to see nursing in its institutional, political and economic context and Melia (1987) describes how the de-contextualized theories unintentionally serve to reinforce an oppression of nursing and nurses.

Focusing on the development of competencies inspired by Dreyfus et al. (1986), Benner (1984) has identified five steps from novice to expert in nursing. In Scandinavia an approach has been developed which builds on and explores the limits of Dreyfus (1986), as well as Lave and Wenger (1991). Nielsen and Kvale (1997), for example, make an appeal for empirical studies in the area of practice in terms of social practice and apprenticeship, and also point to a need for the development of theory. Phenomenology and anthropology are drawn upon in the study and lead to a critique of the dominant scholastic perspective on teaching and learning. However, the issue of whether apprenticeship is or can be a new dogmatic solution to problems in education is also discussed.

Drawing mainly on representations of agents (in interviews, diaries and questionnaires etc.) and on nurses' construction of nursing, (nursing is about taking care of the whole patient) the Scandinavian scholars Löfmark and Thorell-Ekstrand (2000), Löfmark and Wikblad (2001), Ax and Kincade (2001) have shown how student nurses experience lack of continuity in supervision, lack of feedback from nurses as well as lack of practical experience. Bjørk (1999) found that nurses did not develop the practical skills that they were supposed to. From a similar construction, Pilhammar Andersson (1993) finds that student nurses do not develop the 'right views' according to the official criterions in nursing. Lindberg-Sand (1996) and Lindgren (1993) have in different ways shown how individual acting and thinking in institutional and hierarchical systems is to a high degree structured or limited by social, institutional or medical power relations. In particular women, according to Franssén (1997), are affected by their orientation towards family. Inspired by Bourdieu, Jensen (1992) points out that the power relations are also embodied and individual. Based mainly on observations in classrooms, Rask Eriksen (1992) shows how the social dispositions of student nurses are destructed during education, and with inspiration from Lave and Wenger (1991), Heggen (1995) focuses on social dynamics within hospitals and among student nurses, including the need for students to be part of a team as a precondition for experiencing situations that facilitate learning.

As demonstrated the area is involving a broad range of paradigms, but it is dominated by research that focuses on nurses or ideological constructions of nursing and learning. The predominant research is very similar to the paradigm, here called the conventional model. From that perspective nursing is seen as substance, as an object for research 'in itself', and practice training is seen as a 'deficit' related to fulfilling or implementing the goals of education. Research that is based on experiences of key persons, collected through interviews, only accounts for what should have happened or have been said by the nurse or the student. Practice serves the function of being the institutional place (physically different from the school), where students apply theory, while reflecting; and the time is seen as part of the progression in the students' education (first the students learn about normative theories, then they learn how to implement theory). At the same time, nurses and students are designated as *the* actors and critical, problem-oriented or reflective conversation is seen as *the* way of learning.

Descriptive analyses based on objectifying observation of practical training on the basis of theory encompassing de-learning and a variety of possible teachers and teaching are to a large degree absent in research. There is likewise a lack of research focusing on the performance of actions, i.e. manifested training that sees (observation) these actions as necessary (Bourdieu, 1999) in relation to the socially constituted position of actual people (agents with certain habitus (dispositions)) in the institution in the medical field. From this perspective the researcher should think in principle, 'that could be me'. That does not imply romanticising training or the people involved. The intention of research is first and foremost to describe or explain actions. Prior to reforming education, one must know which factors come into play and how. One cannot describe an educational programme and improve it at the same time.

Aims and methods

The article is based on parts of a PhD study, Learning in practice - known and mis-recognized perspectives (Larsen 2000). The study, which both tests hypotheses and is explorative, focuses on practice training within the 3-year nursing programme. The study, which is primarily micro oriented but which includes a macro perspective, tries to integrate qualitative and quantitative dimensions and takes the perspective of progress and comparison. The progress relates to development and performance of qualifications from the start to the end of the programme. The comparative part, which is not discussed here, relates to the possible effects of different educational planning at two nursing schools in Copenhagen, Denmark.

The study is inspired by the sociologist Pierre Bourdieu (1977, 1999, 2000) and Bourdieu and Passeron (1977), especially the outline of a theory of practice that encompasses the notion of learning through the body, primarily without being conscious of it. Bourdieu's work is also relevant in pointing out the need in research to break with spontaneous, official or professional constructions of the object and instead make a theoretic construction of the object explicit (see also Broady (1997)). Maurice Merleau Ponty (1994) and Ludwig Wittgenstein (1995), who give philosophical inspiration to the work, and Donald Schön (1983) are all represented in the work in the formulation of different ways of thinking about learning in the education of nurses. Inspiration is drawn from Schön's description of practice as unique, complex etc., and not his levels of reflection. The aim is to develop knowledge about learning within practice training, and conventional assumptions (doxa about education) are discussed. These assumptions, which are studied intensively in a reflected way by the Dreyfus brothers (1986) and Patricia Benner (1984), consider practice training as an application of theory. One might say that practice is viewed as a practiced idea and theory, legitimized by its degree of applicability in practice by practitioners. According to this view, there is a straight line from the practitioners' practical practice to knowledge (rules) in the domain of science (Callewaert 1999). The conventional assumptions bring a cognitive element and accumulation of knowledge into focus for each individual and transmission of knowledge is primarily explained to be verbal. That position as mentioned previously; also looks upon learning, as an activity between legitimate agents, i.e. teachers/mentors (the nurses) and the receivers (the students) of knowledge. These explicit and implicit assumptions are discussed in this study.

Based upon studies of literature, personal and other researchers' empirical work, nursing is constructed as an activity primarily aimed at the administration of medical treatment activity in a medical field inspired by Petersen (1998) and Heyman (1995). Direct, non-participating, objectifying relational observation of specific chosen nursing activities is used in the following areas of focus:

- The students' relations and participation in administrative functions.
- The students' relations to patients experiencing pain and crises.
- The students' relations to technical tools and measuring instruments.

The research questions are:

What kind of knowledge does the student use when she is nursing and from whom or what does she get the knowledge: (who or what is the teacher)?

In this work relational observation is elaborated as criticism of implicit substantialistic observation. It implies that the genesis of practice of the student is seen as part of or integrated in the physical localities (the architecture of the hospitals – the medicine rooms, offices, corridors and wards) and integrated in artefacts and tools (i.e. medicaments, sphygmomanometers, food and bedside tables). The genesis of practice of the students are also seen and explained as integrated in relation to at least 25 other agents such as doctors, nurses, other students, patients etc. When a student is observed, other actions and verbal remarks from many other agents are registered at the same time. The study is inspired by Bourdieu's way of working but adapted especially to the present object of research.

Data

The questions are answered through observations and interviews of nursing students at different stages of their practice training. Eight students in particular have been observed during their practice training for approximately 80 days during a period of eight months on medical and surgical gastrointestinal wards at two Copenhagen hospitals. The observations lasted four to five hours followed by 1-1½ hours of interview concerning specific parts of the focused areas. The observations included quantitative registration of time and activity. The researcher (the author) wore a uniform and followed the students in the hospital. Most parts of the verbal communication and the sounds between and around the agents 'in action' were taped and then transcribed.

The study also includes data from the students' evaluation talks with the nurses and those responsible for the education programme, as well as observation in classrooms and demonstration training, clinical verbal teaching, transcriptions from the students' diaries, documents from the programme with descriptions of purpose, administrative documents etc. The following is an outline of the principles used in the study, the so-called *alternative* model, which is differentiated here from the *conventional* model.

A brief introduction to nursing education in Denmark

Nursing education in Denmark is state-financed and students receive a nominal allowance during the course of their studies. Most students have completed primary and secondary school (a total of 13 years of formal education) prior to starting the nursing programme, and are on average 23-24 years of age. Often, they have gained some experience through work in social or health sectors (e.g. in homes for elderly people, child day care institutions).

Nursing is a three-year educational programme comprising 55% theory at a nursing school and 45% practical (clinical) training mainly in a hospital setting. However, a small proportion of students do their training in the primary care sector (e.g. home care services). The theoretical (school) part of the programme has a duration of 6-18 months and is followed by a clinical training period of five to eight months.

When interviewed in the middle of their education, the student nurses experienced that in 90% of their references, the source of their knowledge originated from formal principal teachers (Larsen 1994), e.g. teachers of nursing education (32%), nurses (42%) and textbooks (16%).

Findings

Acting in defiance

The students feel and are looked upon as novices on the hospital wards, but in objectifying observations they seem knowledgeable and pre-adapted and are able to function in the medical field. Despite their lack of theory and mentors, and their limited general view and compulsion to act, the students generally succeed in intervening with adequate practices. They do not seem to remain passive despite their lack of theory etc. It is the conventional view that the students try to implement theory, but on a basic unconscious level they seem more oriented towards trying to *avoid making mistakes*. In other words, the students seem oriented towards a precautionary principle: They would rather avoid intervening than intervene in an unfamiliar situation.

As a dimension of the students' disposition for acting, in many situations it seems as if the students are not given the opportunity to nurse rather than they cannot nurse. This may be the case if there is a patient who is in pain and in crisis and who has a close relation with a nurse. In such a situation the student is not in control, she is excluded and physically closed, insecure etc.

Figure 11.1

Nurse, patient and student in relations of crisis

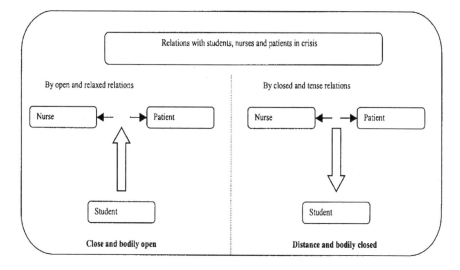

According to the educational system, the new nursing students who have not studied psychological crisis theories and who are in their first clinical training period cannot handle interaction with seriously ill patients or those patients suffering from pain who are in a crisis situation. During interviews on the topic, the new students express these same beliefs. However, when the nurses are not present in a patient's room, the students nevertheless master the situation in an adequate way, attending to and interacting with the patient.

The nurse, the patient and herself force the student to the periphery of the social surroundings. She knows, for example, that she is supposed to follow the events at a distance. From a sociological point of view, it is the nurse who plays the active role in taking care of the situation. The professional dynamic at a micro level means that the student, although she is perfectly capable of doing so, does not get a chance to hold the patient's hand. The hierarchical relations among the personnel are constitutive for the learning process. The opportunity to act is defined according to whether the hierarchy is present physically. When the nurse is present she is 'in charge'; when she is not present, the position is given to and taken on by the student. Nursing students compromise themselves and others as little as possible. This is seen as an unconscious and bodily strategy directed towards gathering capital (in this case knowledge relevant in the sub-field of medicine) in Bourdieu's terms. The body of the student knows how to act, basically without thinking about it, when it takes place. Slowly, however, the student is 'allowed to' act and she 'takes over'.

The analysis shows that the capacity to deal with patients who are in pain, in crisis, or in tears has to do with *social positions* in the concrete patient relation, which also has to do with the degree to which the student is *integrated* into the hospital world as part of the environment. This is in turn related to the degree to which the student and patient *know* each other. The immersed body knows how to manage. Fundamentally, this is not a cognitive issue or question; these factors are more important than the student's *level* of education in the formal nursing education system, i.e. whether she is taking part in her first, second or third clinical internship periods, whether she has received classroom instruction in crisis management, whether she has taken the subsequent school examination etc.

The point is that in the clinical setting, the student does not apply a crisis theory. It is rather intuition acquired through approximately 24 years of life experience with pain, suffering, grief, etc. on a personal level or within her close family that enables the nursing student to confront situations, including situations with suffering, crying or depressed patients. This does not mean that the students do not learn anything about crises while working in the hospital. They learn, for example, to maintain a certain professional distance to the patient's grief, so that this grief does not become their own grief.

Learning from below, from patients and other students

Especially at the beginning of their education students have very high regard for their mentors. They may say, for example, that they learn from the questions the researcher asks them, or that they learn from listening to patients etc. However, in the course of their studies, students refine their perception of their mentors. The professional (social) hierarchy grows in significance and influences the students' awareness of who are the legitimate mentors, i.e. the nurses, contact nurses, nursing teachers and doctors. From the middle to the end of their studies, a student may say: 'I have learned nothing the last couple of weeks ... my nurse has been sick and she has been on evening duty.... I have been all alone'. At the same time, observations reveal that she has been embedded in situations of learning and has acquired knowledge.

Learning through the body and in architecture

The practice is transformed (learned) through the body and is mostly non-verbal. The students are embedded in practice. The architecture of the hospital is, or can be seen as, a kind of an unpaid teacher. The division between productive and reproductive rooms of medical treatment, and between central and peripheral medical rooms are not neutral volumes. The physical room, the furniture and how it is organized as well as the smells and odours constantly communicate and point out through social agents directions for what to do in the room and the way to do it.

There is a kind of *dialogue between room and body* and back again. This is very much inspired by the work of Merleau-Ponty. For instance, the corridors act as practice rooms. Medically taboo areas (i.e. infections) can be talked about and discussed here. This is not possible in the medically, architecturally and mentally central rooms such as the office areas.

In office areas patients are manipulated in words and in the minds of nurses and students. The staff talks about patients. In this room, a heavy patient is hard work with regard to administration, whereas in patient rooms a heavy patient is physically heavy. Two students are needed to turn him around in the bed. In patient rooms, patients are physical manipulated, washed, dressed and so on. Students touch, sense, feel and smell patients. To a large degree you can see the feelings of the patient by looking at the body of the student. Few words are spoken, especially when something important takes place. It can be said that it is the architecture produced by human beings and again producing human activities that sets the tone and shapes the bodily activity and sometimes gives rise to verbal bodily activity, which eventually calls for reflection on the part of the involved persons. This is opposed to, or rather expands the ideas of Schön (1983), who sees reflection as being initiated by actions and things that surprise the agents. His analysis is more focused on a level of consciousness. The students can also be said to be in a bodily dialogue with the raw (but sensed) presence of artefacts and tools. The presence of a thermometer on a patient's bedside table is a kind of invitation to measure of temperature. The tool calls for application.

Student-nurses' activities, speaking and reflection are not determined by architecture, artefacts, tools, smells and sounds, but even when students carry out a simple task, the surroundings to some degree capture and manipulate the student.

Often, one or two nurses in each ward have been appointed to be teachers and mentors for the students and to help them integrate theory in practice, but unlike the ideology about mastership the students do not have one personified master at their disposal. Often the nurse and the student do not start work at the same time for several days. However, the students are not as alone as they perceive themselves to be. Mastership relations can be described as mutual for all agents. Students make use of and are involved in distinct mutual helping systems or back-up systems especially in peripheral medical rooms, such as corridors and wards. The help they can give each other and receive here is more related to problems in the ongoing work than to educational questions. They frequently contact and assist each other without verbal requests. Practical questions call for practical help in the ongoing daily work, and often students do not remember having asked for assistance or having received it. Students are part of a mutual back-up mastership system in which they continuously and within seconds change between a master position and a student position. Within certain frames such positions are convertible. It is evident that the students learn from many situations that can be described and documented as instructive, although they may fail to appreciate it. They misrecognize it. The concept of misrecognizing deals with the fact, for example, that certain insights or type of knowledge are no longer perceived by the agents and that 'selected forgetting' carries a social function. This is briefly developed in the following lines.

Education as part of social and cultural reproduction

The basic sociological perspective of the study is that education is not something substantial. Education and certificates are based on social differences and are active parts in re-producing such social differences. The education system contributes to a comparatively limited amount of technical knowledge, but has great social effect.

In a modern society, we all, on a pre-conscious level, know and have to believe that medical doctors 'cure' patients by using evidence-based medical knowledge. The social and the economic position of doctors in the medical field are established and produced at a distance from, and by making a distance to, paramedics and practitioners of so-called alternative medicine, who 'heal' patients on the basis of superstition, undocumented knowledge or common sense. From the relational (and power) perspective, the position of a medical doctor is constituted and continuously sustained by and in relation to other positions in the field. Being a doctor in a medical field is nothing 'in itself' (substance). It is only something (a position) because it is distinct to and different from other positions in the field (relational perspective).

Examples of misrecognized teaching situations and mentors

Other students as teachers

Student nurses may feel that they are on their own with the patients, but it becomes apparent when observing them that they are never alone. They always work closely with representatives from other (semi-) professions and not least, with other students at different levels in their education. The students often work together with one patient or they have one each in the same room. As they work the students invent an adequate practice in the situation and while doing so, they integrate on the spot and to a high degree each other and each other's knowledge. A student nurse can ask another student a question and learn from the response, without losing credit within the group of nurses. Often they tend to ask downwards (other students) rather than upwards (nurses), except when it is possible to ask nurses questions that demonstrate how much they (the students) know.

During a specific and short nursing sequence the performance of well over 22 specific tasks was observed involving a nursing auxiliary student teaching another nursing student. In the subsequent interview the nursing student says:

> Interviewer: You have been on the ward for about two hours. Do you think you have learned anything?
> Student: No, not really.
> Interviewer: No?
> Student: I don't mean that she made a lot of mistakes, or that I could not make the same mistakes ... Because you make a lot of mistakes during the day.

Interviewer: ......
Student: But I also learned from her mistakes, right?

The nursing student is instructed and taught both through the explicit and implicit pedagogics of the situation as a whole and by the nursing auxiliary student. But the students' progression in their course of studies also involves progression in the misrecognizing of certain teachers. From a theoretical and practical perspective it is an adequate analysis to say, 'I did not learn from the nursing auxiliary student'.

Patients as teachers

Another important element in the education of nurses is that the patient also teaches the student. Below, an example is presented involving a patient with Chrohn's Disease:[1]

Objectively: First of all, the patient *is* the disease: She is weakened and skinny, she often goes to the toilet etc. The disease, Chrohn's Disease, is a part of her body and soul. The body and its constitution have objectively become a pattern of physical scars on the stomach after many operations, the vestiges of a fistula on the skin from the sick intestine, and possibly a 'moon face' after adrenal cortex treatment[2] or loss of weight after several blood and protein losses and severe stomach pain. The patient as a body, as flesh, is in a certain way related to repeated hospitalizations on medical and surgical wards.

Subjectively: The patient verbally interprets her own subjective story as a variation within the generalized disease construction learned from books. The student receives this verbal story (about active and passive periods, change of medicine, food, hospitalizations etc.) through the physical and verbal contact with the patient. The patient is an open book.

Here follows a short description of a specific professional task involving the student changing a bandage on the patient's (P) left ankle. This includes bodily (materialised and verbal) communication between the student and the patient. The student did not remember or see this situation as being something she could learn from. The student (E) cuts some gauze bandage.

P: You should cut a piece gauze bandage about 15 cm long, OK?
E: Yes, ok, I'll do it. [Finds the scissors and cuts]
P: You should put two layers of Vaseline on it, remember, and then gauze swabs on it afterwards, allright?

---

[1] Chrohn's Disease is a chronic illness in the small intestine. The patients often experience diarrhoea and pain, they are tired and lose weight. The treatment is both surgical and medical.

[2] Often students refer to their knowledge about pain, pain relief and adrenal cortex treatment in statements like: I know, what a 'moon face' is, because I have read about it in a book. The student fails to appreciate that she with her own body first and foremost read the patient's body and 'moon face'.

[P constantly tells E what she should do and in what sequence. E takes some saline solution.]

P: No, not saline solution.. The others use soapy water now.

[E uses the soapy water first.]

[E removes the Vaseline by slowly rinsing the area with soapy water. While doing so, she asks the patient whether it hurts. E continues to wash the wound with the soapy water while P corrects her. E then administers, according to the patient's instructions, Vaseline, the gauze swabs and finally the tube gauze. P insists that the tube gauze is still too short. She says that E must cut a longer piece. E cuts a longer piece and puts it on, while P holds a few fingers on the gauze swabs.]

P: The others normally cut the gauze and then tie a knot so it stays in place.

[E does as directed and P is satisfied.]

Of course the medical construction, classification and logic can be learned to some extent through literature studies and can help the student to 'see' a disease. However unlike learning in the educational system and in contrast to Dreyfus' perspective, the disease is basically learned through the student's own body and the learning is more closely related to the patient than to the books. Furthermore, the patient acts like an ill person long before the disease has been diagnosed. The fact is that the patient is the disease and everything else is secondary (historical and genetic factors and what occurs during the learning process). To sum up:

The students are taught and instructed both verbally and to a high degree non-verbally and unconsciously through practical mastership, i.e. on the ward. The students learn by using the techniques or concepts that an unappreciated teacher has taught them.

The body-interaction includes an entire system of reciprocal bodily signals and ways of moving the body, facial expressions, the voice, etc. When, for example, a student helps a patient put on a hospital gown, an entire network of bodily actions is involved. The student's and the patient's bodily dialogue, including the guidance and teaching which can be said to lie in the patient's bodily actions in interaction with the student, is massive and drives forward the actual interaction between them, though this is not acknowledged in the student's consciousness of the interaction or in the context of education.

Summary

Student nurses have different social background which in terms of Bourdieu, is called different dispositions (habitus) and they perceive and act different in this field of work (sub-field of a medical field). But this chapter focuses on the dominant structures, that tend to structure and homogenize practice in the field. From this perspective it is obvious that learning in this field of work to a large extent is a social process, and only secondarily a process of developing technical and cognitive competencies. Or rather, these processes are integrated.

The alternative model provides the possibility to produce 'break' knowledge about learning in this field. It is clear that students receive, explicitly and implicitly, instruction at the nursing school by the nurses on the wards, and that they learn from reading the textbooks. This teaching by the official pedagogical authorities in the area, however, is viewed as *the* teaching of the students. In this study and from the theoretical perspective taken in it, it is shown that the students learn more and other things than they can give an account of. Sometimes they even learn things and ways of doing things that stand in contrast to what they spontaneously experience.

They misrecognize the fact that they first and foremost take advantage of their own physical and life experience in generating adequate practice in the hospitals. Students do not lie when they account for their own learning. Repression of certain mastership relations is an integrated dimension of learning the professional knowledge and functioning in the field. Progression in professional learning processes is closely related to the fact that the position (the student) as part of capturing the inside position has to repress – or better misrecognize – certain types of knowledge and mentors. The diagrams below give a rough outline of transformations in and around the students during their education. It is organized according to type of activity, students' subjective experiences with learning and three levels in education.

Table 11.2
**Patterns of behaviour in different phrases of the student nurses'
learning**

Type of activity	Start-up phase	Mid-way phase	Terminating phase
Dominant attitude, degree/type of involvement	Interesting and attentive.	Involved and distanced.	Involved and occupied (preoccupied).
Position in relation to the activity	Outside Student – Observer.	On the way in. Patient's advocate.	Inside. The system's (medical) advocate.
Dominant statements about those being hospitalized in connection with pain **Various positions concerning pain (perspectives on pain)**	Personal name: 'Christine Anderson has a stomach ache!' 'I didn't feel good that she was lying there and was in pain because of constipation. It's too bad for her. I have talked with her.'	Last name and placement of bed; 'Mrs. Anderson in room 2, bed 3 has abdominal pains!' 'I attended a proctoscopy. Through the proctoscope you could see the condition of the intestine. It's too bad that it has to be so painful for the patient.	Disease and placement of the bed; 'The Chrohn woman in room 2, bed 3 has abdominal pains!' '...eight morphine tablets were prescribed to deal with the pain.'
Dominant tasks and activity in relation to ideological view of care and of caring work, 'patient care'	Executes caring work. Patient care like washing in bed or shower of patient + dressing. Work with, looks on and touches the sick body. Calls for help. Speaks with sick people.	Partly executes caring work. Along the way plans and looks on that others execute patient care. Calls for help. Speaks with and about sick bodies.	Plans and monitors that others execute caring work. Writes and speaks about medically related aspects of care in the office. Is called upon as 'expert'. Speaks about sick bodies.

Note: The outline illustrates the principles only and is not directly linked to concrete movements by individuals throughout the educational process.

Table 11.3
Student nurses' subjective experiences with learning

Student nurses'subjective experiences with learning	Start-up phase	Mid-way phase	Terminating phase
Types of references used in self-study	Secondary source of references. Creative and nu-anced.	Formal, primary source of references.	Formal, primary source of references. Conformative and conventional.
Items identified as learning sources	Patient-related events and experiences. Patients' various reaction forms, their wounds, pain.	Medically-related actions and events. Ward-rounds, coloscopy, change of stoma, sterile technique, injec-tions.	Medical and admin-istrative events. Discharge procedure, securing home care nursing service, the card index system.
When learning is achieved	Learning at all times.		Learning when events and teachers are present.
Student experience of teachers	Teachers point to everyone. Other students, patients, self, nurses, etc.	Teachers selectively.	Teachers exclu-sively. By nurses and doctors.

A student in the beginning of their education is on the outside and at the bot-tom of the professional hierarchy. She is nothing, and she has nothing to lose. She (the position) can see the game as an illusion and say/think that she is learning all the time through all senses, through her own experience. She experiences learning from patients, from other students etc. These kinds of references are to a great de-gree *un*thinkable for a student who is halfway through her second practical training session (internship). At this time, it is inconceivable for the student to refer down-wards – it would simply not occur to her to do so any more. The position inside believes in the game, its value and its efforts. With Bourdieu, I characterize the 'inside' position with the term illusio. Gradually the students are taken seriously and they take things seriously. A student at the end of her education knows who and what is considered and regarded as important in the field. Through hard work she has captured professional capital including certain and distinct ways of walking and thinking. At the same time she has learned to reject certain aspects of what is going on in the field, why etc. Patients, nursing auxiliaries and student nursing auxiliaries are no longer seen as mentors, although they may be described as such. Progression in technical knowledge calls for certain behavioural patterns and perceptions. Social and technical learning are integrated.

In general, the educational system contributes to the reproduction and reconstruction of: learned person/layman, expert/client, teacher/student, nurse/student relations. As part of earning their nursing authorization a student must be able to incorporate (or rather consolidate) these dichotomies. Increasingly she becomes 'unlike' or 'distinct from'. Bit by bit she will have to learn that:

1. She is *not* a nursing auxiliary or doctor
2. This makes a big difference
3. The difference can be attributed to education, diligence and talents.

Consequences and future perspectives

In this study, practice training has been regarded from a perspective that reduces the significance of the cognitive, accumulated, individual and verbal learning from the legitimate teachers. For Bourdieu and others, the body is in focus. This type of research is oriented towards raising awareness of and answering basic questions about nursing practice and learning. The research is humanistic or society-oriented and attempts to describe and understand the issue. It does not attempt to improve education or educational programmes or to give didactic principles to teachers, clinical nurses or student nurses. Rather, the insights elucidate the complexity of practical training in nursing education, and this may capture central aspects within other educations and their practical training. This is confirmed by some tendencies in the research on the education of junior doctors; (Bayer; Henriksen; Larsen and Ringsted 2002), specialists (Bach; Bayer; Brinkkjær; Larsen and Pallesen 2004), and pre-school teachers (Bayer 2001). This research presents new ways of thinking about and describing practical training, and by doing so, serves to challenge and inspire students, principal teachers and designers of educational programmes.

The practice is transformed (learned) through bodies in architecture, in rooms with specific furniture, artefacts, tools and smells. The students are embedded in practice and they are parts in an ongoing mutual back-up mastership system in which they learn a great deal. Patients, students and other professional groups are principal teachers for nurse students, but they are not perceived as such. This study, contributes to a critique of Dreyfus' hierarchy learning theory, the conventional model and also to reflections upon the used observational method, the lack of knowledge about the individual strategies of the students, the limits of the theory of Bourdieu etc.

However, this insight implies that nursing is not 'in itself' a research object. It is a sub-field in a medical field. And it implies the need to redefine other relationships within and outside of the nursing (wannabe) profession such as theory and practice, concept and action, the theorist and the practitioner, the teacher and the student. Today these relationships are separated and hierarchically arranged in Western modern welfare societies. Recognizing patients, other students and professional groups as principal teachers for student nurses presents a challenge not only on a didactic level but also towards the prescribed cultural and historical power relationships. To see patients as principal teachers is perhaps possible now that so-called post-modern thinking is challenging the modern, but the findings are not new, like; 'not yet known'. The insight is a kind of misrecognized knowledge in daily practice and to a great extent within pedagogical research. I think it makes sense that research strives to make explicit things that 'go without saying', pushing back the limits of doxa and exposing the arbitrariness of what is taken for granted, the so-called 'natural world'.

References

Ax, S. and Kincade, E. (2001): 'Nursing students' perception of research: usefulness, implementation and training', in: *Journal of Advanced Nursing*, 35 (2): 161-170.

Bach, B., Bayer, M., Larsen, K. and Pallesen, I. (2004): *Speciallægeuddannelsen i Danmark* (The specialist doctor education in Denmark). Copenhagen: The Danish University of Education Press, (in print). *www.dpu.dk*.

Bayer, M. (2001): *Praktikkens skjulte læreplan; Praktikuddannelse – empirisk undersøgt i pædagoguddannelsen* (The hidden curriculum of practical training. Practical training education – an empirical study of the social educator programme). Copenhagen: The Danish University of Education Press.

Bayer, M., Henriksen, A.H., Larsen, K., Ringsted, C. (2002): *Turnuslægers praksislæring* (The learning of practice by medical students doing compulsory graduate terms in hospital service). Copenhagen: The Copenhagen Hospital Corporation Postgraduate Department of Medicine (H: SPMI).

Benner, P. (1984): *From novice to expert*. Menlo Park, California: Addison-Wesley Publishing Company.

Bjørk, I.T. (1999): *Hands-on nursing: new graduates' practical skill development in the clinical setting*. Oslo: University of Oslo.

Bourdieu, P. (1977): *Outline of a theory of practice*. Cambridge: Cambridge University Press.

Bourdieu, P. (1999): *The weight of the world: social suffering in contemporary society*. Cambridge: Polity Press.

Bourdieu, P. (2000): *Pascalian Meditations*. Cambridge: Polity Press.

Bourdieu, P. and Passeron, J C (1977): *Reproduction in education, society and culture*. London: Sage Publications.

Broady, D. (1997): 'The epistemological tradition in French sociology', in: Gripsrud, J. (ed.): *Rhetoric and epistemology: papers from a seminar at the Maison des sciences de l'homme in Paris, September 1996*. Bergen: Department of Media Studies, University of Bergen.

Callewaert, S. (1999): 'Towards a general theory of professional knowledge and action', in: *Journal of Nordic Educational Research*, 19 (4): 209-222.

Carr, W. and Kemmis, S. (1986): 'A critical approach to theory and practice', in: Carr, W. and Kemmis, S.: *Becoming critical: education, knowledge and action research*. London: Falmer Press.

Colliere, M.F. (1986): 'Invisible care and invisible women as health care-providers', in: *International Journal of Nursing Studies*, 23 (2): 95-112.

Cox, H., Hickson, P. and Taylor, B. (1991): 'Exploring reflection: knowing and constructing practice', in: Gray, G. and Pratt, R. (eds.): *Towards a discipline of nursing*. Edinburgh: Churchill Livingstone.

Dreyfus, H.L., Dreyfus, S.E. and Athanasiou, T. (1986): *Mind over machine: the power of human intuition and expertise in the era of the computer*. Oxford: Basil Blackwell.

Eriksen, T. Rask (1992): *Omsorg i forandring* (Care in change). Copenhagen: Munksgaard.

Franssén, A. (1997): *Omsorg i tanke och handling: en studie av kvinnors arbete i vården* (Caring in thought and acting: a study of women working in nursing). Lund: Arkiv förlag.

Ghaye, T. and Lillyman, S. (2000): *Reflection: principles and practice for healthcare professionals*. Dinton, Wilts: Quay Books.

Heggen, K. (1995): *Sykehuset som 'klasserom': praksisopplæring i profesjonutdanninger* (The hospital as a class-room: Practice learning in profession educations). Oslo: Universitets-forlaget.

Heyman, I. (1995): *Gånge hatt till: omvårdnadsforskningens framväxt i Sverige: sjuksköternes avhandlinger 1974-1991* (The emergence of nursing research in Sweden. Doctoral theses written by nurses 1974-1991). Göteborg: Daidalos.

Hickson, P. (1990): 'The promises of critical theory'. Unpublished paper presented at Embodiment, Empowerment, Emancipation conference, Melbourne.

Jensen, K. (1992): *Hjemlig omsorg i offentlig regi: En studie av kunnskapsutvikling i omsorgsarbeidet* (Nursing at home in public framework: A study of development of knowledge in nursing). Oslo: Universitetsforlaget.

Lave, J. and Wenger, E. (1991): *Situated learning – Legitimate peripheral participation*. New York: Cambridge University Press.

Larsen, K. (2000) *Praktikuddannelse, kendte og miskendte sider: et observationsstudie af praktikuddannelse inden for sygeplejerskeuddannelsen* (Apprenticeship, known and unappreciated aspects: an observation study on apprenticeship in nursing education). Copenhagen: University Hospitals Centre for Nursing and Care Research.

Larsen, K. (1994): *Teori og praksis i sygeplejerskeuddännelsen: en empirisk undersøgelse af forholdet mellem teori og praksis i sygeplejerskeuddannelsen* (Theory and practice in the education of nurses: an empirical study of the relationship between theory and practice in the education of nurses) University of Copenhagen, 1993. Published by *Danmarks Sygeplejerskehøjskoles Skriftserie* (The Danish College of Nursing's publication series), no. 16.

Lindberg-Sand, Å. (1996): *Spindeln i klistret: den kliniska praktikens betydelse för utvecklingen av yrkeskompetens som sjuksköterska: et etnografisk-fenomenografisk studie* (The spider in the glue: the impact of clinical training on the development of professional nursing competence: an ethnographic-phenomenographic study). Lund: Lund University.

Lindgren, G. (1993): *Doktorer, systrar och flickor: om informell makt* (Doctors, nurses and girls: on informal power). Stockholm: Carlssons.

Löfmark, A. and Thorell-Ekstrand, I. (2000): *Evaluation by nurses and students of a new assessment form for clinical nursing education*. Scandinavian Journal of Caring Sciences, Vol. 14, no. 2, 2000: 89-96.

Löfmark, A. and Wikblad, K. (2001): 'Facilitating and obstructing factors for development of learning in clinical practice: a student perspective', in: *Journal of Advanced Nursing* 34 (1): 43-50.

Melia, K.M. (1987): 'Conclusions and beyond', in: Melia, K M: *Learning and working: the occupational socialization of nurses*. London, Tavistock.

Merleau-Ponty, M. (1994): *Kroppens fænomenologi* (Phenomenology of the body), Translation of the chapter 'Le corps' in: 'Phénoménologie de la perception'. Copenhagen: Det Lille Forlag.

Newton, J.M. (2000): 'Uncovering knowing in practice amongst a group of undergraduate student nurses', in: *Reflective Practice* 1 (2): 183-197.

Nielsen, K. and Kvale, S. (eds.) (1997): *Journal of Nordic Educational Research*: Vol 17, No 3: special issue: *Apprentinceship - learning at social practice*. Oslo: Scandinavian University Press.

Petersen, K.A. (1998): *Sygeplejevidenskab: myte eller virkelighed: om genese og struktur af feltet af akademiske uddannelser og forskning i sygepleje i Danmark* (Nursing science: Myth or reality: About genesis and structure of the field of academic education and research in nursing in Denmark). Viborg: Viborg County.

Pilhammar Andersson, E. (1993): *Det är vi som är dom: sjuksköterskestuderandes forestallningar och perspektiv under utbildningstiden* (Now we are them! Registered nurse students' perceptions and perspectives during the nurse training programme). Göteborg: Acta Univetsitatis Gothoburgensis.

Schön, D.A. (1983): *The reflective practitioner: how professionals think in action*. New York: Basic Books.

Schön, D.A. (1987): *Educating the reflective practitioner: toward a new design for teaching and learning in the professions*. San Francisco: Jossey-Bass.

Street, A. (1990): *Nursing practice: high, hard ground, messy swamps and the pathways in between*. Geelong: Deakin University.

Thompson, J.L. (1987): 'Critical scholarship: the critique of domination in nursing', in: *Advances in Nursing Science* 10 (1): 27-38.

Wittgenstein, L. (1995): *Philosophical investigations*. Oxford: Basil Blackwell.

Conclusion

Continuity, Change and Dilemmas

Tine Rask Eriksen and
Hanne Marlene Dahl

State feminism and new public management

Often the Nordic welfare states are understood as a heaven on earth for women. They are described as 'potentially women friendly' (Hernes, 1987), or as carriers of state feminism. State feminism is understood in a wide sense as feminism from above (social and equal opportunity policies), from below (women's mobilization through, for example, social movements) and through the feminization and support of welfare state professions (Hernes, 1987; 1998). Hernes understands these professions as being staffed increasingly by women creating professional, regulated and safe jobs for women.

More specifically, it is possible to understand a welfare state profession such as home-helpers as having partly been generated and supported by the Nordic welfare state(s) in line with what Henriksson and Wrede have labelled *'democratic professionalism'*. Democratic professionalism can be interpreted as an untraditional professionalism, which tries to alleviate the social divisions shaping the occupational structure. The concept was originally developed by Hugman (1991) as a contrast to the more orthodox form of professionalization but has been redefined by Henriksson and Wrede who shift the focus upon the recipient of care (the user) to a focus upon state strategies towards the care givers – in particular less developed professions. It overlaps somewhat with the concept of an 'alternative professionalization' introduced by Johansson in a study of the Swedish care profession (1995) that, as mentioned in the introduction, referred to female, mass and subordinate professions as opposed to the 'more' classical, male and elitist professions.

In their contribution to the present volume Henriksson and Wrede show that the Finnish welfare state is increasingly moving away from such a political and moral commitment to democratic professionalism, since there is a return to more traditional forms of professionalization processes. As in other Nordic welfare state(s), New Public Management (NPM) inspired policies have brought various changes to state regulated home care for elderly people in the 1990s. NPM has resulted in a reconfiguration of home care work, where some nursing groups have improved their professional opportunities (in managerial work) whereas other professions have suffered from a weakening of their position as a result, for example, of the brief training period home-helpers receive. An increasing number of the home care workers work on a less regulated, and temporary basis due to their employment in the private sector, or their status as private entrepreneurs in the care sector. With the genesis of new professions, and de-professionalization of the home-helper, new inter- and intraprofessional divisions have been the result of introducing NPM in Finland. Whereas Henriksson and Wrede focus upon the changes in the organization of work and the professional boundaries, there are other elements of NPM inspired policies such as those concerning the financing and the provision of care.

In her analysis of developments within pre-school care and elderly care in Sweden, Szebehely shows that the Swedish model is moving away from the universalist model, especially within elderly care, in relation to financing, provision and its work organization. Szebehely analyses the effects of policy changes (legislation and administrative practices), and does not analyse the ideological developments such as the elements of NPM that have been implemented. However, it is obvious that Sweden has implemented NPM inspired ideas in its call for *privatization*. These are identified in the three areas where change has taken place that Szebehely discusses in her contribution to the present volume: *the financing of care, provision of care and the work organization of care.*

Concerning the financing of care, user fees have been introduced in Sweden. They have changed the relation between public and private responsibility understood as encompassing the market and civil society. Concerning the provision of care, there is no longer a unity or continuity of the care provided, since care is also provided by private firms subsidised by the state. Finally, the concrete organization and exercise of care has been influenced by the market-inspired organization leading to a decline in staff continuity and a thinning out of domestic support.

In her analysis, Szebehely exposes the similarities between the developments in the two policy fields of pre-school and elderly care, but also notes the differences. Whereas child-care has moved towards increased accessibility, i.e. an increased universalism, elderly care has become more selective, since there is *decreased universalism* in this field. Elderly people in Sweden with a low educational background rely to a larger extent upon informal help than do their fellow citizens with a higher educational background who can afford to purchase assistance privately.

The Swedish and the Finnish case are remarkably similar in regard to three developments, namely, the retrenchment of the welfare state, a refamilialization of care obligations, and a marketization of care services. The developments in Denmark and Norway will be discussed below, but from a slightly different angle.

Explicit and implicit power, normalization and quasi-quality

Both Christensen and Dahl discuss the issue of power and regulation. Drawing on different traditions of power, they both conclude that there has been an increase in the regulation in the field of care for elderly people in their own homes in both Norway and Denmark. There is less room for developing the professional judgement of the home-helper and for the care relation between the home helper and the elderly.

In a new model of power relations, Christensen argues that the historical development of Norwegian care services can be broken down into three phases: *traditional, modern and late modern* outputs there occurs a gradual strengthening of the legal and ideological control of the field. There is a change from implicit to explicit power in state regulation. This development means a formalization and standardization of the home-helpers' work, reducing their flexibility and reducing the possibility for good care. Christensen states that there 'exist important care dilemmas between what is needed in the care relational praxis and what is possible in the light of structural conditions'.

In a study of the development of the political-administrative discourse in Denmark, Dahl argues that recent welfare state reforms in elderly care have been ambiguous. On the one hand there has been a discursive retrenchment in the obligations acknowledged by the state and on the other, the state simultaneously extends its disciplinary power. The retrenchment concerns a paradigmatic shift in the way that it is possible to think and talk about care in the politico-administrative discourse, where some needs are prioritized whereas others become silenced examples of these are relieving distress, relieving loneliness or even cleaning. The discourse pictures the good life (for an elderly person) as one of change, being self-reliant and capable. The focus is upon creating wellbeing, growth and enabling life-realization. This will to the pleasant is becoming dominant in the discourse simultaneously with a tyranny of transformation, where elderly people continuously are expected to develop in a 'reciprocal developing co-operation' with their home helpers. Development and change becomes self-referential. In short, the ideal of care changes with an ambiguous twist, since elderly people are increasingly expected to behave in line with this new normative ideal. There is an increase in the subtle forms of power, where a normalization and a moralization occur. This form of power is more implicit, since it regulates behaviour through normative ideals, neither through sanctions nor economic incentives.

Superficially it seems as though Christensen and Dahl present opposing interpretations of the developments in Norway and Denmark, since Christensen argues that regulation is increasingly explicit, whereas Dahl argues that there is an increase in the subtle, more implicit forms of power. However, the differences stem from their different approaches to power and their different terminologies. Both developments happen simultaneously, since there is in both an increased, explicit regulation, and in the Danish case an increase in the more indirect, and subtle forms of power.

Apart from such differences, there is an agreement in the contributions by Christensen, Dahl, Henrikson and Wrede, Szebehely and Wærness upon the negative effects of recent welfare state developments for the persons providing care and the recipients of care. The conditions for caregiving work have changed. Wærness perceives good care to be increasingly taking place in spite of the institutional conditions. Quoting Slagsvold (1995), Wærness asserts that recent attempts to improve the quality of care might have unintended effects such as decreasing the quality of care, and instead produce *quasi-quality*. NPM and a legalistic rationality lead to this rather paradoxical development. An increasingly rights based legislation contrary to its intentions results in quasi-quality.

Late modernity, self-realization and care

There are changes in two conditions for state regulated care, namely the above-mentioned change in public policies as well as the change from modernity to late modernity. In late modernity, according to Giddens (1991), the formation of the self changes. The increased self-reflexivity of the self is closely related to the lessened importance of traditions and norms, and to the disembeddedness of time and space. This increased self-reflexivity also contains an intimization and a drive for self-realization (Giddens, 1992) that can create new paradoxes in state regulated care. Self-reflexivity and the drive for self-realization, means high and rising expectations, where users are surfing on the internet achieving complex information and questioning traditional authorities. A paradox arises between high expectations compared to poor structural conditions for providing good care. Or as Hochschild puts it, based on the US context, 'Ideologically, "care" went to heaven. Practically, it's gone to hell' (Hochschild, 2003: 2).

Deeply embedded in late modernity is a re-articulation of the private and the public. This has implications for both our ways of dealing with death and dirty work in health care policies as argued in the contributions by Timm and Dahle. In later modern society, there exists a space of acting in relation to death and dying that is markedly different from that of modern death and dying where death was hidden and doctors were the experts. The Danish expert discourse on death and dying has been a compromise between various groups: experts (the doctors) and the social movement for hospices in Denmark. The result was a discourse on the good death that particularly suited well-educated middle class people as is shown in the example of Peter who was dying of cancer and was himself trained as a psychologist. The private experiences become public, since death becomes a subject of conversation, scientific training of nurses and doctors, and increasingly also a scientific subject. This expert discourse, however, is biased in relation to class and education, since it cannot grasp the wishes, pains and needs of Karl, an invalid working class pensioner also dying of cancer.

Dahle argues that the body is deeply ambiguous in late modernity, since there is both public exposure of the body and simultaneously an increasing privatization. The private and public are transcended and simultaneously reproduced. The ambiguity is also found among nurses in their attitudes to dirty work involving such close contact with bodily secretions where they experience shame as well as necessity. Interestingly, dirty work has varying status depending upon the context, i.e. whether a scientific context such as the treatment of a disease or the essential daily work performed by nurses or auxiliary nurses. Context matters – and is gendered in divisions of work and the status assigned.

Globalization, justice and the status of care

As mentioned in the introduction, ideas travel today through international organizations like the OECD. In addition, people travel increasingly, not just for holidays, but in the form of migration. There has occurred an increase in migration, especially the female part (Kofman, 2003). The bounds of the nation state have in this sense dissolved, and we increasingly experience that migrants take up low paid jobs in institutional or in private care (Isaksen, 2001). This is not a development particular to the Nordic welfare state(s), as Hochschild argues that care is increasingly embedded in *chains of care* (2003). Care has become a 'pass-on' job, where, often, well-educated women migrate to the first world to work in care jobs and leave their own children behind. In this sense, globalization has had a negative impact upon the value associated with care where, according to Hochschild (2003: 196), the status of care has fallen lower yet.

One can ask whether the description of such a development of decreasing status and misrecognition of care and caregiving work is fair. Are not all persons worthy of respect and recognition for whatever work they provide? Asking such a question in a perspective of justice enables us to consider care, not just as an ethical question of how we ought to behave in relations with other people, but rather in considering what marks a good and fair society. In our framing of this question we rely on recent developments in theories of justice such as advocated by the American feminist philosopher Nancy Fraser (1997) (Fraser and Honneth, 2003), where justice is seen to refer to, among others, recognition (Dahl, forthcoming 2004). The lack of recognition (status) is due to paid care work being inscribed within a division of labour[1] signifying femininity and masculinity and the corresponding differences in status including the pay for the work (Tronto, 1993).

Seen from such a perspective, the Norwegian Commission on Values has taken a courageous step forward, since it has introduced the status of care on to the political agenda in the following way:

'Within politics attention to care has been sparse. The Commission on Values believes that this fact must be challenged and changed. Only in so far that we understand care as a political issue is it possible to change the cultural value assigned to those who provide caregiving work' (Verdikommisjonen, 1999: 45, quoted from Fjørtoft, 2002: 41, our translation).

Politically there seems to be some hope of a changed status of care and caregiving work due amonmg others to the emerging recruitment problem in domestic care and nursing such as mentioned by several of the authors in this volume.

However, we also believe that research into care needs to reflective more upon the consequences on care, informally as well as formal, of globalization in its widespread use of the nation state (or group of nation states) as a frame of reference. Considering both migration and the changed demographic picture of for-

---

[1] This division of labour is also based upon a reproduction of various dichotomies like public vs. privat, production vs. reproduction, clean vs. unclean, treatment vs. care, professional vs. non professional and the 'masculine' versus the 'feminine' that are at play together with hierarchies of more or less valuable activities.

merly relatively homogenous populations, new research questions enter the field concerning both the needs of recipients of care and the qualifications of the care givers (their ethnicity, gender, class and age).

Conditions for the paid care work in modern care bureaucracies

Modernization initiatives in the public sector have, as shown above, contributed substantially to a number of *changes* in the conditions and content of paid care work. In Denmark, hospital expenses are rising whilst the number of hospital beds is decreasing. At the same time, the number of employees in the health sector has increased (Eriksen 2000). The articles by Dahle, Eriksen, and Timm in the section on Dilemmas in the Professions and Users in Public Health show, in different ways, how the *changed* conditions affect social relations between professionals and users/patients in large modern care bureaucracies in the Nordic countries.

Dahle demonstrates how bodily, dirty work is understood and interpreted in the Norwegian public sphere, and she illustrates how the body is rendered increasingly private. She thus describes how the work with others' bodies and different forms of intimacy affect the patients and the professionals. The dirty work manifests itself in the relations between the sick and the female-dominated care professions. This dirty work forms part of a comprehensive bodily, gendered, and hegemonic system of meaning in paid care work. Eriksen's studies of the Danish case illustrate how conditions of the cancer field influence the care relations between the sick and the professionals, since structural conditions of the field promote the establishment of technical and standardized care relations. Furthermore, the female care workers accept the productive, masculine logic of the field. Their female care experiences are thus with time *transformed* into a masculine logic: to verbalize care. The professionals thereby become communicators of a symbolic power in the relational work, instead of accommodating the patients' biological, gendered, and class-differentiated needs for care.

According to Bourdieu (1996), the most brutal power relations are symbolic relations where one submits to and obeys a given power. One might submit to, for instance, certain ideas about how the world should be viewed and understood in a given field. In the cancer field, the forms of symbolic power are defined in a masculine universe, where the relationship between *power and gender* (Widerberg 1995:13) is important in order to understand the circumstances that structure paid care work. Masculine supremacy thus forms part of the symbolic power in the cancer field, as its cognitive structures dictate that professionals and patients often must function through a rational and masculine logic.

Professionalized care work and its knowledge forms

The dramatic *change in work communities* have also been discussed by Danish pedagogue Kristian Larsen. He demonstrates how the architecture, professionalization, and efficiency maximization of care work affect social relations. Thus, a number of the anthology's articles uncover how the *dichotomy* between the conditions for paid care work and paid care work's subjective content has become more marked in the Nordic welfare states. This is a dilemma that the sociologically inspired research on care often presents as a dichotomy between the private and the public. In the anthology's introduction, the dilemma is approached through the human sciences in order to provide a more nuanced exposition. This is a scientific approach of the human's realization as a human, where the person becomes what it is through its conditions and experiences (Kjørup 1996). Here the *dichotomies within care abilities* in the post-modern Nordic care institutions are exposed as gendered, experience-based, bodily, emotional, and practical knowledge, but also as knowledge where the conditions for paid care work produce other types of care knowledge in which the bodily and emotional elements are reduced.

The anthology's contributions can thus be criticised for lacking explanatory power in regards to the subjective aspects of care work. Wærness touches on the subject from a sociological perspective by emphasizing the growing dichotomy between motherhood and paid work. Timm and Eriksen suggest that the relations between professionals and the sick are marked by a range of 'non-meetings'. Timm's culture-sociological knowledge universe possesses no subjective explanatory power of the relational elements. Likewise, Eriksen's use of the concept of habitus attempts to explain the relational elements, but the explanatory power does not transcend the gendered and class-differentiated agent level. Their culture-theoretical reconstructions of the sick's action-patterns reveal them to be gendered as well as socially and bodily differentiated. The sick are recipients of standardised care services; the professionals in the cancer field transform the sick person into a sick, objectified, and labour divided body, which is primarily an object of treatment and secondarily a recipient of care and nursing.

In her studies of the work of home-helpers, Karen Christensen from Norway has developed an empirical concept of other-orientation (Christensen 1999: 56). Here, the care recipient in the role of the other is seen as the most important factor in regards to the content and performance of care work. The concept is drawn from Alfred Schutz's everyday-life theories, and its content has clear parallels to e.g. Løgstrup (1956) and Noddings (1984), which were mentioned in the introduction. Schutz describes other-orientation as a basic precondition for social relations. One must be able to view the other as a conscious person and see and feel that there are levels of intensity in this orientation. Christensen demonstrates, like Eriksen, that other-orientation is often developed through the socialization women are subject to during childhood. Both authors hint that there can be found parallels, although in other forms, to this orientation in the professionalized knowledge forms of care work; it is a *stable aspect* of care abilities. But it is an aspect that is *weakened* in paid care work, as it is intensified, rationalised, and made into an instrumental service.

The *contradictory knowledge forms* of professionalized care work are presented indirectly in Part II 'Dilemmas in the Nordic Welfare States and their Provision of Care'. The documented insight here should be communicated as forward-looking *political strategies* for paid care work in the primary health sector (private homes and elder care institutions). On the basis of the *new insights*, care researchers can communicate there insights into political contexts (as manifests), in order to, if possible, limit the continuous regulation of paid care work; a regulation that is based on a wish for productivity and quality. This is in part sought achieved through increased documentation and a securing of patient rights. Care work is thereby sapped of subject-substance, and there is, as mentioned earlier, a risk of creating quasi-quality. We must, at the same time, draw attention to the class struggle in care work in the Nordic countries. This is seen when the most educated (e.g. nurses) attempt to set the agenda (in continuation of the masculine hospital logic) for other lower positioned groups of care workers in e.g. elderly care.

Rendering care educations academic in Nordic countries

The Nordic educational system and thereby the care educations have from the 1990s until today undergone *marked changes*. Dybbroe illustrates, through a case study of Danish pre-school pedagogues, how students' life historical knowledge of care is displayed in the educational space. Further, it is illustrated how the conditions of the classroom are influenced by modernization initiatives and by a number of educational factors such as organization, educational plans, the students' qualifications, the teacher's position, and the given power relations. In the classroom, for instance, a dismissal of the personal and bodily experiences of practical and moral character takes place, thus resulting in the students developing lower self-esteem and less potential for action.

In their article, Jensen and Tveit show how the decreasing amount of applications to the nursing education and the high dropout rate leaves the profession in a difficult situation. This is put into perspective by research on new youth cultures that shows that young people's identity is moving *away from the values* that have traditionally been appreciated in the nursing profession. Jensen and Tveit's empirical investigation demonstrates the gap between youths' self-understanding and the image that is produced in four different training degrees in the health services from the beginning to the end of the educational course. The survey is based on interviews collected at a one year.

The extracted patterns suggest that young people consider their own needs and wishes as the most important considerations in regards to their career choice. The findings raise the question of whether nursing schools are able to strike a balance between the energetic and motivated students and a reflection of certain (care) values that are sought established in the education. A new survey from Denmark shows otherwise: students that in 2002 sought entrance to the professional bachelor's degree in nursing had a lower social status, less schooling, and were from families with a more traditional division of labour than was the case 15 years ago (Eriksen 2004).

Medium length care educations in Nordic countries have during the last 15 years been transformed from practical schooling into an academic education. This educational transformation should be understood in relation to modernization initiatives that result in *education policy directives*. They are reinforced by the care professions' wish to position themselves better in the struggle for (knowledge) resources, where professionalization becomes a part of the strategy. These struggles have been decisive for the mentioned shift from a predominately practical knowledge to a mostly formal knowledge (Mathiesen 2000) in regards to the most educated care providers. This is an education strategy that, at the same time, has affected the less educated or non-educated care providers that have been submitted to a scholarly educational strategy.

Rendering care educations academic thus *reinforces* the already established cognitive and linguistic knowledge forms of care work, since reflective learning processes are the medium and the goal of a rendering academic. The aim is to study theory and via reflective learning processes to contribute to the development of knowledge (Bengtsson 1998). For female students this means that they must establish a division between the life historical care experiences and a scientific theory universe (Søndergaard 1996). The rendering academic of the female-dominated care educations thus contributes to a production of 'forms of repression' of life historical care experiences (Eriksen, 1999). These reflective processes at the same time create a distance to acting in practical situations.

The documented insight of the section on Different Forms of Knowledge and Dilemmas of Care Education should be communicated in a didactics for care educations. The care didactical strategies must fetch inspiration from learning theories that contain a bodily, experience-based, intuitive, and cognitive knowledge of care. A knowledge form that according to Merleau-Ponty (2000) presupposes pre-scientific, bodily, as well as scientific insight into the care initiatives that promote curative and educational processes (Haavind 1987).

New research approaches to the understanding of paid care-work

Profession-based care research, as mentioned in the introduction, does not possess adequate explanatory power in regards to *the nature and conditions of care work*. In the Nordic countries, this research is primarily developed within different care professions in *non-university institutions*. It is characterised by *normative descriptions* of how care works, and relations between the professionals and the users *should be systematized, organized, and executed*. Alternatively, it is displayed as empirical research that quantitatively maps out work procedures and routines in a given profession. It is a form of research that intends to be instructive in regards to how the professionals should handle a profession's content. These ideological profession theories often define users in relation to the professions' self-understanding, just as the users are ascribed the needs that professionals can meet. This profession research should be understood as a *modernizations strategy*, where science is determined by the market as a political strategy, and where it results in administrative problem solving techniques 'dressed in scientific garments'.

This is in contrast to Wærness' point that Nordic research on care has not had any power in regards to practical care work. This point should be elaborated upon by showing that ideological and profession-internal research on care 'has a form of life' in practice, and that the profession-external and university-based research on care 'lives disassociated from practice'. Therefore, the university-based research on care should establish greater consciousness of the explanatory power it must have in order to comprehend *what actually goes on both at the professional and the educational levels.*

We agree with Kari Wærness on this critique of university research on care. She states in her contribution the rather sad fact that:

> The knowledge from feminist inspired research has not hitherto had any effect on the structure of care organizations. The public discussion on how the health and welfare services should be changed is still dominated by academic experts who mainly use a language based on economic, technical and legal rationality.

This fact is also documented by Dahl in a study of the Danish elite discourse on care (Dahl, 2000). Although dominated by technical, economic and legal ways of thinking, there is also a struggle between these rationalities about the proper way to define the political problem of elder care. In this sense, the elite discourse in not homogenous and contains potentials for change.

Despite the lack of impact upon the structure of care organizations, Wærness ends her article by pointing to some promising fields of research that might have an impact upon policy makers in the future such as feminist economics that has developed close ties with some feminist ethics of care. Wærness thus develops a *forward-looking research strategy* inspired by the collaboration between philosopher Martha Nussbaum and Nobel Prize winner in Economics Amartya Sen. She writes that such collaborations should also take place in care research, in order to develop collaboration between different discourses. She also argues that researchers on care should attempt to gain influence on the care educations in order to promote the students' awareness of how the conditions of care work affect care values and vice versa.

As suggested in the section on professionalized care work and its knowledge forms, the sociological research on care lacks a certain explanatory power in regards to the concrete meeting between the little ones, the sick and the elderly, and the professionals in a given institution. It is necessary, for instance, to increasingly employ psychological and perhaps psychoanalytical theories in the science of care. Care researchers in the Nordic countries as well as internationally thus face a paradigmatic challenge (Kuhn 1962), since the existing research on care is unable to absorb important aspects of paid care work. One such example is the *dichotomy* between the nature of care (that we are vulnerable and dependent as humans, and that we are exposed to others) and the routine care services of public institutions. It is similarly a problem that the nature of care is both verbal and non-verbal; the theories students in care educations are exposed to have *considerable problems* in regards to explain what happens in an actual situation of care between a professional and someone in need of help. In order to meet such paradigmatic challenges

(Eriksen 2001) a forward-looking research strategy could cover the following areas:

- What is it (female) professionals do, and what are their conditions in paid care work?
- Which care qualifications and care abilities does it demand?
- How are learning processes, educational courses, and work conditions developed in order to promote good care relations and relevant care abilities?
- What specific positions of understanding and scientific methods can help us gain insight into the paid care work in post-modern institutions?

Such a new strategy for research on care must simultaneously be able to relate to normative theories about good care that are neither de-contextualized nor carried forward exclusively by professional interests (Dahl, 2000b).

At the Nordic seminar on care, which constituted the starting point of this anthology, there was a large scale attempt towards asking new questions and working with new research approaches and strategies, thus aiming to achieve deeper insights into the *stable aspects* of care work and the *changes* that form the conditions of paid care work today.

References

Bengtsson, J. (1998): 'Vad är refleksion?', in: *Fenomenolologiska utflykter*. Stockholm: Daidalos.

Bourdieu, P. (1996): *Symbolsk magt*. Oslo: Pax Forlag.

Christensen, K. (1999): 'Andre-orienteringen & offentligt omsorgsarbejde', in: *Social Kritik* no. 63, Copenhagen.

Dahl, H.M. (2000a): *Fra kitler til eget tøj – diskurser om professionalisme, omsorg og køn*. Århus: Politica.

Dahl, H.M. (2000b): 'A Perceptive and Reflective State?', in: *The European Jounal of Women's Studies*, 7 (4).

Dahl, H.M. (Forthcoming 2004): 'A View from the Inside: Recognition and Redistribution in the Nordic Welfare State from a Gender Perspective', in: *Acta Sociologica*, no. 4.

Egeland, C. (2001): 'Kønsforskellenes monstrøsitet. Kønsbarriere i Akademia – et ugyldigt problem', in: *Kvinder, køn & forskning*, 10 (4).

Eriksen, T.R. (1999): 'Akademiseringen af de praktiske fag – er vi på rette vej?', in: *Dansk Pædagogisk Tidsskrift* no. 3.

Eriksen, T.R. (2000): 'Det moderne plejearbejde og omsorgsbureaukratierne', in: *Grus* 21.

Eriksen, T.R. (2004): 'Gendered professional identity and professional knowledge in female health education – put into perspective by a follow-up study (1987-2002)', in: *Nora* 4.

Fraser, N. (1997): *Justice Interruptus*. London: Routhledge.

Fraser, N and Honneth, A (2003): *Recognition or Redistribution?* London: Verso.

Fjørtoft, K. (2002): 'Omsorg og rettferdighet', in: Cathrine Holst (ed.): *Kjønnsrettferdighet*. Oslo: Makt- og demokratiutredningen.

Giddens, A. (1991): *Modernity and Self-Identity – Self and Society in Late Modern Age*. Stanford: Standford University Press.

Giddens, A. (1992): *The Transformation of Intimacy*. Oxford: Polity Press.

Haavind, H. (1987): *Liten og stor. Mødres omsorg og barns utviklingsmuligheter.* Oslo: Universitetsforlaget.

Hermann, S. og Kristensen, J.E. (2003): 'Kompetenceudviklingens nye sociale spørgsmål – det sociale som investeringsobjekt', in: *Dansk Pædagogisk Tidsskrift,* no. 4.

Hernes, H. (1987): *Welfare State and Woman Power – Essays in State Feminism.* Oslo: Universitetsforlaget.

Hernes, H. (1998): 'Skandinavisk kvinners medborgerskap i velferdsstaten', in: Nagel, A.-H. (ed.): *Kjønn og velferdsstat.* Bergen: Alma Mater.

Hugman, R. (1991): *Power in Caring Professions.* London: Macmillan.

Hochschild, A.R. (2003): *The Commercialization of Intimate Life.* Berkeley: The University of California Press.

Isaksen, L. Widding (2001): ' 'Kommer din praktikant også fra Lithauen'. Om nye løsninger på gamle problemer', in: *Kvinneforskning,* 25 (2).

Jensen, K. and Aamodt, P.O. (2002): Moral motivation and the battle for students: The case of studies in nursing and social work in Norway. *Higher Education,* no. 44.

Johansson, S. (1995): 'Introduktion', in: Johansson, S. (ed.): *Sjukhus og hem som arbetsplats.* Stockholm: Bonnier/Universitetsforlaget.

Kofman, E. (2003): *Women Migrants in Europe.* Paper given at a conference arranged by The European Commission and the OECD, Brussels January 21-22.

Kjørup, S. (1996): *Menneskevidenskaberne. Problemer og traditioner i humanioras videnskabsteori.* Roskilde: Roskilde University Press.

Kuhn, T. (1962): *The Structure of Scientific Revolutions.* Chicago: The University of Chicago Press.

Mathiesen, A. (2000): 'Uddannelsernes sociologi'. *Pædagogisk Forum.* Copenhagen: Christians Ejlers Forlag.

Merleau-Ponty, M. (2000): *Kroppens Fænomenologi.* Copenhagen: Det lille forlag.

Slagsvold, B. (1995): 'Kvalitet og kontekst', in: Thorsen, K. and Wærness, K.: *Blir omsorgen borte?* Oslo: Ad Notam Gyldendal.

Søndergård, D.M. (1996): *Tegnet på kroppen. Køn koder og konstruktioner blandt unge voksne.* Copenhagen: Museum Tusculanum.

Tronto, J.C. (1993): *Moral Boundaries.* New York: Routhledge.

Widerberg, K. (1995): 'Sociologiens makt – maktens sociologi', in: *Sociologiske Forskning* no. 4.

Index